Contents

Part I   Cover Letters

Chapter 1: Cover Letter Writing Essentials / 1

Chapter 2: Phrases to Use When Responding to Postings / 8

Chapter 3: Phrases to Use When Contacting Targeted Employers / 38

Chapter 4: Cover Letters to Employment Agencies and Search Professionals / 53

Chapter 5: Cover Letter Phrases to Use When Networking / 65

Chapter 6: Cover Letter Phrases to Use for Special Situations / 80

Chapter 7: 25 Things Not to Say in Your Cover Letter / 99

Chapter 8: What to Say in Follow-Up Communications / 103

Part II Resumes

Chapter 9: Resume Writing Essentials / 109

Chapter 10: Phrases for Your Resume / 119

Chapter 11: 25 Things Not to Say in Your Resume / 161

Chapter 12: Buzz Words and Action Verbs for Your Resume / 164

Appendix A: Job Board Giants and Niche Sites / 240

Appendix B: Effective Action Verbs and Adverbs / 241

Index / 246

What to Write
to **Get** the
Job That's Right

PLUS **50**
PHRASES
YOU SHOULD
NEVER
USE!

The
RESUME
and
COVER LETTER

PHRASE BOOK

NANCY SCHUMAN
CSP, VICE PRESIDENT OF LLOYD STAFFING
AND **BURTON JAY NADLER**

A adams media
Avon, Massachusetts

Published by
Adams Media, a division of F+W Media, Inc.
57 Littlefield Street, Avon, MA 02322. U.S.A.
www.adamsmedia.com

ISBN 10: 1-4405-0981-6
ISBN 13: 978-1-4405-0981-0
eISBN 10: 1-4405-0993-X
eISBN 13: 978-1-4405-0993-3

Printed in the United States of America.

10 9 8 7 6 5 4 3 2 1

Library of Congress Cataloging-in-Publication Data
A cup of comfort for couples / edited by Colleen Sell.
p. cm.
ISBN 978-1-4405-0200-2
1. Couples. 2. Man-woman relationships. 3. Love. I. Sell, Colleen.
HQ801.C84 2011
306.7092'2—dc22
2010038484

Contains material adapted and abridged from *The Everything® Cover Letter Book,
2nd Edition*, by Burton Jay Nadler, copyright © 2005 by F+W Media, Inc., ISBN
10: 1-59337-335-X, ISBN 13: 978-1-59337-335-1; *The Everything® Resume Book,
3rd Edition*, by Nancy Schuman, copyright © 2008 by F+W Media, Inc., ISBN
10: 1-59869-637-8, ISBN 13: 978-1-59869-637-0; and *Resume Buzz Words*, by
Erik Herman and Sarah Rocha, copyright © 2004 F+W Media, Inc., ISBN 10:
1-59337-114-4, ISBN 13: 978-1-59337-114-2.

Part I

Cover Letters

Chapter 1

Cover Letter Writing Essentials

WRITING A COVER LETTER is often an annoying and sometimes difficult step in the job application process. For many people, finding the right words to introduce themselves and their experiences to a potential employer is stressful. However, writing a cover letter that lands you an interview can be achieved more easily than you think. Following the RIGHT formula, discussed in the next paragraph, can get you started. It also helps to familiarize yourself with the different types of cover letters used to contact potential employers. You'll also want to understand the basic components of a cover letter—each paragraph in the document seeks to communicate specific strategically targeted and job-function-focused information that you don't want to accidentally leave out.

Write Your Cover Letter the RIGHT Way

Writing your cover letter is as simple as following a five-step process. Just think of the acronym R-I-G-H-T. It stands for Review, Identify, Generate, Hone, Transmit:

▶ 1. Review Samples, Postings, or Descriptions

To inspire initial efforts and motivate actions, review sample cover letters and postings as well as job descriptions. Think about the phrases or special language used in these items. Key phrases in job postings must be transformed into the best paragraphs in your cover letters. If imitation is the most sincere form of flattery, it can be the best cover letter–writing strategy.

▶ 2. Identify Resume Key Points

Look at your resume and think about how it relates to the job for which you're applying. Identify key points that you wish to highlight in your cover letter. These should be field-focused qualities as well as directly related academic, employment, or co-curricular achievements. What is it about your resume that you think is most strategically linked to targeted career fields and the specific job or particular functional areas of an employer? What two resume entries do you want the cover letter reader to examine in detail?

▶ 3. Generate a Draft

Keep your first draft to one page if possible, but don't worry too much about length. Later, you'll edit to the desired word count. Use the examples in the Sample Cover Letter Phrases section for inspiration, but don't copy word for word any of the samples that inspire you. Just get some ideas down on paper or on screen. Don't feel pressured to generate your final draft first.

▶ 4. Hone a Finished Version

This is when you'll edit the content to achieve maximum effectiveness and impact. The finished version should not contain typos or any major grammatical or style errors. Remember, this is your first writing assignment for your prospective employer.

▶ 5. Transmit via E-mail or Fax, Then Mail

Once done, don't delay communication. There truly is no reason to wait. Never procrastinate. Proceed to the next section to learn details regarding cover letter format, content, and specifics to completing the five steps to cover letter success.

When to Send Which Letter

The lists within this section define different types of cover letters, the circumstances for which they are appropriate, and to whom they are sent. Later, you will review samples phrases to include in each type of letter.

▶ **Letters of Application Used When Responding to Postings**
These letters target:
- **Confidential Postings** (when employers are not identified). These letters must focus on the job descriptions and the skills you possess to succeed in the position.
- **Employer Identified Postings** (with the employer clearly noted, yet a contact name may not be given). These letters should reveal research on the company. If you don't have someone to address letters to, use memo format.
- **Employment Agencies** (when employers are not identified). When your letter is sent to a search professional, use the phrase "judge my candidacy worthy of an interview for this position with your client's firm."
- **Executive Search Firms** (when employers are not identified). As with positions posted by employment agencies, focus your letter on motivating the reader to support your candidacy and forward documentation to the client who is the hiring organization, with a recommendation to interview. These firms deal with more senior positions.

▶ **Letters of Introduction Addressed to People and Places**
These letters are transmitted:
- **As Broadcast Letters.** These letters are very popular yet least effective if done as opened and unfocused letters sent to hundreds of employers. They can be effective if they identify specific career fields, functional areas of interest, and particular firms. Be sure to cite the employer's name in these letters.

- **As Cold Communiqués.** These letters target individuals or companies with whom the writer has no true connection. These might be addressed to lists of senior executives on websites, names in professional association membership directories, or those in specialized, field-focused directories.
- **In Advance of On-Campus Interviews.** These letters request an interview or set the scene, impressing employers that you communicated after being selected to meet.
- **In Advance of Career Fairs.** In these cases, the letters set the scene and increase your chances for being granted an interview for post-baccalaureate jobs or internships.
- **To Targeted Employers.** These letters are best sent to a particular person, although they can be effective if sent generally to Human Resources when uploaded or e-mailed through a company's website. It's recommended to direct such letters to the attention of a particular person or a connection of some kind.

▶ Networking Notes

These are brief e-mail or faxed messages sent to advocates and network members. In these notes, you ask for consideration, referrals, or support. Resumes are attached, and reference is made to a cover letter that will be sent later. While some people still believe these should be handwritten, e-mail and faxing is faster and, now, most appropriate.

Content of the Cover Letter

The cover letter should, in most cases, be one page. Cover letter content almost always consists of the following three elements:

1. Introductory focus paragraph. Remember what you once learned about the five-paragraph essay? Begin with a clear thesis statement supported by two paragraphs and end with a conclusion. Cover letters should include the same. The initial paragraph cites job title or functional area of interest, and requests an interview. This first section can identify the foundations upon which you will rest your can-didacy. Is it education? Is it work experience in general, or one or two particular accomplishments? Is it a specific project that matches the position's stated requirements?

2. Qualification and motivation paragraphs. These two paragraphs (sometimes presented in bullet-point lists) detail qualification and motivation connections. They identify examples from your past that project abilities to perform in the future. This is where you apply the first two of the five steps. What key resume points will you present here? How can you connect achievements to job requirements? Be specific! The more you use the language of the field you wish to enter, special phrases and keywords, the better. Talk the talk to walk the walk. Use appropriate language to ensure that you will soon walk into an interview with confidence. Keep in mind that today many employers read the Twitter streams, blogs, and Facebook pages and other social networking site links posted by candidates. Many times these are used to uncover negative information about a candidate, but you have a real advantage if your blog or Twitter stream is timely to your industry and has relevant information that suggests you're a subject matter expert. Call attention to this in the body of your letter.

3. Closing paragraph. Restate your desire for an interview, per-haps suggesting a phone interview as a convenient next communi-cation. State that you will follow up to confirm receipt of the letter and accompanying resume. If you wish, you can close with the most critical point you wish to cover during the interview. Of course, also say thank you.

▶ Special Circumstance Statements

These can be added as Post Scripts or in the last paragraph. You may share with the reader that you anticipate being in a particular city on a particular date, that you have an offer in hand and limited time to conduct interviews, or that you have also enclosed supporting documents such as writing samples, letters of recommendation, or other materials.

Your Cover Letter, Not Theirs

When writing cover letters, too often candidates wonder, "Is this what employers want to see?" Frankly, you should ask, "Is this what I want employers to see?" You cannot read the minds of potential employers, but you can conduct field-, function-, and firm-specific research to be very focused. Cover letters are most powerful when they are targeted and clearly present performance potential. Here are a few more questions to ask and answer about cover letters:

- Have you identified samples that you wish to model? Do they match your goals or do they appeal to your sense of style?
- Do these samples have objectives, qualification summaries, or achievement summaries? How are paragraphs presented in the letter? What is first and what is last? Do these samples identify the most significant qualifications in the first two paragraphs?
- Can you state your objectives clearly and concisely? Does the first paragraph of your cover letter focus on a particular job or job function? To whom will you be sending your cover letter, and why?
- Do your most significant achievements appear somewhere on the document, as paragraph text or bullet points? Have you used the cover letter to connect past achievements to future performance potential?
- Can you describe the job you are seeking? What qualification connections would be associated with this position? Do you have a collection of keywords associated with your field- or job-focused goals?
- Have you typed a cover letter draft? Is it longer than one page? Did you do spelling and grammar checks? Did you have someone else proofread and comment on the draft?
- Will you e-mail, fax, mail, or hand deliver your cover letter? Do you have a cut-and-paste e-mail friendly version of it?

If you answered mostly "Yes" or "Sure," you are ready to draft and then finalize a powerful cover letter.

Now it's time to do the dirty work—you need to start drafting your cover letter. The following chapters contain sample phrases taken from different types of cover letters that can help jumpstart the writing process for you. The samples are broken down into six categories:

- Phrases to use when responding to postings.
- Phrases to use when contacting targeted employers.
- Phrases to use when contacting search professionals.
- Phrases to use for networking letters,
- Phrases to use for special situations.
- Phrases to use in follow-up letters.

We devote a chapter to each of these.

Chapter 2

Phrases to Use When Responding to Postings

THIS SAMPLE COLLECTION OF COVER LETTER PHRASES reveals some of the best ways to respond to job postings. Responding to printed or web-based announcements is an important part of your job search. Here, the samples are organized by paragraph type (introductory, qualification and motivation, and conclusion).

Phrases for Introductory Paragraphs

These phrases convey a strong sense of enthusiasm and interest.

▶ **Administrative Assistant**
Upon reading the advertisement in the *Jackson Review*, I was inspired to contact you immediately and offer this cover letter and attached resume to formalize my interest.

▶ **Assistant Curator**
Please consider me a strong, enthusiastic, and focused candidate for the Assistant Curator position recently advertised on *www .evansvillecourierjobs.com*.

▶ **Assistant Editor**

I would like to take all appropriate steps to formalize my candidacy for the position of Assistant Editor. When I reviewed the posting advertised via *www.bostonglobejobs.com*, I wanted to immediately share the attached resume and writing samples.

▶ **Field Finance Manager**

While my current position with Other Company, Inc. is most challenging and rewarding, the opportunity to serve within the capacities described in the posting is professionally exciting.

▶ **Fundraiser**

I hope someday my enthusiasm and professionalism can contribute to the success of your development campaigns and grant application efforts.

▶ **Home Economics Department Coordinator**

It would be with great professional enthusiasm and the pride of an alumnus that I now formalize my candidacy for the Home Economics Department Coordinator position.

▶ **Multimedia Specialist**

Please consider me a strong, enthusiastic, and qualified candidate for the Multimedia Specialist position recently posted on Any Corporation's website.

▶ **Newspaper Intern**

As documented on the enclosed resume, I am currently a junior English major with a strong interest in a journalism career.

The following phrases cite specific numbers that communicate a wealth of experience and track record of success.

► **Administrative Judge**

More than ten years of experience as a litigator and ever-curious student of the judicial system have, I trust, prepared me to be a competent and appropriately confident candidate for the Administrative Judge position.

► **Chief Financial Officer**

Detailed on the attached resume, I have a ten-year record of success managing corporate financial operations for profitable and fast-growing manufacturing companies with multistate and international operations.

► **Claims Adjuster**

During the past fifteen years, I have been with a major insurance company primarily focusing on workers' compensation claims. Accomplishments, all cited on the attached resume, required a sound background in claims management, cost containment, customer relations, employee training, and administrative support. I am proud that annually, for the past five years, I have cost-effectively negotiated well over two hundred claims.

► **Travel Agent**

As the attached resume indicates, I have a decade of progressive responsible experience in the travel and tourism field.

These phrases make a connection between the candidates' skills and the skills listed in the job descriptions.

► **Analyst**

Detailed on the attached resume, my current position as an Analyst at Another Company requires a skill set similar to the one stated as required for your position.

▶ Campus Police Officer

Your advertisement in *Careers in Law Enforcement* notes requirements and capabilities that I possess and would like to discuss during an interview.

▶ Child Care Assistant Director

As a licensed child care provider in the state of Ohio with three years' experience in a private center, the position described in your Child Care Assistant Director posting on *www.toledojobs.com* is exactly what I seek.

▶ Hotel Manager

Each step on my current career path has allowed me to develop qualifications for the Hotel Manager position announced via the Hospitality Association Newsletter.

▶ International Buyer

As I read the position appearing on Any Corporation's website, I identified a number of specific qualifications I posses that match those you seek.

▶ Park Maintenance Supervisor

As a current town employee, it would be a wonderful and logical next step to serve within roles that would ask me to manage, motivate, hire, and train others to perform efficiently and professionally.

This sample calls attention to a portfolio that can be accessed online, which is convenient and easy for the recipient to review.

▶ Associate Desktop Publisher

In support of my candidacy for the Associate Desktop Publisher position on your firm's website, attached is a copy of my resume. Also, please review my portfolio at *www.csmith.com*.

These phrases demonstrate how to call attention to materials you are submitting in addition to your resume.

▶ **Cosmetologist**

Attached please find my resume, a list of references, and a letter of recommendation. While these documents do inform you of my professional experiences and capabilities, through an interview I can learn more about your vision for Any Boutique, what you expect of the Cosmetologist, and the nature of your clientele.

▶ **Director of Public Works**

Attached is a resume, a list of references, and performance reviews from the previous two years. All reveal past achievements.

▶ **Editor**

I am very interested in the Editor position listed on *www.dallas morningnewsjobs.com*. Attached, please find my resume and a writing sample, both offered to support my candidacy and request for an interview.

▶ **Meeting Planner**

I would like to be Any Corporation's meeting planner. After reading your announcement in the *San Francisco Chronicle*, I was eager to share qualifications via the attached resume and letters of recommendation. After evaluating these documents, I hope you would allow me the opportunity to interview for this exciting opportunity.

These phrases show how to word a request to keep your application confidential.

▶ **Dental Hygienist**

I would like to interview for the Dental Hygienist position you advertised in the *Times-Union*. My concerns for current patients are such that I must ask that my candidacy remain confidential. While I am eager to interview, share my motivations and qualifications, and provide you with references, I ask you to please keep our communications private.

► **Event Planner**

Current circumstances require that my interest in this position remain confidential, but please be assured I am most definitely ready to interview and accept an offer if one were given.

These phrases mention crucial keywords that immediately make the applicants stand out.

► **Photographer/Writer**

Detailed on the enclosed resume and illustrated via samples of my work, I am an accomplished photographer with over ten years' experience in commercial and industrial photography, portraiture, and wedding photography. Published writings include *A Shutterbug's Notes* and *Picture Your Pet,* and I have broad experience creating printed and online newsletters, which involved all copy and graphics.

► **Production Quality Control Manager**

After seven years of progressively responsible experience in production, electro-mechanical assembly, soldering, testing, and total quality management with a precision manufacturing operation, I feel I have all the qualifications you require for the Production Quality Control Manager position.

► **Program Coordinator**

I am particularly qualified for this opportunity as a result of my double language major, my current enrollment in two language-proficiency certificate programs, as well as past experiences within tutorial and teaching roles.

▶ Site Location Supervisor

During the past fifteen years, my experiences as a developer, general contractor, owner, and property manager of residential, commercial, and industrial projects have been extensive. In conjunction with these projects, I was actively involved in investment analysis, whole loans and structured transactions, and financial control to assure quality completion within schedules and budgets.

▶ Technical Writer

As detailed on the attached resume, I am currently a Technical Writer and Senior Project Administrator at Rizzo Associates. Within these capacities, I complete all research, drafting, editing, and finalizing of documentation for a defense contractor.

This sample mentions a personal connection within the company that may help the applicant get his or her foot in the door.

▶ Senior HVAC Technician

At the suggestion of Donald Lee of your HVAC department, I am requesting an interview for the Senior HVAC Technician position recently posted on Any Corporation's website. Donald is well aware of my background, so he encouraged me to share my resume and request consideration for this opportunity.

These phrases can help you out if you're responding to a confidential listing. Note that each one mentions where the listing was found, and many focus on education, current employment, and professional achievements.

▶ Applications Programmer

After reviewing your posting in *www.softwarejobs.com*, I seek to become an active candidate for this position by submitting the attached resume via this web-based system.

▶ Assistant Personnel Officer

I would like to interview for the Assistant Personnel Officer position recently advertised in the *Washington Post*. As the attached resume indicates, I have extensive experience in personnel, including my most recent position as Assistant Staff Manager at Virginia General Hospital. To succeed in this capacity, I recruited and trained administrative and clerical staffs, ancillary and works department staffs, and professional and technical staffs. I also evaluated personnel, conducted disciplinary and grievance interviews, signed employees to contracts, and advised staff on conditions of employment, entitlements, and maternity leave.

▶ Biomedical Engineer

As I recently earned my undergraduate biomedical engineering degree, it is with great enthusiasm that I now seek to interview for the Engineering Trainee Position recently posted on *www.biojobs.com*.

▶ Business Consultant

I am responding to your advertisement for a Business Consultant in the *Wall Street Journal*. It is likely that my consulting experience with large and small businesses matches the requirements for this position.

▶ Legal Associate

Please consider me a strong candidate for the Legal Associate position advertised in *Lawyers Weekly*. Upon reading this announcement, I wanted to provide you the enclosed resume, recommendations, and transcripts. As you will note from my resume, I hold a Juris Doctor degree and recently received a Master of Tax and Accounting, with a concentration in estates and trust. Described on each of the supporting documents, my career started as a general practitioner, and, with time, become more involved in estate planning activities. Thus, it is with a comprehensive foundation of knowledge and professional experience that I now seek to interview for and, I hope, serve within the capacities of the Legal Associate.

▶ **Librarian**

I would like to apply for the position of Librarian advertised on *www.libraryscience.com*. In addition to an MLS degree and ALA accreditation, I have experience in varied settings. Professionally, my experience at the Kathryn Bell Library for the past eight years focused on patron services and education, my work within circulation and my reference desk roles enhanced the above capabilities. Prior, working within a private secondary school, I addressed issues pertinent to faculty, students, and parents. In all capacities, and via academic training, including a graduate degree in library science and undergraduate English major, I nurtured research, acquisition, as well as book manuscript, journal, and dissertations archival and retrieval efforts.

▶ **Operations Manager**

I would like to interview for the Operations Manager position recently posted in the *Arkansas Democrat-Gazette*. While the announcement does reveal some of what you are seeking, during an interview I can learn more about what you would expect of the next Operations Manager and target specific capabilities accordingly.

▶ **Pharmaceutical Sales**

After success selling tangible products and software services, it is with great focus and confidence that I now seek to interview for the Pharmaceutical Sales position recently posted on *www.pharmjobs .com*.

Phrases for Qualification and Motivation Paragraphs

These phrases communicate current and past job responsibilities by describing key tasks the applicants have performed. Notice how these phrases include strong action verbs and adverbs to grab the recipients' attention. Important job-specific keywords are also used.

▶ **Administrative Assistant**

By prioritizing tasks, managing time efficiently, and communicating effectively with those to whom I reported, as well as those who reported to me, I maximized the output and customer service efforts of a very demanding office.

▶ **Administrative Judge**

In this position, I utilized legal knowledge as well as research, analytical, and writing skills in addition to trial and negotiation talents to yield among my office's highest conviction rates.

▶ **Analyst**

I have monitored and analyzed accounts receivable and accounts payable, and I have worked with internal accountants to complete monthly, quarterly, and annual reports.

▶ **Assistant Curator**

As the Classical Music Listings Coordinator for the *Complete Musical Almanac* summer and fall supplements, I updated a comprehensive database and oversaw creation of a system that stores and retrieves past editions, using keywords, dates, composers, and genre.

▶ **Associate Desktop Publisher**

Ten years of progressively responsible computer experience, all detailed on my resume, include researching, developing, and documenting the operational procedures of a software seller. I was responsible for all aspects of the design, creation, and dissemination of many, user-friendly, yet state-of-the-art, manuals. I also coordinated and published the sales and marketing of a newsletter distributed to key accounts and sales representatives.

▶ **Campus Police Officer**

Described in detail on the attached resume, in my present position I maintain the highest possible site and operations security for a defense contractor. Prior, for almost a decade, I served in the United States Army, maintaining peak law enforcement/security alertness and the welfare of all personnel. In that capacity, I received numerous letters of commendation for superior job performance.

► Case Manager

Noted on my resume, I have guided at-risk youth as well as inmates through individual counseling and structured programs. This involved extensive case documentation, referrals, and goal identification, as well as communication and interaction with boards of trustees, agency personnel, and others. All cases were clearly, concisely, and professionally tracked and documented, so appropriate groups, including psychologists, teachers, judges, and parole boards, could review them.

► Dentistry Department Manager

Through efficient tracking and control systems, budget planning, and administration, I have, and can continue to, generate cost savings and greater profit margins.

► Features Reporter

While earning dual degrees in Journalism and Fine Arts at Mount St. Mary's, I worked as editor-in-chief of the yearbook and as layout editor and reporter for the school's weekly newspaper, where I became proficient in desktop publishing.

► Hospital Administrator

I am a strong organizer, enthusiastic speaker, capable leader, and team player who can interface effectively with you, your Any Health Resource colleagues, medical professionals, as well as support staff and vendors.

► Legal Assistant

This fall and past summer, I interned for a small general practice firm, where I was entrusted with a great deal of responsibility. In paralegal capacities I researched, wrote, and proofed appellate briefs; composed memoranda pertaining corporate, contract, and criminal law; and drafted complaints and answers. I was an active participant in attorney-client conferences, interviewing clients, and addressing how the law affects clients' suits, as well as raising potential consequences of varied legal outcomes.

▶ Occupational Health Manager

I am a certified occupational health nurse with twenty-one years of experience developing and implementing occupational health programs. Each related position required sound knowledge of OSHA and general occupational health issues in manufacturing, research, and healthcare settings. I have served within diagnostic, patient care, physician support, education, training, and regulatory compliance roles.

▶ Photographer/Writer

Academically, I hold a Bachelor of Arts in English from Reed College, where relevant coursework included feature writing, photojournalism, and news reporting. I have attended seminars and workshops through the Fred Jones Workshop and the Winona School of Professional Photography. My photos have appeared in the Winona course catalog, BBI Printing Company's catalog, and numerous Smithco publications (including annual reports and newsletters). I wrote all copy for the above-cited books.

▶ Political Staffer

Currently, I am an Administrative Assistant at the State House in Providence, RI. In this role, my primary responsibilities include writing press releases, researching and drafting legislation, and consistent constituent contact. I have also worked with various committees and legislators regarding an array of legislative issues. Prior, I worked as an intern at the Lieutenant Governor's office and I actively worked for several political and social causes on campus and in the Boston, MA, area.

▶ Product Developer

I have more than ten years of experience in manufacturing R&D, management of new product development, and existing product redevelopment and upgrade. I am especially experienced with complex composite materials, precision metal castings, and PC board industries. In addition, I have extensive experience both as a teacher and a lecturer at several well-known universities; and have earned a PhD in Materials Science Engineering and completed undergraduate studies in Mechanical Engineering.

▶ Publisher's Assistant

As a current temporary assignment worker with Alltemps in Topeka, KS, I have become highly computer literate in both Macintosh and Windows operating systems and software programs. To accomplish all that is cited on my resume, I was organized and accurate, mastered new information rapidly, communicated effectively with supervisors, peers and subordinates, and I work well with diverse individuals.

▶ Restaurant Manager Trainee

I have held positions of responsibility in banquet and special event catering, function management, and restaurant food service operations. I have additional experience in front-desk operation of a conference facility. Within each position, I nurtured ever-improving organizational, leadership, training, and supervisory skills in settings dedicated to providing quality service and performance in high-volume operations.

▶ Television Camera Operator

At L.A. Productions, I was involved in all aspects of video production, supporting writing, direction, production, and editing efforts associated with three short 8-mm films and several music videos which were shot and edited using digital equipment.

The following phrases direct attention to specific sections of the applicants' resumes. Taking this approach is helpful when certain aspects (and not necessarily all aspects) of your professional or educational experience directly correlate to the job for which you're applying.

► Assistant Hospital Supervisor

Recently, I took a sabbatical and finished my Masters of Public Health at Emerson College, so I am now actively seeking opportunities to build upon academic and employment skill sets. Please focus particular attention on the summary of qualification section of my resume, for all competencies and potential to succeed as your Assistant Hospital Supervisor are clearly noted.

► Conference Coordinator

When making determinations regarding interviews, please focus attention on accomplishments associated with my roles as Director of Volunteer Services, specifically those related to planning and implementing annual educational, fundraising, and community-awareness events.

► Gemologist

The summary of qualification section of my resume highlights retail and manufacturing gemology experiences as well as previous public relations, sales, promotions, and retail achievements.

These phrases state how the job in question can help the applicants grow professionally.

► Athletic Director

Recently, I became responsible for running Yale University's boathouse and two national secondary rowing competitions. Over the past two seasons, I addressed all ordering, budgeting, donation solicitation, parts inventory, and travel arrangements for crew teams. I now wish to continue my relationships with secondary coaches and educators within administrative roles.

► Child Care Assistant Director

As AnyCenter's Assistant Director, I will continue my passionate commitment to children, yet expand my efforts to support the professional growth of my colleagues as well as effective marketing, parent relations, and management undertakings.

These phrases cite continued education and training these applicants have pursued. Including this information in your cover letter lets the recipient know how you've stayed current in your field.

▶ **Chief Financial Officer**

I have been a Certified Public Accountant for over two decades, completing continued professional studies required of updated certification. I have earned an MBA in Finance and a Bachelor of Arts in Accounting. Most important, I have always supported the educational and professional development of my staff and hired those committed to continued learning and professional excellence.

▶ **Home Economics Department Coordinator**

Academically, in addition to earning a BS in Home Economics and Nutrition Education, I completed supplemental professional development with each employer since graduation. Additional training now includes specialized seminars in preventative nutrition, community outreach, and budget management, all taught by faculty of a well-respected teaching hospital.

▶ **Senior HVAC Technician**

I possess nine years of experience in after-warranty maintenance, preventive maintenance programs, and complete overhaul of major heating, air conditioning, and ventilation systems. I have successfully installed and repaired systems within varied buildings and work settings, often in facilities that are challenging and requiring creativity as well as technical know-how. I have also completed extensive and continuous education and training on the latest and most cost-efficient energy and control systems.

These phrases point to figures that support the candidates' successes in their current jobs.

▶ **Customer Service Manager**

During my tenure, 55 percent of the entry-level staff I trained advanced to managerial positions within Fortmiller. I instilled within these men and women that customer service excellence does sustain loyalty, enhance sales, and, ultimately, yield profitability.

▶ **Director of Public Works**

As featured on my resume, I am an effective manager and budget administrator; and I have the ability to work with individuals and groups in construction/public works environments where concentration is on community services, safety, the environment, and constituency concerns.

These phrases provide some insight into the applicants' interests and clarify why the applicants are seeking out these positions considering their work experiences to date.

▶ **Park Maintenance Supervisor**

For the past twelve years, I have held positions within the Youngstown Fire Department. Although my current position is secure and rewarding, it is strictly administrative and does not allow me to physically participate, as I have in the past, in actual firefighting or other hands-on activities that provide the outdoor work environment I most enjoy. The Park Maintenance Supervisor position described in your advertisement matches motivations and qualifications presented on my resume and in this letter.

▶ **Pharmacist**

Since graduating from the University of the Pacific School of Pharmacy, I have successfully completed all professional roles and responsibilities while working within a hospital setting. While my experiences at the David Grant Medical Center were challenging and rewarding, I now seek a position that will allow me to continue my career development within a retail pharmacy setting.

▶ State Administrator

While my previous positions have been challenging, rewarding, and broad in scope, I now wish my expertise to be utilized to by Any Organization. Your mission to provide lobbying and financial support for those individuals and groups committed to the education of deserving students is one I seek to transform into record-breaking fundraising, dynamic public relations, and effective policy papers.

The following sample shows phrases used to communicate interest in a job posting with a regional focus, as well a willingness to relocate to the specified region.

▶ Travel Agent

Relocation to Connecticut motivates me to respond enthusiastically to your posting. Recent efforts coordinating all travel and accommodations for those attending a major conference held at the Mohegan Sun have enhanced my relationship with the Greater Connecticut Convention and Visitor's Bureau and the Connecticut Chamber of Commerce and heightened my awareness of this region. I now strongly believe in my potential to market services to people traveling to and from Connecticut, for business as well as personal reasons.

The phrases that follow share a common trait: They are organized in bullet points. Using bullet points in your cover letter communicates information quickly and effectively. That's especially important when you're competing against hundreds of other applicants for the same job. The phrases you use in bullet points need to be short and direct. This is another situation where the use of clear action verbs and adverbs is key.

▶ **Assistant Editor**

Through internships, co-curriculars, and practical experience, I now offer Any Corporation:

- Writing, editing and layout skills gained as features editor, art editor, graphic artist, and reporter for various college publications.

- Knowledge and technical skills gained from courses and projects associated with advertising art and desktop publishing.

- Experience using PageMaker, Word, WordPerfect, Excel, PowerPoint, and varied graphics software to draft, edit, and finalize publications and presentations and to create dynamic graphics.

▶ **Associate Desktop Publisher**

Successful completion of the projects detailed on my resume require skills that match those stated as required of the Associate Desktop Publisher post. These qualifications include:

- Experience transforming research abilities into factual, detailed, and accurate copy and graphics.

- Record of success planning, overseeing, and delivering projects on time and error free.

- Comprehensive graphic and text editing talents, and capacities to maximize the efforts of writers, graphic artists, designers, and freelancers.

- Proficiency using, supporting, and teaching others Word, PageMaker, PhotoShop, PhotoShow, Visual Studio, Picture It, QuarkXPress, Illustrator, Front Page, Print Shop, and Publisher.

▶ **Claims Adjuster**

In summary, my qualifications, motivations, and achievements include:

- Over fifteen years of progressively responsible claims experience, encompassing life, health, and auto, but specializing in workers' compensation.

- Knowledge of laws and regulations pertaining to claims and potential outcomes of litigation.
- Experience conducting extensive research, working with investigators, and appropriately interacting with policyholders, physicians, healthcare practitioners, and legal professionals.
- Record of success coordinating detailed data and negotiating effectively with claimants, professional peers, corporate management, and others to arrive at mutually favorable solutions.
- Experience training, establishing goals for, monitoring, and supervising claims professionals.

▶ Clinical Research Nurse

As a result of patient care- and research-related experiences, I have nurtured the skills stated as required in the posting. These include:

- Past experience in clinical research.
- Capacities to develop and follow detailed protocols, procedures, and database-collection efforts.
- Commitment to flawless patient record keeping and confidentiality.
- Knowledge of issues pertaining to AIDS and experience working with this patient population.
- Experience working in research contexts, supporting clinical trials and laboratory research efforts.
- Graduate and undergraduate studies in nursing, including anatomy and physiology.

▶ Cosmetologist

Now, at the Other Boutique, I am proud to say that I have:

- Developed a strong and loyal clientele.
- Introduced an exciting new and profitable line of cosmetic products.
- Expanded bridal- and wedding-party business.
- Accounted for sales in excess of $4,000 for 14 months.

▶ **Dental Hygienist**

Summarizing all that appears on the attached resume, I offer:

- Current experience as a Hygienist, Surgical Assistant, and Assistant Office Manager.
- Success in providing state-of-the art prophylaxis treatment to adults and adolescents.
- Capacity to perform pre-surgical, surgical, and postoperative care roles.
- Progressively responsible experience as a Hygienist, Assistant, and Office Administrator.
- Sound knowledge of medical terminology and clinical procedures.
- Certification in first aid, cardiopulmonary resuscitations, and electrocardiography.

▶ **Editor**

Detailed on my resume, specific abilities and achievements of mine that match the stated requirements include:

- Over two years of experience within book acquisition, editorial production, and marketing roles.
- Special knowledge of youth and adult markets, focusing on lifestyle, sports, and leisure.
- The commitment to blend creativity with profitability.

▶ **Event Planner**

I am confident my six years of experience in public relations with a focus on event planning have prepared me to succeed in the position described in the posting. I offer you and your Any Corporation colleagues:

- Experience planning annual marketing, promotions, fundraising, and volunteer recognition events.
- Proven abilities to negotiate and liaise with catering, hotel, and travel professionals.
- Capacities to generate corporate partners and individuals willing to share event costs.

- Record of success using events to mobilize and motivate others and, ultimately, have bottom line impact on sales or donations.

▶ Field Finance Manager

It would be with great focus and confidence that I would:

- Develop new and enhance existing relationships with dealers who use Any Corporation financing.
- Monitor existing accounts and provide detailed weekly, monthly, quarterly, and annual reports to senior managers and field representatives.
- Hire, train, and motivate field representatives.
- Focus on profitability, risk management, and underwriting.

▶ Loan Officer

Qualifications, capabilities, and achievements all detailed on the resume include:

- Outstanding record of achieving sales goals as Branch Manager; successfully conducting residential and commercial mortgage acquisitions and personal and commercial loan transactions.
- Extensive experience developing commercial lending packages for private clientele, including financial restructuring, REFI, equipment financing; coordinating activities with COMIDA, GCIDA, IBDC, and ESDC, and attorneys, appraisers, title companies, and governments.
- Capacity to train, supervise, and motivate others to achieve maximum performance.
- Expertise to develop marketing strategies and collateral, internal management programs, and professional business plans through utilization of Word, Excel, and PowerPoint.

▶ Office Receptionist

In summary, my receptionist and administrative skills include:

- Experience using multiple phone lines and serving as telephone and in-person receptionist.

- 70 wpm typing speed and proficiency using word processing programs and spreadsheet applications.
- Strong worth ethic and record of success within corporate, medical, and retail settings.

► Public Relations Associate

I would like to touch on particular aspects of my background that should be of interest to you. These include:

- Over five years progressively responsible campaign development experience.
- Undergraduate Public Relations degree from one of the nation's top communication programs.
- Capacities to successfully address needs and achieve goals of corporate and not-for-profit clients.

► Purchasing Agent

When starting my career, as purchasing clerk and now as a Senior Buyer who wishes to become your next Purchasing Agent, I have learned to:

- Clarify the needs of end users.
- Source and communicate effectively with vendors and suppliers via phone and Internet.
- Create detailed spreadsheet cost-benefit analyses of potential purchases.
- Communicate with end users and negotiate with suppliers and vendors with great focus.
- Track, store, and retrieve all purchase documentation, delivery dates, warrantees, and installation agreements.
- Use purchasing, budgetary, and related software systems

► Social Worker

Previewing and reviewing what appears on the resume, I offer the following:

- Capabilities to serve within comprehensive social work capacities in school or healthcare settings.
- Experience creating and implementing treatment plans for clients with psychosocial, behavioral, and health-related disorders.
- Capacity to manage cases, maintain accurate case records, and create detailed reports.

▶ Technical Writer

Summarizing what appears on the attached resume, the capabilities and abilities I will use to succeed at Any Tech include:

- Proven abilities to structure technical writing projects and motivate others to complete components accurately and on time.
- Capacities to transform technical information into detailed illustrations and documentation.
- Sensitivities related to creation of classified training and support materials for military hardware.
- Security Clearance Level IA.
- Project- and team-management skills nurtured via observation and experience.
- Capacities to identify specific task components and set realistic deadlines, then monitor and motivate others.
- Expertise associated with the use of Word, WordPerfect, PowerPoint, Lotus 1-2-3, Excel, and CAD.

▶ Telemarketer

My achievements to date include:

- Induction into performance clubs and earning of multiple recognitions over the past three years.
- Personal responsibility for over $500,000 FY annual sales.
- Record of consistently reaching or exceeding established goals for over four years.

Qualifications, gained with ESP Telecom and the Test Review Education Group include:

- Outstanding selling and closing capabilities illustrated by a proven track record of exceeding goals.
- Active listening techniques, nurturing conversations through appropriate questioning.
- Drive and focus required to meet contact and sales quotas, meeting self- and other-established deadlines.
- Confidence in cold calling and direct sales roles, marketing services and products to businesses and clients.
- Pride associated with using earnings as a telemarketer to pay for college tuition and expenses.
- Knowledge, concepts, specialized techniques, and vocabulary gained from Business administration, public speaking, persuasive writing, and marketing courses.

Phrases for Closing Paragraphs

These phrases show how you could handle wording the request for an interview.

▶ **Administrative Assistant**

I hope you will give me the opportunity to discuss the available position with you.

▶ **Administrative Judge**

I welcome the opportunity to discuss my qualifications with the selection committee.

▶ **Assistant Curator**

I have often relied on the resources available at Any Music Library, and I would welcome the opportunity to join your curatorial staff. I would be happy to discuss the position with you further.

▶ **Assistant Editor**

I hope you will give me the opportunity to discuss your expectations for this position and the above bullets, point by point.

▶ **Assistant Hospital Supervisor**

I would be interested in speaking with you further regarding this position.

▶ **Associate Desktop Publisher**

I will be visiting Richmond next week, and I would be happy to meet with you at your convenience.

▶ **Campus Police Officer**

I would like to discuss my qualifications and outline the potential I have to be a strong member of your security force.

▶ **Case Manager**

I would welcome a meeting to discuss my academic as well as professional background and to learn more about the undertakings of Any Agency.

▶ **Child Care Assistant Director**

During an interview I can elaborate upon qualifications cited in this letter and the Summary of Qualifications on my resume. Ideally, we might also discuss the inspiration I gained and sought to give as the author of the children's book *Home We Go!* I would appreciate the opportunity to speak to you further about this position.

▶ **Claims Adjuster**

I hope I can share my qualifications for the Claims Adjuster position with Any Insurance. My salary requirements are appropriate for the position, so please let's discuss my desire to become a strong contributor to your claims efforts.

▶ **Customer Service Manager**

It would be with enthusiasm and confidence that I would interview for this exciting opportunity. I do hope that after you review my resume, as well as the attached training memos, that you will wish to discuss my customer service experience.

▶ **Dental Hygienist**

I look forward to meeting with you and further discussing my desires to join your team.

▶ **Dentistry Department Manager**

Through a telephone or in-person interview, I can detail information regarding the above accomplishments and learn more about your visions for the dentistry department.

▶ **Director of Public Works**

I am confident of my ability to direct an efficient, cost-effective, and productive department. In order to translate this confidence into performance-focused outcomes, I must convince you and your selection committee colleagues of my potential to serve as the next Director of Public Works. I will call your office next week to see if it would be appropriate to schedule a meeting.

▶ **Editor**

I do hope to have the chance to expand upon the above bullets and describe how much my efforts at Books R Cool prepared me to succeed at Any Corporation.

▶ **Event Planner**

I welcome the opportunity to meet with you to further discuss my qualifications and your expectations for Any Corporation's next Event Planner.

▶ **Film Archivist**

I will call soon to confirm receipt of this e-mail and, I do hope, to arrange a telephone or in-person interview.

▶ **Fundraiser**

I look forward to speaking with you about my qualifications and your expectations for the Fundraiser who will be joining you and your Any Organization colleagues.

▶ **Gemologist**

After you have reviewed my qualifications, I would appreciate interviewing with you for this position. Perhaps an initial telephone conversation could be followed by a lengthier in-person discussion?

▶ **Home Economics Department Coordinator**

I will be in Seattle next week. Would it be possible to meet to discuss my qualifications for this position?

▶ **Hospital Administrator**

Through a telephone or in-person interview I can reiterate the qualifications presented in this letter and on the accompanying resume. Most important, during our meeting I can learn about your goals for Any Health Resource Corporation and your expectations for the next Hospital Administrator.

▶ **Hotel Manager**

I would welcome the chance to speak by phone or in person regarding this position. I will be attending the Hospitality Association Conference next week. If you will be there, perhaps we could meet then?

▶ **International Buyer**

I do hope that you will allow me the opportunity to expand upon the attached resume via an interview.

▶ **Legal Assistant**

During an initial telephone interview and, subsequent to my relocation, via an in-person meeting, I would be happy to detail my qualifications and motivations to join Any Law Firm as a Legal Assistant.

▶ **Television Camera Operator**

I look forward to sharing my tapes with you and interviewing for this position. I hope to hear from you regarding a mutually convenient meeting.

These phrases express the candidates' intentions to make future contact.

▶ **Meeting Planner**

I will call to discuss your thoughts regarding an interview and, ideally, to creatively share ideas about your next events.

▶ **Multimedia Specialist**

Of course, I will call to discuss your thoughts regarding my candidacy.

▶ **Newspaper Intern**

I will call your office next week to confirm receipt of my resume and inquire about the possibility of an interview.

▶ **Office Receptionist**

I will call to discuss your thoughts regarding next steps.

▶ **Pharmacist**

I will call to confirm receipt of this e-mail and to arrange either an in-person or telephone interview.

▶ **Political Staffer**

I will call to discuss your thoughts regarding my candidacy and, if you believe appropriate, to arrange an interview.

▶ **Production Quality Control Manager**

I will call to confirm receipt of this fax (originals to follow in the mail) and to discuss your assessment of my background.

▶ **Public Relations Associate**

I will call to confirm receipt of this letter and, if you judge it appropriate, to arrange an interview at a mutually convenient time and date.

▶ **Publisher's Assistant**

I will call in a week to schedule a convenient time to discuss my qualifications and your expectations.

▶ **Researcher**

I will call to confirm receipt of this letter and to discuss your thoughts regarding whether a phone or in-person interview would be appropriate.

▶ **Restaurant Manager Trainee**

I will call to confirm receipt of this fax (originals will follow in the mail) and to arrange a mutually convenient time and date for an interview.

These phrases show how you might indicate that a reference will be in touch or that transcripts and/or a letter of recommendation is forthcoming.

▶ **Biomedical Engineer**

I will e-mail a copy of my transcript and a letter of recommendation soon to further support my candidacy.

▶ **Operations Manager**

In addition, soon I will be forwarding a reference list and letters of recommendation to support my candidacy. I trust all documentation assists you with your deliberations.

▶ **Preschool Director**

To assist with your deliberation, I asked the first person listed on the attached reference page to contact you regarding my abilities.

▶ **Translator**

Also find enclosed letters of recommendation.

These phrases very simply thank the reader of the cover letter for their consideration. There are many ways to word this, although the message is more or less the same.

▶ **Pharmaceutical Sales**

I appreciate your reviewing the attached documents, and I look forward to hearing from you soon.

▶ **Purchasing Agent**

I appreciate your consideration of my candidacy and look forward to your reply. Thank you.

▶ **State Administrator**

I appreciate your time and look forward to speaking with you.

▶ **Store Manager**

Thank you for reviewing my credentials. I look forward to speaking with you.

Chapter 3

Phrases to Use When Contacting Targeted Employers

THESE PROACTIVE COVER LETTERS ARE SELF-INITIATED, meaning you're not sending them in response to a specific job listing. While review of web-based information or printed materials may spark interest, nothing has fueled the flames of reactive efforts. In this section, sample phrases are divided between two types of cover letters:

1. Cold contact letters. When making cold contact in the form of a cover letter, you are not responding to a posting or contacting someone at the advice of others. These cover letters can be effective. The more focused they are, and the more you reveal knowledge of the job and employer, the better. In these cover letters, company-specific information must be changed letter to letter.

2. Broadcast letters. These are distributed to many employers, and they are less focused. Their format may appear similar to other letters, and it is most important to have the company name appear prominently early. While less company-specific information is contained, you must still show readers that you know the organization's name and the nature of the business. Broadcast letters can be good first efforts and momentum builders if you maintain appropriate expectations and follow up effectively.

When broadcasting your availability, share with readers potential titles and functional areas of interest. They must be dynamic *Here I am, here is what I do best, and let's talk about how I can succeed* letters.

Cold Contact Letters:
Phrases for Introductory Paragraphs

When you contact a potential employer without responding to a specific job posting, it's important to begin your cover letter by clearly stating your intentions. The phrases that follow contain examples of how individuals have expressed their interest in working for the companies they've contacted. Notice how many examples show that the candidates possess some knowledge of each company's present or future business plans.

▶ Administrative Assistant

Upon review of Any Corporation's website, I am motivated to share my availability for an Administrative Assistant position. While no specific opportunities were posted, I want to express my strong desire to meet with you to share motivations and qualifications and to seek consideration for current or anticipated openings.

▶ Admissions Counselor

Now, through this letter, I seek consideration for a position within your office.

▶ Advertising Sales Associate

Given past sales achievements and a desire for a future career in advertising, I would like to explore opportunities at Any Station.

▶ Associate Editor

Ideally, you will find my background strong enough to warrant consideration for an editorial post at Any Publishing. Specifically, I am seeking a position as an Associate Editor, Project Editor, or equivalent in new book or journal development.

▶ Audiovisual Specialist

To initiate consideration for audiovisual opportunities with your company, attached is a resume for your review.

▶ **Chef**

As Any Hotel completes its renovations and will soon expand wedding-planning efforts, I seek to join your team and, as your mission statement cites, "blend customer service and culinary excellence with profitability."

▶ **Computer Software Designer**

I do hope Any Corporation is now recruiting or will do so in the near future. I understand you and your colleagues are now working on major government contracts for specialized applications, next generations of your popular and profitable Any Software programs, and numerous research and development projects.

▶ **Editorial Assistant**

I would like to interview for an assistant position or an internship in the editorial department at Any Magazine. It would be wonderful if I could utilize existing skills and knowledge within the context of my goal to work for a music- and lifestyle-related publication.

▶ **Elementary School Teacher**

It is with great enthusiasm for, and commitment to, elementary education that I inquire about teaching positions at Any Private School.

▶ **Financial Analyst**

Now, as I seek to relocate to the St. Louis area, it is with great excitement that I wish to discuss my potential to contribute to the finance area of Any Corporation.

▶ **Marketing Director**

It would be with continued professional pride, ambition, and goal-direction that I would serve as a Marketing Director, Brand Manager, or related title at Any Corporation. Please grant me the opportunity to discuss my hopes for the future, as well as your goals for your organization during an interview.

▶ **Mutual Funds Broker**

Described with pride and in detail on the enclosed resume, I have over a decade of experience within the financial services area. Now, as I look ahead to future challenges and, of course, rewards, I seek to focus on a specialized area of expertise—mutual funds. Therefore, it is with great confidence gained from a history of success and the enthusiasm of seeking new opportunities that I seek consideration for a brokerage position at Any Brokers.

▶ **School and Community Counseling**

In anticipation of relocation to Dallas, I have researched a number of facilities and become particularly intrigued by Any Center's offerings. Therefore, I would welcome consideration for a full-time counseling position.

Phrases for Motivational
and Qualification Paragraphs

In these sample phrases, the candidates describe their interests, experiences, skills, and accomplishments as they relate to the companies' businesses. You might feel a little awkward talking yourself up, but remember—you've reached out cold to a company that doesn't know anything about you. You need to make yourself stand out.

▶ **Administrative Assistant**

Most recently, I worked as a receptionist with Other Consulting, where I gained exposure to all facets of administrative support, specifically for a firm like Any Corporation that markets and provides state-of-the art information technology services. I am well aware of Any Corporation's commitment to "excellence in specialized customer service," as stated in your mission statement.

▶ **Advertising Sales Associate**

I believe the ratings and demographics of the station could be effectively marketed to both large and small local, regional, and national businesses, focusing on youth and male target audiences. The newly acquired WWE programming should be an Advertising Sales Associate's greatest asset.

▶ Computer Software Designer

I am confident I can be a successful Computer Software Designer at Any Corporation. I have considerable experience with DBMS packages, like Oracle, Ingres, DB2, FoxPro, and OS/2 Data Manager.

Competencies include Unix, C, SAS, Pascal, and a variety of other programming languages, including (but not limited to) SUNOS, DOS, and VAX operating systems. I have used, taught, and provided user support for graphics, spreadsheet, database, desktop publishing, word processing, and telecommunication applications.

▶ Elementary School Teacher

As you prepare to dedicate the new Blake Entertainment Center I am confident that you and your Any School colleagues, parents, and students anticipate expanded music instruction, choral, and performance offerings. I would like to discuss how my background could address these special goals, as well as those associated with traditional classroom instruction.

▶ Financial Analyst

Any Corporation's growth over the past years, including expansion to Canadian and Mexican markets and the aggressive acquisition of smaller competitors, requires strong financial oversight and flow of information to key decision makers. I am confident in my ability to set up and manage financial analysis and credit leveraging systems, procedures and controls, and employee-training programs that will address Any Corporation's expanding needs.

▶ Fundraiser

Fulfilling Any Organization's mission "to enhance the potential for young men and women to maximize educational and career opportunity" would be a personal and professional passion.

▶ Management Consulting Analyst

Ideally, I will contribute to the following practice areas: financial analysis, management strategies, and business development. Detailed in the attached resume, I detail my fine-tuned research, analysis, and writing capabilities.

▶ Marketing Director

Qualifications for a related position with Any Corporation, a manufacturer and marketer of optical scanning and mapping devices, are all cited on my resume, along with details of all achievements.

▶ Public Relations Assistant

Media relationships were developed as I selected and placed models for television commercials. I have the skills to coordinate creative programs and innovative functions involving clients and the general public, and, clearly, I feel confident I could successfully apply my experience to a position in your firm.

▶ School and Community Counselor

I have counseled clients ranging in ages from four to twenty-four and specifically addressed ADHD, ODD, and learning disabilities within a team context, including teachers, parents, outside professionals, and the student in planning and implementation. So, it would be an ideal next professional step to work at Any Center with adolescents dealing with many of the issues cited and using a rational emotive and behavioral approach to treatment.

▶ Television Production Assistant

Last summer, and most relevant to my request to interview for a PA position, I worked as an intern for KBZT-TV's "Island Beat." In this capacity I had the opportunity to co-produce a local talk show, which required that I pre-interview and schedule guests, handle financial and transportation details, and research show topics. I also networked resource organizations to locate potential guests and panel members. I wish to bring all the talents, ambition, and commitment I nurtured as an intern and a student to Any Station. While most interested in PA opportunities, I would welcome consideration for an internship as well.

In some cases, it will be appropriate to describe your accomplishments using a list. The following lists show what the candidates hope to accomplish, what type of work interests them, and what type of work they are qualified to perform. The lists are short in length, and each bullet point is concisely written.

▶ **Admissions Counselor**

I would like to become associated with Any University and educate potential applicants, parents, and guidance counselors regarding:

- A curriculum that allows students to learn what they love, and love what they learn.
- Specialized offerings like the Early Medical Scholars, Take 5, Study Abroad, Internships, The Senior Scholar Program, 3-2 Programs, and Certificate programs.

▶ **Audiovisual Specialist**

It would be with great focus and confidence that I would like to assist Any Corporation with:

- Creating and maintaining multimedia presentations as well as web-based presentations.
- Purchasing, scheduling, and setting up equipment as needed.
- Providing user support for all who develop presentations and use related equipment.

▶ **Mutual Funds Broker**

Highlighting all I wish to discuss during an interview, my qualifications include:

- More than a decade of progressively significant roles and achievements within planning portfolio management and client services.
- Personal responsibilities for more than $210 million in client assets
- Recognition for outstanding asset-based performance and customer services.
- Service as trainer and curriculum developer after completion of the ABC Financial Consultant Sales Training and Advanced Training.
- Licensed Series 6, 7, 63, and health and life insurance.

Phrases for Closing Paragraphs

In this section of your cover letter, your goal is to secure an interview by making yourself appear available and interested. You're reinforcing everything you said in your first and second paragraphs. Naturally, you'll close by thanking your contact for his or her consideration and review.

▶ Admissions Counselor

I will call your office to confirm receipt of this e-mail (originals to follow in the mail) and, I hope, to arrange either a formal employment interview or informal discussion regarding anticipated opportunities.

▶ Advertising Sales Associate

I want to discuss your reactions to this letter and accompanying resume and assess your thoughts regarding adding a new sales professional to your team.

▶ Associate Editor

I will be relocating to the New York area later this summer, so I will be available to begin employment anytime thereafter. I will be in New York next week. Could we meet then?

▶ **Audiovisual Specialist**

The nature of your manufacturing and marketing of consumer products, specifically all promotions, sales, and marketing efforts, requires a variety of audiovisual needs. I look forward to speaking with you about how I can creatively and enthusiastically address those needs.

▶ **Chef**

Perhaps we could begin discussions of potential opportunities by phone. I will call to confirm receipt of this letter and to discuss next steps.

▶ **Computer Software Designer**

Please, let's talk soon about current or future opportunities at Any Corporation. I look forward to hearing from you and meeting you.

▶ **Editorial Assistant**

I will call to confirm receipt of my resume and, at your convenience, to arrange an initial phone interview and in-person meeting. Chicago is home, so I am actively exploring opportunities in the area, and I will be visiting for interviews regularly.

▶ **Elementary School Teacher**

Please, let's meet to discuss your assessment of my potential to be a strong member of Any School's instructional team.

▶ **Financial Analyst**

I would appreciate the opportunity to discuss your visions for the finance area of Any Corporation and how I might contribute as an analyst.

▶ **Investment Banking Analyst**

I would welcome the chance to discuss my qualifications for an Analyst position when you visit campus. If it would be more convenient for me to visit New York City, I would be happy to do so.

▶ Librarian

Could we arrange an interview to discuss how I may best contribute to the staff of Any Library? I will call to confirm receipt of this e-mail and arrange a meeting when we can discuss any current or anticipated openings for a librarian.

▶ Mutual Funds Broker

Please, let's talk about my potential to succeed at Any Brokers, about my desires to either expand your business on the island, and, if more appropriate, about my willingness to relocate to Southern California.

▶ Public Relations Assistant

Please allow me the opportunity to directly share motivations as well as qualifications via an interview. I will be in Los Angeles at the end of the month and wonder if it would be possible to arrange for an interview?

▶ School and Community Counseling

I hope we can meet to discuss anticipated openings and how my background might match Any Center's needs.

Broadcast Letters

Phrases for Introductory Paragraphs

You're writing a broadcast letter, which means you're probably sending it out to quite a few companies. You'll want to create a descriptive statement about your experience that you can use in most of your letters. For that reason, it should be general enough that it can apply to almost any cover letter you send out, and it should be specific in a way that catches the recipient's eye.

▶ Administrative Assistant

Are you currently in need of an Administrative Assistant with over a decade of experience and a commitment to supporting the needs of patients and supervisors, and working effectively with peers? If yes, please review the attached resume and consider my candidacy for a position with Any Company.

▶ Admissions and Enrollment Management

I trust the enclosed resume, specifically the Admissions Achievements section, highlights my capabilities for an Admissions and Enrollment Management position. Within professional capacities I have held titles of Senior Assistant Director and Director of International Recruitment, as well as Assistant Director and Counselor.

▶ Chiropractor

I am a certified chiropractor currently exploring affiliations with established practices. Cited on the attached resume, I have worked in the Chicago area for over twenty years and, as a result, my reputation for quality care is well known.

▶ Credit Manager

I am seeking a position as Credit Manager, to which I bring many years of successful credit management experience.

▶ Freight Supervisor

During the past thirteen years, I have been actively involved in positions as field manager of container operations and night operations supervisor of freight stations and service centers, dealing with domestic and international freight deliveries.

▶ Senior Vice President (Banking)

As you know, because of our regular interactions as members of the Missouri Bankers Association, I am currently a Senior Vice President at Central St. Louis Bank. The recent acquisition of CSB necessitates my communicating with other financial institutions, actively seeking consideration for a SVP position.

Phrases for Motivational and Qualification Paragraphs

This is where you need to expand on your brief descriptive statement that you used in the intro paragraph. You've hooked your reader, now tell them why you're right for the job.

▶ **Administrative Assistant**

Detailed on the attached resume, I have worked in a hospital setting where I learned all critical terminology, how to address specialized billing and support issues, and what is required to support the needs of physicians, nurses, and healthcare practitioners. I now am actively seeking the opportunity to return to a challenging and rewarding medical setting.

▶ **Admissions and Enrollment Management**

With the assistance of colleagues, I doubled the number of international candidates completing applications and interviews and those receiving offers to enroll at Seton Hall University. In-depth knowledge of admissions and enrollment strategies and processes and appreciation for how academic, athletic, co-curricular, and residential communities can be marketed make me an enthusiastic and qualified candidate for a position at Any School.

▶ **Chiropractor**

Currently, I work as a chiropractic therapist with the Chicago Chiropractic Center, a position I have held for the past fifteen years. In this capacity I provide spinal manipulation and handle necessary musculoskeletal needs of sports injury patients, alleviate pain in elderly and work-related patients, and assist the industrial-accident-injured in regaining strength and stamina.

I, like you and your Any Practice colleagues, am an active member of the American Chiropractic Association, Illinois Chiropractic Society, Chicago Chiropractic Society, and Sports Injury Council of the American Chiropractic Association.

▶ **Credit Manager**

During the past ten years, as credit manager with a $20 million manufacturing and distribution firm, I have successfully set up and enforced credit controls, resulting in reducing DSO from sixty days to thirty-three. I am continually involved in training personnel in credit and collection policies and procedures, troubleshooting and resolving sales and customer disputes, and making credit and collection decisions to reduce bad debt risk and increase cash flow.

Based on my past contributions to the credit profession, I received recognition, through NACM New England, as Credit Executive of the Year in 2010 and was elected the president of the same professional credit association for the 2009–2010 term.

▶ **Freight Supervisor**

In addition to supervising day-to-day operations, my experience encompasses hiring, training, and supervising drivers and office and support personnel, and providing cost-effective, quality service within a multiple-service network. I have sound knowledge of computer systems for freight movement management and I am skilled in both troubleshooting and resolving problems relative to the movement of materials and the people to make these activities possible.

▶ **Marketing/Sales Executive**

During an interview I will share how past successes below required skills that will lead to future achievements with Any Corporation. Sales and marketing accomplishments to date include:

- Developing sales programs and new businesses to increase penetration, market share, and revenue, using advanced, technically sophisticated systems-management services.
- Participating in development and marketing teams for new service products for a service business generating $3.7 billion worldwide.
- Assuming P&L responsibility for an added-value services business generating $90 million.
- Establishing a record for producing positive bottom-line results in a high-tech, service-oriented business with worldwide markets.

▶ **Optics Researcher**

Noted on the attached resume, I will be graduating in December from the University of Rochester. I have experience working as a researcher and as an optical engineer. Specifically, through experiences at Sine Patterns, I developed qualifications applicable to Any Corporation, including:

- Abilities to operate microlithography and photographic equipment.
- Capacities to transform stated needs of customers into completed products including optical masks, resolution charts, reticles, and custom film.
- Knowledge of product management and quality control issues.
- Specialized skills associated with team and independent tasks and projects.

Phrases for Closing Paragraphs

Keep it simple. The key phrases used in closing paragraphs don't vary much among different types of cover letters. In the case of a broadcast letter, you're requesting to hear from the company based on whether they have a position available that your expertise could serve.

▶ **Admissions and Enrollment Management**

I will inquire soon to confirm receipt of this letter, to learn if you are currently expanding your operation, and to identify appropriate next steps.

▶ **Chiropractor**

I look forward to hearing from you if my qualifications are of interest.

▶ **Credit Manager**

I look forward to hearing from you if you have a suitable position available, or if you have any referrals.

▶ **Freight Supervisor**

I would welcome the opportunity to discuss whether Any Corporation has a need for someone with my background and whether you would be willing to consider me for immediate or future employment.

▶ **Marketing/Sales Executive**

I am well qualified to direct areas that are key to achieving your sales and profit objectives. If you have such a position open, I look forward to hearing from you.

▶ **Optics Researcher**

Because I will be available to start immediately after receipt of my degree, around January 1, I would certainly appreciate the opportunity to speak with you soon regarding your anticipated hiring needs.

▶ **Senior Vice President (Banking)**

Although my present position is challenging, and I have a record of success within these capacities, my future is with another organization, like Any Bank. Ideally, my next position will addresses both national and international banking markets and I will be called upon to continue an accomplishment-filled career as a leader, motivator, and achiever. Let's discuss your reactions to my request for consideration.

Chapter 4

Cover Letters to Employment Agencies and Search Professionals

THE COVER LETTER PHRASES IN THIS CHAPTER are directed to employment agencies and search professionals.

Employment agencies most often deal with temporary, temp-to-perm, or entry-level opportunities. In truth, they don't find jobs for people, they find candidates for jobs posted with them. Search professionals, or headhunters as they are called, regularly source candidates and they also seek retainer or contingency relationships with potential employers. Once employers post, these professionals screen information from candidates to determine those who match. Most often, search professionals deal with management or executive level candidates and opportunities or with very specialized fields.

Search professionals also don't find jobs for people, they find people for jobs that have been posted with them. Cover letters must inspire search professionals to interview and, ultimately, select you as worthy of referral to an employer. If they believe you will get an offer, they envision their contingency or retainer payment already earned, so they are motivated to advocate on your behalf.

Cover Letter Phrases to Use When Contacting Employment Agencies

Phrases for Introductory Paragraphs

What can a staffing/search firm do for you? For the recipient of your cover letter to know the answer to that question, you need to be direct about what type of job you're looking for, and you need to present yourself as a go-getter.

► **Accounting Manager**
The enclosed resume outlines my diverse and in-depth experience in accounting and finance management. I am in search of an appropriate opportunity in the greater Missouri area.

► **Bookkeeper**
If one of your clients is in need of a highly motivated bookkeeper with the experience and enthusiasm needed to handle the day-to-day details necessary to insure smooth operation, I would appreciate your consideration of my candidacy on behalf of that client.

► **Claims Processor**
As a qualified and motivated candidate with a record of past achievements, I now seek opportunities to continue an accomplishment-focused career in claims with a firm that has now posted an opportunity with Any Staffing Firm. I trust you recall that a number of years ago I communicated with you and your colleague, Francis Williams, regarding my interest in claims, and you placed me at Marifield Rehab. Now, I seek your professional assistance again.

► **Chef**
I will be moving to the Dayton area and I would like the assistance of Any Staffing Firm as I search for exciting new positions.

The advertisement in Today's Cook is most appealing; I would like to be considered for this particular position. Your announcement also inspires confidence that you will have other client postings that match my qualifications.

▶ Dental Assistant

I am conducting a search for a full-time or part-time position in the Indianapolis area. I have heard about your agency's placement record through several colleagues, so I am very enthusiastic that you may now or soon have client postings that match my professional abilities.

▶ Executive Assistant

Currently, I am seeking appropriate career opportunities in the corporate arena. This particular posting seems ideal, but I would also welcome your consideration for any other client postings you believe match my background.

▶ Legal Administrator

I have recently relocated to Florida and I would like the assistance of Any Staffing Firm to locate a court or paralegal-related Administrator position with one of your clients.

▶ Research and Development Position

I will be relocating to your area next month and I would be interested in a position in which to apply my chemical, electromechanical, and mechanical research skills. I believe I would be a good match for a progressive, technically oriented company seeking support in research, manufacturing, or production. Your professional views and assistance with my job search would be most welcomed.

▶ Sales/Customer Service Representative

I enjoyed our brief conversation at the New Jersey Sales and Marketing Expo. As you now know, I am actively seeking new, challenging, and rewarding sales or customer service opportunities. I am now formally requesting the assistance of your agency with my search.

Phrases for Motivational and Qualification Paragraphs

In these paragraphs, you'll describe your practical experience. Mentioning your current salary is appropriate here because it will help a recruiter make a better match for you. Be honest about your skills and experience; the more accurately you can communicate your strengths, the better chance you'll have of finding work through a staffing/search firm.

▶ Bookkeeper
Although my preference is to stay in Hawaii, I would consider relocation to California, so referral to one of your California offices would be welcomed. Salary, benefits, and future opportunity for growth will influence my enthusiasm for particular opportunities that may now be available via Any Staffing Firm. My present salary is $38,000, so I am motivated to maximize my earnings and increase this amount by at least 10 percent.

▶ Chef
Areas of expertise include all aspects of food preparation and presentation, as well as kitchen management including ordering, hiring, and training. I now work at the McGuiness Inn and I will leave this establishment with positive references and a history of planning seasonal menus, overseeing all preparation of traditional American cuisine. In addition to cooking to order, I perform in scheduling, controlling inventory, and customer relations roles.

▶ Dental Assistant
Highlighting all that is detailed on the resume and revealed through the attached letter of recommendation, my qualifications are as follows:

- Over six years of experience as a dental assistant, contributing to direct patient care and patient relations.
- Recognition from National Education Center as dental assistant honors graduate.
- Certification in first aid, cardiopulmonary resuscitation, and electrocardiography.
- Additional experience as receptionist/secretary with an executive search/management consulting firm, a financial management company, and realty firms.

▶ Executive Assistant

In addition to five years of staff experience at Bradstreet and Associates, I have worked for three years as Executive Assistant to the president and to the executive vice president of a software development company.

▶ Legal Assistant

As described on the enclosed resume, in Washington, D.C., I was a Legal Assistant for a well-respected law firm. There my responsibilities included completion of legal research, drafting and proofing documents, interviewing witnesses and clients, and preparing documentation needed to support litigation activities of attorneys.

As a result I have highly refined technical and organizational skills, including comprehensive computer expertise. I have extensive experience working on multiple projects and meeting deadlines in a team-oriented legal environment.

▶ Research and Development

Some colleagues identify my greatest strengths as related to building and maintenance of testing equipment, prototypes, and maintenance of manufacturing equipment.

▶ **Sales/Customer Service Representative**

My current ambition is to gain management and supervisory responsibilities. I am willing to travel and I would be interested in a salary in the $35,000 to $45,000 range.

▶ **Security Guard**

For the past three years as a bank Security Guard, I was responsible for ensuring the safety and security of customers, bank employees, and bank assets. My compensation for that position was about $30,000. I am an experienced, motivated, and well-trained professional. I do hope that Any Staffing Firm has current clients, and related postings, that match my background.

Phrases to Use for Closing Paragraphs

When writing to a recruitment/talent acquisition firm, a strong closing paragraph requests a meeting (or at least suggests future communication) and communicates confidence in your candidacy for a position that matches your interests. Always be sure to thank the agency for their time and review of the materials you submit.

▶ **Accounting Manager**

I do hope that you judge me qualified for one or more searches being conducted by Any Employment. After we speak, I trust you will refer my candidacy to employers who have posted those opportunities with you.

▶ **Claims Processor**

I would very much like to discuss all of my professional and personal goals, including salary, with you or one of your Any Staffing Firm partners.

▶ **Chef**

Perhaps we could meet to discuss my ambitions and qualifications? Ideally, you now have employers in search of candidates and

I could also interview with them during my upcoming visit. Also, please be aware that I would welcome consideration for positions within an hour commute from Dayton.

▶ Dental Assistant

I am available to start as soon as needed, and relocation is easy to arrange. Please, let's talk by phone regarding appropriate next steps, and should you judge appropriate, arrange an in-person meeting. I would be happy to travel to Indianapolis to meet with you or one of your clients whenever necessary.

▶ Executive Assistant

I hope you identify my candidacy as worthy of referral to those who posted the Executive Assistant position, and to other clients. I do believe Any Staffing Firm can help me with my overall job search.

▶ Legal Administrator

I hope you will find me a qualified candidate for the position posted and refer me to the client seeking to hire the Legal Administrator. I also hope you have additional clients who have engaged you to find candidates for immediate full-time or part-time opportunities.

▶ Research and Development

Please, let's discuss by phone your thoughts regarding my candidacy and whether Any Staffing Firm might help. Do you know of any openings that match my qualifications? Would you refer me to an employer interview? What are the appropriate next steps?

▶ Sales/Customer Service Representative

I would be interested in further discussing my candidacy and identifying any employment opportunities you feel would be applicable to my skills. Please do keep my candidacy confidential and I respectfully request that you or any prospective employers only contact references cited in the contract.

Cover Letter Phrases to Use When Contacting Executive Search Firms:

Phrases for Introductory Paragraphs

These letters begin much like letters to employment agencies. If anything, your introductory paragraph may focus more heavily on your work experience. Check out these samples to see how you might start this cover letter.

▶ **Director of Information Services**

During our meeting at the Minority Professional Recruiting Expo, we discussed opportunities with your client firms that are of great interest to me. As we discussed, I am currently seeking a challenging environment where I can apply my combined technical knowledge, experience, and ability to create and implement innovative concepts for greater information systems efficiency.

▶ **Management Consultant**

To date, I have played a key role in designing, implementing, reorganizing, and managing a variety of functions—including operations, manufacturing, materials, engineering, and quality assurance—for nationally and internationally recognized corporations. The attached resume documents past achievements. My contact with you reveals ambitions for future challenges and rewards.

▶ **Operations Manager**

Any Search Firm is well known within the industry, so I am confident that ours will be a positive and mutually beneficial relationship. I am actively seeking a new and challenging position and I am confident that, ultimately, you will find me a candidate easy to place.

▶ Plant Manager

During the past ten years, I have held positions ranging from production supervisor to plant and operations manager with a $16 million manufacturer and importer of electrical products. I am now seeking a new position where I can contribute to a company's cost-effective, quality operation and profitability.

▶ Senior Accountant

The varied accounting, finance, and general management experience gained over the course of my career should be of interest to you as you conduct current or future client searches. As you may recall, you once contacted me regarding a Senior Accountant position, but at that time I was not ready to seek new opportunities. Well, now I am ready, willing, and eager to do so.

Phrases for Motivational and Qualification Paragraphs

Why are you qualified for the type of job you seek? What are your areas of expertise? What have you accomplished in past positions? You must highlight this information in your cover letter, specifically in these paragraphs

▶ Director of Information Services

Qualifications, all detailed on the resume attached to this e-mail, include the following:

- Thirteen years of experience with MIS corporate information systems.
- Experience operating and supervising administrative functions of several UNIX systems.
- Skill communicating with domestic and international networks, mainframes, and network system support.

- Ability to work as a team member, team leader, and/or independent contributor, working offsite via modem and data network, to assist users in sales, finance, manufacturing, and production.
- Ability to generate positive results in a company's information systems and networks by streamlining systems and improving user training and performance.

▶ Management Consultant

Currently, I am seeking a position within management consulting. I strongly believe this firm, and their clients can benefit from my twenty years of progressively responsible management experience. Areas of expertise, and those that can ultimately yield value-added assets within consulting roles, are diverse and include the following:

- Five years as director of operations for a $60 million manufacturer.
- Over six years as materials manager with a multi-plant, multi-warehouse, $10 million manufacturer of industrial rubber products.
- Over nine years as manufacturing coordinator with a toy manufacturer, with responsibilities related to expansion of existing manufacturing and support facilities, setup of new facilities, manpower planning, union relations, and capital equipment investment and materials purchases.

▶ Operations Manager

Because of diversity of past achievements, I am able to transfer skills to marketing, manufacturing, distribution, and service of other products. In addition to a strong marketing and sales background, I have also established a record for setting up, staffing, and managing top-producing, profitable district sales and service operations.

▶ Plant Manager

In my current position as plant manager, I developed a stable workforce and environment following a restructuring. Under my direction, the company has benefited from efficient supervisory staff and support personnel in all phases of plant operations, including production, purchasing, inventory control, warehousing, distribution, and maintenance of a 325,000-square-foot facility.

▶ Senior Accountant

As a manufacturing plant controller, I managed accounting activities of a $35 million manufacturing plant. Accomplishments include:

- Preparing, analyzing, and presenting P&L, balance sheet, departmental expense, manufacturing variance, and other operating reports.
- Preparing $2 million annual departmental operating budgets, analyzing results, initiating required operational improvements, and preparing forecasts.
- Developing annual strategic and operational improvements, resulting in a 15 percent increase in efficiency.
- Overseeing human resources, purchasing, payroll, and other plant administrative functions.
- Maintaining quality accounting operations by implementing internal controls testing programs.

Phrases for Closing Paragraphs

If you're planning a move (or are currently in the process of relocating) or need to keep your search confidential, now's the time to say so. Set the agency's expectations. This includes salary requirements. It should be noted that this is one of the rare times when discussing salary in a cover letter is acceptable. Request a response from the agency, and as usual, be sure to say thank you.

▶ Director of Information Services

Relocation is not a problem, target cities remain Chicago, Boston, and San Francisco, and my compensation requirements are in the low $70,000 range. Please keep my candidacy confidential and do let's continue our conversations regarding opportunities as they arise.

▶ Management Consultant

Please review your current contingency and retainer client relationships to determine those that might match my strengths. I would greatly appreciate your consideration and, ultimately, your referrals for interviews with one, or more of these consulting organizations or with a firm seeking to hire an internal consultant.

▶ Operations Manager

Should you be aware of an advanced marketing and development position in the $100,000–$150,000 range, please consider me an eager and qualified candidate. I would welcome your assistance with my search efforts and I would be happy to discuss my background with you or one of your client firms at any time.

▶ Plant Manager

I would welcome the opportunity to apply my proven track record to one of your client firms. Relocation is not a problem. While salary and compensation is negotiable, my current salary is in the low $70s, so I would anticipate a new position to offer an increase or the potential to earn more. Please, let's discuss my candidacy and how Any Search might assist me with my search.

▶ Senior Accountant

While my prime interest is securing a position on the East Coast, I am willing to relocate for the right opportunity and compensation (ideally $85,000–$95,000, annually).

Chapter 5

Cover Letter
Phrases to Use
When **Networking**

THE SAMPLE COVER LETTER PHRASES IN THIS SECTION illustrate the best ways to solicit and use referrals, use past contacts, and make new ones. Two types of letters are highlighted here: networking letters and networking notes. Here's how they differ:

1. Networking letters. These are actual solicitations for particular positions or, in some cases, requests for referrals. Most often, these are proactive documents addressed to people who can grant consideration or offer names of others who might also consider candidates for employment. Occasionally, they are reactive documents, when a particular person's name is cited as supporting your candidacy for a specific job. These are regularly the same length as any cover letter, and their format and content may appear quite similar to the samples you have already read. Persuading the recipient to review the attached or enclosed resume is clearly the main purpose of these letters.

2. Networking notes. These are brief and personal notes that are intended to begin a process that will build momentum with each subsequent communication. Typically, they are brief (one or two paragraphs) and do not contain detailed summaries of qualifications. Resumes are attached or enclosed to share biographical information quickly, not to solicit consideration formally. These notes are most often e-mailed, but sometimes, still, they are handwritten and faxed or mailed when convenient. Do keep yours concise, focused, and enthusiastic.

When you network, you're engaging in person-to-person communication for specific purposes. Successful job seekers respond to postings, contact places on their hit lists and, of course, communicate with people, expressing desires to interview and find a great job. To be more successful at networking, consider these tips:

- Don't limit networking to existing contacts.
- Do expand your network via personal referrals, membership directories, or other listings.
- Don't ever be deceptive and ask for information about a career field when you really want consideration or referrals.
- Do honestly and clearly present goals or desired assistance of all you contact.
- Don't be presumptive, thinking all your contacts will respond immediately and positively.
- Do be persistent, patient, and enthusiastic when e-mailing, calling, faxing or mailing.
- Don't appear impersonal or as if you are conducting a mass-mailing networking campaign.

Upon review of the sample phrases that follow, you will be inspired to transform these dos and don'ts from words into successful actions.

Networking Letters

Phrases for Introductory Paragraphs

Networking is all about connections, so be sure to mention who gave you the contact information for the person you're reaching out to. If you established the connection on your own, remind him or her how you met (for example, perhaps you met at a conference or were seated next to each other on a plane). Be clear about why you're making contact. These phrases show a variety of ways to initiate a networking letter.

▶ Administrative Assistant

Recently, Francis Williams suggested I contact you regarding my job search. I am currently seeking a position that would use my legal, administrative, and office management knowledge and experience.

▶ Auto Salesperson

During a recent visit to Rochester, NY, my long-time friend Francis Williams mentioned your name as a contact in the field of auto sales. I understand that your corporation has contracted Bill's agency several times to promote your regional dealerships. I would like to take this opportunity to ask for any assistance or, ideally, consideration you might be able to provide with my job search.

▶ Bank Manager

Francis Williams, a colleague of mine at United Bank in St. Louis, MO, mentioned your name as an authority in the Midwest banking industry. Francis met you on a visit to your Omaha, NE, office last month and was impressed by both the reputation and successful operation of your branches. I now respectfully request advice, consideration, or referrals as I seek banking opportunities in the Omaha area, where I will be relocating next month.

▶ Chief Financial Officer

Ideally upon review of my resume you will feel comfortable identifying a few individuals, perhaps corporate clients of Any Bank, who I can present my candidacy to, as well as search professionals who specialize in my field.

▶ Customer Support Representative

I met with Dennis last week while on a business trip to Pittsburgh, PA, and he suggested that you might have an opening within the customer support department of your corporation and that as a result of your active involvement in the Pennsylvania Association of Customer Service professionals that you might have some suggestions regarding others I can present my candidacy to.

▶ Editor

John Curran, whom I saw recently at the ABA convention, spoke highly of your creative, market-sensitive approach to publishing and the tremendous impact you have had on Any Publishing. He also said you might have plans to expand your editorial team and suggested that I write you.

▶ Finance Manager

Kelly Monroe, of First Avenue Bank, informed me that Any Bank might be expanding its professional staff. Kelly once worked for me and can attest to my past performance and potential for future success. Based on my comprehensive experience in the field of finance, all detailed in the attached resume, I can offer your bank a broad range of management and technical skills.

▶ International Controller

It was a pleasure meeting you last month when we were both visiting the Maximillians at their home in Austin. As you may recall, I was then working as international controller of Other Company, a multi-division manufacturer of automatic test equipment. Recent ownership changes prompted me to seek a new position in finance management. When I spoke with Francis Maximillian regarding my search, I was strongly encouraged to request your assistance.

▶ Marketing Assistant

It was a pleasure talking to you during our flight to Chicago last April. I hope you enjoyed your trip! As you may recall, I was then a senior at Harvard University studying marketing and sales. You were kind enough to give me your business card with instructions to contact you once I was "liberated from the demands of academia." Finally, that day has arrived.

▶ **Marketing Specialist**

Thank you for taking the time to speak with me after your sales presentation last Thursday. As you may recall, I am now actively seeking consideration for a marketing position within Any Corporation. I have applied for a Marketing Specialist position via the online system, but your advice and support would be much appreciated. Are there individuals to whom I should send my resume and cover letter directly?

▶ **Mortgage/Loan Officer**

Francis Williams, one of your branch office managers and fellow alum of Any University, thought you might be interested in someone with my qualifications. I am currently seeking a new position with a bank or specialty lender as a mortgage loan officer. When I shared my goals with Francis, I was strongly encouraged to contact you immediately.

▶ **Nurse**

Kelly Williams, a nurse in your pediatric unit, suggested I contact you regarding the currently posted Nurse position at Any Hospital. Kelly believes that I have the qualifications, motivation, and special qualities needed to join her as a member of your care-focused nursing team, or "family," as she called it.

▶ **Payroll Supervisor**

I received your name from a mutual friend, Francis Williams. I was employed at Francis's bank several years ago and we worked closely on several projects. In a recent conversation, Francis mentioned that you were actively recruiting candidates for a payroll specialist. I hope upon review of the attached resume, that you will judge my candidacy as worthy of an employment interview.

▶ **Production Manager**

As Francis Williams may have informed you, as a result of a dramatic downsizing my production position was eliminated, so I am immediately available to interview for the Production Manager position now posted on Any Corporation's website. Francis is familiar with my managerial style and accomplishments, for he started his career in production under my supervision.

▶ **Publicist**

Francis Williams suggested I write you with regard to opportunities in advertising, public relations, and promotions. I would appreciate any information, advice or consideration you can provide as I search for Publicist or related positions.

▶ **Secretary**

Francis Williams suggested I apply for the Secretarial position recently posted on your company's website. As a current employee of Any Corporation, she is well aware of the qualifications and motivations you seek in administrative support professionals. As a past coworker, she is very familiar with my potential to join her on the Any Corporation team. I hope, after reviewing the attached resume you will find that my abilities and capabilities suit your needs and that I will be invited to interview for this position.

▶ **Staff Accountant**

It was a pleasure meeting you at the alumni luncheon last Monday, and kind of you to offer your assistance with my job search for a new and challenging accounting position. As you suggested, and following the instruction on the handout provided, I did register for and now have access to the online posting system and electronic alumni directory. Any additional assistance, advice, or referrals would be most welcomed.

▶ Telecommunications Specialist

A few years ago, I was your son Dan's classmate at the University of Miami. When I bumped into him last week in Billings, Montana, he informed me that you deal closely with several leading specialists in the telecommunications field and suggested I contact you immediately. At present, I am interested in joining a company where I can contribute strong skills and education in communications.

Phrases to Use for Motivational and Qualification Paragraphs

In these paragraphs, you can describe your experience and point out key skills or achievements listed on your resume. It's also okay to ask your contact for advice or assistance with your job search. The main objective, however, is to give your contact a reason to think of you first—above any other candidate—when he or she becomes aware of an open position that matches your experience.

▶ Auto Salesperson

Due to recent downsizing, I am seeking a new, long-term association with an aggressive, fast-paced dealership.

▶ Bank Manager

As my resume indicates, I am a skilled professional with over ten years of relevant experience. In addition to an MBA degree (Executive Program), I have five years' loan officer experience, and a BA degree in Economics and Finance.

▶ Marketing Assistant

Enclosed is a copy of my resume for your reference and referral. I am wondering if there are any Chicago-based individuals whom you would encourage me to contact. In particular, I would like to contact someone at Leo Burnett or Quaker Oats. Could I use your name in my correspondence with these persons? In addition, I would like to request consideration for a position with Any Corporation.

▶ Marketing Specialist

Detailed on the attached resume, during the past five years, my experience in my present marketing position focused on product management, strategic planning, marketing, and the sale of equipment, systems, chemicals, and related products and services. I am a strong contributing member of the team responsible for the worldwide marketing of bio-instrument chemicals sold to biotech markets, pharmaceutical markets, and research laboratories.

▶ Mortgage/Loan Officer

My current position as a senior collections specialist has provided me with the opportunity to accomplish and exceed a set objective of reducing delinquent loans from $24 million to $10 million within six months. At this point, I feel I have successfully surpassed both company and personal goals and am searching for new and greater challenges, particularly those that would involve marketing and client–relationship building responsibilities.

▶ Payroll Supervisor

My background encompasses eleven years of progressively responsible and sophisticated hands-on experience, including serving as a union benefits coordinator and human resources administrator. Most significant, in my present position as payroll administrator, with a special emphasis on the day-to-day details of related financial and MIS operations, I have gained particular expertise required of a Payroll Supervisor.

▶ Production Manager

As you can see from my resume, production-related experience extends throughout the last two decades. After completing a BS in Management, I entered the Other Company's management development program and found operations and production to be my greatest strengths. Several titles, progressively responsible positions, and promotions later I amassed supervisory and Production Management experience with the same large, Washington, D.C.–based corporation. While the firm is now downsizing, I remain eager to continue an accomplishment-filled career with Any Corporation.

▶ Publicist

As you will see after you review this document, I possess comprehensive experience supporting a successful direct-mail fundraising effort of a major university. Training and expertise also include publicity and public relations, staff training and supervision, program coordination, budget management, market research, copyediting, and management.

▶ Secretary

I now offer Any Corporation, skills I possess include:
- Administrative and customer service achievements spanning over six years.
- Abilities to use, support, and teach others Word, Access, Power-Point, Excel, and Internet applications.
- Bilingual Spanish–English abilities that have been used on the job.

▶ Telecommunications Specialist

My qualifications, all detailed on the enclosed resume, are as follows:
- A Bachelor of Arts in Communications that included courses, projects, and case studies addressing marketing, public relations, web design, and advertising issues.
- Experience with all planning and implementation areas of marketing, public relations, advertising, and sales.
- Bilingual German–English skills, and experience living and studying in Europe.

Phrases to Use for Closing Paragraphs

Don't be shy—ask for a meeting, a referral, or consideration for an existing open position with your contact's company. Here are some tactfully worded examples that show how you can express your interest and enthusiasm.

▶ Administrative Assistant

Should you know of any related openings or contacts I should forward a resume, I would appreciate your advice and referrals. Of course, if your firm were in need of a person with my background, your consideration would also be much appreciated.

▶ Auto Salesperson

I will be visiting the Rochester, NY, area next week and I would like to meet with you if your schedule permits. Your insight into the market, as well as any specific advice or contact names, would be very helpful.

▶ Bank Manager

During a brief telephone or in-person conversation, I could gain contact names within Any Bank, or within other area financial institutions, as well as any search professionals you think might be of assistance. Of course, if Any Bank would find my candidacy attractive, I would also welcome your consideration.

▶ Customer Support Representative

Could we meet so that I can further outline my qualifications and how I could contribute successfully to your firm? And, if appropriate, could you provide me with a list of additional contacts? I look forward to your advice, referrals, and, ideally, consideration for employment with Any Corporation.

▶ Finance Manager

I am confident I could contribute my expertise to the continued success of Any Bank and would welcome the chance to discuss career opportunities. My desire to relocate to the New York City area is strong, as is my willingness to travel, solicit new business, and become an accomplishment-driven professional on the Any Bank team.

▶ International Controller

Also, I will be visiting Austin, TX, again in two weeks. Should your schedule permit, I would like to meet, perhaps for lunch or dinner. This would allow me to thank you properly and personally for your assistance, and provide me the opportunity to gain additional insights you might have regarding my search efforts as they focus on Austin.

▶ Marketing Specialist

I appreciate your advice, consideration, and support of my candidacy and I look forward to speaking with you regarding appropriate next steps.

▶ Mortgage/Loan Officer

Thank you for your consideration. Of course, feel free to communicate with Francis or anyone on my reference list regarding my potential to be a performance-driven and very successful Loan Officer.

▶ Nurse

I trust you will agree with Kelly's views regarding my candidacy, and grant me the opportunity to interview for this position and support my credentials in person. Of course, I did complete the online application, but I wanted to personalize my candidacy via this letter, accompanying resume, and letters of recommendation.

▶ Payroll Supervisor

I look forward to speaking with you in detail about your expectations for the person who becomes Any Corporation's next Payroll Supervisor and regarding my qualifications for this position.

▶ **Secretary**

I look forward to interviewing for the Secretarial position now available at Any Corporation. Thank you for your consideration.

▶ **Staff Accountant**

If you know of Any Corporation in need of an experienced Accountant, in addition to those now posted on Any College's online system, I would appreciate your letting me know. Your idea of contacting all past on-campus recruiters was a good one and I look forward to receiving the listing from you. And, I will of course begin to network with other alumni in the accounting field to conduct, as you called it, "a proactive networking blitz."

▶ **Telecommunications Specialist**

I would greatly appreciate any advice or referrals you might be able to provide. A listing of firms and contact names would be wonderful, and I would of course cite your referral in any communications with these individuals.

Networking Notes

As previously mentioned, any networking notes that you write will be short. In this section, each sample is presented in whole instead of being broken down by paragraph type.

▶ **To an Alumnus**

Ms. Smith:

As an alumna of Any College, I thought you might be able to assist me with my efforts to find a Public Relations position in the Chicago, IL, area. Attached is a copy of my resume that clearly projects my qualifications for these positions. Any contacts within your firm, within other firms in the city, or with search firms specializing in public relations and communications would be appreciated. Of course,

I would send a more detailed cover letter with my resume to these individuals. While I do hope your firm might consider my candidacy, any referrals to other firms would be welcomed. In advance, thank you for your assistance.

Chris Murphy

▶ To a Faculty Member

Dear Ms. Smith,

With commencement near, I wanted to gain your insights and referrals regarding potential employers. As you know, my interest in marketing and promotions is quite strong, and I am very proud of my accomplishments in your Marketing Cases and Strategies course. Our final project is prominently detailed on the attached resume and I hope someday soon I will describe it to prospective employers during interviews. Are there particular companies, contacts, or alumni you would encourage me to communicate with? And, can I use you as a reference? I will call to follow up on this e-mail, but because you are so busy, continuing our communications electronically would be fine. Thank you.

Chris Murphy

▶ To a Friend of the Family

Mr. Worth:

It does seem a bit awkward asking you for assistance with my job search, but mom and dad inspired me to overcome my concerns and do so anyway. As you may know by now, via communications with my family members, I am actively seeking new Property Management opportunities that will allow me the chance to relocate to the New York City area. Do you know of any companies now seeking someone with my real estate background? Are there individuals you would encourage me to contact and send a copy of the attached resume? Are there particular posting sites I should utilize or local professional organizations I should join? Last, and most ideal, would Any Corporation consider my candidacy?

Your answers to these queries would be most welcomed and appreciated. A few minutes of your time over the phone would be great. When I am next in New York, for interviews or pre-relocation activities, please allow me to purchase you and your family dinner or lunch. Thank you for your assistance now and, sincerely, for being a great family friend for so long.

Sincerely,

Chris Murphy

▶ To a Past Employer

Ms. Smith:

I am very proud that my accounting career began as an Intern and, after, as an Audit Trainee with Any Corporation. As you know, when I left Any Corporation to earn my MBA at Any University in Boston, MA, my performance record was strong and my friends within the organization many. While my post-graduate school achievements with Other Company have been fulfilling, and all documented on the attached resume, your assistance with my efforts to relocate "home" to the Rochester, NY, area would be most welcomed. Do you know of any companies now seeking someone with my finance, auditing, cash flow, and strategic planning expertise? Are there individuals you would encourage me to contact? Are there particular posting sites I should utilize or professional organization members I should network with? Last, and most ideal, would Any Corporation consider my candidacy?

Your answers to these queries would be most welcomed and appreciated. A few minutes of your time when I next visit Rochester for a pre-relocation trip, would be wonderful. Also, please convey my regards to all of my old Any Corporation colleagues. Thank you.

Sincerely,

Chris Murphy

▶ To a Professional Society Colleague

Ms. Smith:

It was good seeing you at the Association of Computer Professionals conference. As we discussed briefly, I am now actively seeking new software design opportunities. Would you feel comfortable sharing some contact names with me? Of course, in addition to the attached resume, I will provide each individual a detailed cover letter and cite your referral. You know of my background and abilities, and I am very appreciative of our friendship and respectful of your professional reputation, so I will handle all communications appropriately. Again, the names of contacts, as well as e-mail, fax or mailing addresses, would be most well-received and appreciated. Thank you.

Chris Murphy

▶ To a Professional Society Officer

Alice:

As the Vice President of Membership for Women in Advertising I thought you might be able to assist me with my efforts to begin a post-baccalaureate career in the field of advertising. Does WIA offer any specialized posting or networking services to members? Are there particular members in the San Francisco Bay area who you would encourage me to contact? Because I will be graduating in June, I would welcome consideration for a full-time, part-time, or internship position.

The attached resume is intended to quickly inform you of my background, not to solicit consideration. Of course I will forward an appropriate and detailed cover letter when I send this document to Women in Advertising members you recommend. Your assistance with my efforts would be most appreciated. Thank you.

Sincerely,

Chris Murphy

Chapter 6

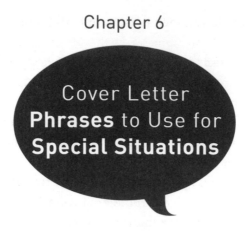

Cover Letter
Phrases to Use for
Special Situations

ARE YOU A RECENT COLLEGE GRAD, looking for your first job or internship? Are you looking to get back into the job market after some time at home? Are you trying to overcome being fired or laid off? Or are you simply motivated to get that next big opportunity?

Almost every job seeker perceives his situation as special, involving unique circumstances and challenges. In reality, your situation may not be so unusual, and you should find inspiration from the sample phrases in this section.

Phrases for Introductory Paragraphs

No matter what your situation, you want to begin your cover letter by alluding to your strengths and stating why you are capable of fulfilling the role for which you're applying. The following samples can help everyone from those who have been in the workforce for decades to those who are just starting out.

As a candidate with decades of experience or an employment history at only one company, you have the opportunity to highlight a variety of accomplishments while demonstrating a serious interest in your industry. Use it to your advantage. Here are some phrases you might include in your introductory paragraph.

► **All Employment at One Company (Materials Manager)**

Described with great pride on the attached resume, during the past eighteen years I have progressed rapidly in positions of responsibility at This Hospital. As the supervisor of patient transportation, manager of warehousing/distribution, and within my current position as senior buyer and manager of inventory control, I have met budgetary goals and provided efficient and mission-driven services.

► **Fifty-Plus-Years-Old Job Candidate (Product Manager)**

Are you and your colleagues in need of a motivated professional with comprehensive product management experience spanning decades? I would like to continue my achievement-filled career with Any Corporation as a full-time, part-time, or contract-based employee. Through this letter, the attached resumes, and ideally an interview, I can present my qualifications for your consideration.

This sample shows how you might present your candidacy for a job within the company where you're currently employed. Be sure to outline key achievements to date.

► **Application for In-House Position (District Supervisor)**

In support of my candidacy for the management job posting for District Supervisor, I present my resume and this memo, summarizing my experience with Any Gas Company and other employers in the gas distribution industry.

When your job has consisted of managing the details of life at home for an extended period of time, your cover letter needs to focus on your experience outside the home. It's essential to communicate your enthusiasm and motivation to continue your career and make a positive contribution to the company.

► **At-Home Parent Re-Entering the Work Force (Graphic Designer)**

I would like to meet to discuss freelance assignments or a part-time position in Graphic Design or Production. During this meeting, I can show you my portfolio and discuss how excited I am to continue my career within an industry that is for me a professional passion.

► **Displaced Homemaker (Administrator)**

I am highly motivated and qualified to serve within an Administrative position at Any Corporation. Detailed on my resume, I offer extensive and varied experience in administrative roles in both employment and community service.

How will you take your experience and apply it to a job in a different field? These sample phrases show how candidates have communicated their intent to potential employers.

► **Career Changer (Advertising Assistant)**

I would like to inquire about and ideally interview for a position at Any Advertising Agency. Detailed on the attached resume, I have over eight years' experience in promotion, communications, and administration. Now, it is with great focus and enthusiasm that I seek to contribute as an Assistant supporting client services, traffic, or media planning activities.

► **Career Changer (Marketing Executive)**

As Any Corporation's Dealer Representative, I will utilize my thorough knowledge of boating as well as sales, marketing, and communication skills to inspire those who sell your products, educate salespersons, and promote product lines directly to consumers. As a semiprofessional sailboat racer, I am very familiar with the Any Corporation line.

▶ **Career Changer (Product and Services Developer)**

Currently, I am seeking a career change and opportunity to associate with a progressive bank, where I can effectively apply my creative and innovative talents and capability for developing or increasing and successfully marketing new service products. During the past eight years, I have served as vice president and director of operations of an ever-expanding, quality-driven, function and recreation complex. In these capacities I had total responsibility for creating effective sales programs and assuring the quality of services provided. Last year, we exceeded our goals by 150 percent and grossed more than $1.4 million in sales. Our increased business resulted from an aggressive marketing effort targeting local businesses.

▶ **Former Small Business Owner (Environmental Advocate)**

The article in the May edition of *Save Our Earth* was impressive. In fact, the article and the mission and offerings of Any Environmental, as dynamically presented on your website, have inspired me to seek employment with your agency. Do you currently have an opening for an Environmental Advocate, Public Relations or Volunteer Coordinator, Researcher, or Lobbyist?

As a freelancer, you must show some knowledge of and proficiency in the position for which you are applying. These two samples clearly inform potential employers why the candidates should be considered for work.

▶ **Freelancer (Editor and Writer)**

I am a Freelance Editor and Writer of educational and reference materials targeting college students and adults. Books and articles written or edited to date have been in the areas of careers, self-help, and parenting. Recently, I identified titles by Any Publishing Company that reveal your interest in targeting similar topics and readers as those cited above. Therefore, I would like to learn more about your Freelance Writing and Editorial needs and acquisition process.

▶ Freelancer (Production Assistant)

I would like to apply for the Production Assistant position advertised on the *www.pa.com* website and in the *Miami Herald*. While the attached resume reveals an extensive list of experiences in all aspects of video production, including positions as writer, researcher, director, and editor, only through an interview can you determine if I have what it takes to transform your vision into day-to-day production realities.

If you're a recent grad, your goal in writing a cover letter is to highlight your course work and internships as they relate to the position. You can begin by mentioning a mutual connection who recommended you apply for the position or by stating what type of job it is that you hope to find. Consider the following wording in these introductory paragraphs.

▶ Recent Graduate (Assistant to Museum Director)

During my undergraduate years, I sought to learn within the classroom and beyond. I did so via specific courses and, most important, through practical internships and training. Now, I seek an opportunity to put my newly developed skills and knowledge to use in a position at Any Museum. Perhaps I can do so as an Assistant to the curator or within patron relations, education, or fundraising roles?

▶ Recent Graduate (Legal Assistant)

Justice Ellen Malone of the Allentown Courthouse suggested that I contact you regarding an opening you may soon have for a Legal Assistant. Judge Malone is aware of my desire to find a challenging paralegal-, legal research-, and administrative-focused position, and she encouraged me to immediately seek consideration to join you and your associates at Any Firm.

▶ Recent Graduate (Set Designer)

Lynne Winchester recently indicated that you may have an opening for a Set Designer and suggested that I contact you. I am seeking a position involving stage design for television, theater, and video productions.

If your educational background isn't your strong point, don't worry. Take this opportunity to showcase what real-life experience you have. If you display familiarity with and success in a certain area, it's difficult for a potential employer to overlook that.

▶ Weak Educational Background (Parking Supervisor)

Described on my resume, I am currently the Parking Supervisor for the Parkinson Hotel and Conference Center. This position was a rapid promotion to management after only one year of service as a parking attendant. As supervisor of parking facilities, I oversee all financial collections, maintain customer service standards, resolve problems, and manage a large staff of hourly workers. I also administer work schedules, evaluate performance, coordinate payroll matters, assign duties, and interface with hotel management. While I am so very proud of my achievements to date in an area that requires practical knowledge and experience, I do wish to find expanded challenges and rewards.

Perhaps you've been laid off or fired. Perhaps your employment history has a few holes. The key to writing an effective cover letter in these situations is to convince your potential employer of your trustworthiness, dedication, and focus. Call their attention to your references, and state your desire to follow a particular career path. Consider the following sample phrases.

▶ Fired/Laid Off (Recruiter)

Attached is a copy of my resume, a list of professional achievements, as well as letters of recommendation written by colleagues, clients, and candidates with whom I've worked. I trust that these documents will convince you that I am worthy of an interview and, after you have had the opportunity to evaluate my candidacy, that I could soon become a strong member of the Any Executive Search Firm team.

▶ Gaps in Employment History (Assistant Curator)

I am seeking a position blending museum and gallery experience as well as a keen interest and academic background in fine art. Ideally that will be as your Assistant Curator. Detailed on the attached resume, I have completed two extensive internships for successful galleries in Alabama. In each position, I contributed to all aspects of operations, including artist relations, sales, show planning and implementation, and administrative duties. Responsibilities and accomplishments included assisting customers, setting up displays, and completing mailings for exhibitions.

▶ No Clear Career Path (Accounting)

I am now actively seeking a career-focused position in Accounting that will utilize my experience in both financial management and customer service, as well as my strong academic background. While researching area firms, I learned of Any Accounting's training and development program. This opportunity seems an ideal way to begin and build an accomplishment-filled career with your firm, and a long-term career is exactly what I seek.

▶ Part-Time Employment History (Store Manager)

I would very much like to join the Any Retail Chain's management team. A very strong and clear sense of career focus, previous retail experience, knowledge of your stores and target markets, and a desire for a full-time management position have prompted me to forward the attached resume.

If you've been working in the military or overseas, you need to show how your experience relates to the position for which you're applying. What about your experience makes you an asset to the team you want to join? By linking your current experience to the duties of the job you want, you'll convince employers that your unique background will serve them well.

▶ **Military Background (Transportation Operator)**

Seven of the past twelve years were spent with the United States Army in transportation-related roles and assignments. Since completion of military services I have worked within sales positions. Now, I am very interested in resuming a civilian career in Transportation Operations or in the sale of products or equipment allied to the transportation field. All pertinent experiences are detailed on the attached resume.

▶ **Overseas Employment History (Marketing Assistant)**

Anticipating relocation home to the United States, I am now actively seeking a Marketing Assistant position with Any Corporation. As you review the attached vita, I trust you will conclude that I can effectively contribute to an international, service-oriented organization dedicated, as your mission states, "to expanding international commerce through effective state of the art and traditional marketing strategies." I understand you currently have a number of international clients and anticipate landing new accounts with multinational firms.

Phrases for Motivational and Qualification Paragraphs

This is the part of your cover letter where you need to sell yourself. Tell your potential future employer what you bring to the table. Imagine being asked the question, "What do you have to offer?" Answer it in these paragraphs.

▶ **All Employment at One Company (Materials Manager)**

Most recently, I have been able to reduce the expenditures of all in-house medical and nonmedical supplies substantially each year through cost-effective negotiations, purchasing, and control. I also played a key role in automating inventories and providing a functional layout for warehouse locations that reduced the selection and distribution process for warehoused materials. This also enabled me to provide more stringent controls, reducing shrinkage, damage, and obsolescence—common problems in the healthcare field. Estimated costs and savings are cited on the resume.

▶ **Application for In-House Position (District Supervisor)**

As you know, these positions required the ability to provide technical support, retain personnel, supervise outside contractors, and work with developers and public officials during the joint work programs and projects. My performance reviews during my tenure at Any Gas have all been above average and my current supervisor, Kelly Stevens, has offered to support my desire for this promotion.

As reflected in all past reviews and training evaluations, I have the technical capability to work with and direct company and contractor personnel on all phases of gas distribution systems, from new construction to replacement and operation. Previous accomplishments with Any Gas indicate my strong communication skills and my ability to work with people at all levels of responsibility, including those who would report to and interact with a District Supervisor.

▶ **At-Home Parent Reentering the Work Force (Graphic Designer)**

Professionally, I offer more than seven years' experience in production and traffic areas of Print and Graphic Design and in related fields, including fundraising and direct- and mass-mailings. After a three-year hiatus, with my family well established, I am highly motivated to return to the workforce and contribute to the growth of Any Advertising Agency. In addition to my resume and portfolio, excellent references do support my candidacy.

▶ **Career Changer (Advertising Assistant)**

As owner of a successful and profitable housecleaning service for four years, I designed and wrote all promotional materials, including direct-mail coupons. Immediately after my first promotional campaign, the volume of business tripled, resulting in my hiring and overseeing six people. In addition to supervising employees, I completed all administrative and budgetary tasks, which entailed handling calls, scheduling, billing, record keeping, ordering supplies, and customer relations. Now, having just sold the business, I am seeking a position in advertising.

▶ Career Changer (Marketing Executive)

A career change that will involve a transition from a successful management career to a marketing, promotions, and consumer relations career is most desired. I am confident that my business and boating background will ensure that I have favorable impact on sales, image and continued growth.

▶ Career Changer (Product and Services Developer)

As I will share personally, if you grant me the opportunity to interview for a client services, loan officer, or marketing position, I am adept at making business-to-business contacts, at creating and utilizing promotional advertising and marketing programs, and making effective presentations.

▶ Displaced Homemaker (Administrator)

I offer Any Corporation:

- Experience with staff supervision and motivation.
- A record of success within meeting planning and direction, and activities scheduling.
- Confidence within public speaking situations.
- Excellent phone and correspondence skills
- Bookkeeping fundraising, and promotions talents.

▶ 50-Plus-Years-Old Job Candidate (Product Manager)

Past experience has provided me many opportunities to implement profitable Product Management strategies including those associated with pricing, production, distribution, as well as advertising for existing and new products. Specifically, for pharmaceutical and food products, I have been involved in all aspects of product/protocol development and management to obtain FDA product approval. As a Product Manager for Estrade, Inc., I coordinate all product development for a medical supply corporation with annual sales in excess of $400 million. Prior, I served in similar capacities for Vita Thirst, the manufacturer of healthful drink products. My product designs, production planning, and marketing techniques have been recognized as consistently innovative and, most important, profitable. Over the years, every product I have been associated with met or exceeded annual profit goals.

▶ Fired/Laid Off (Recruiter)

As detailed on my resume, recruiting skills and accomplishments were nurtured over seven years while recruiting high technology, support staff, and marketing personnel. Much of this experience involved extensive travel, training program development, and networking prospective clients. In addition to a record of success and a well-earned reputation, I possess valuable contacts within the management information systems, software development, and engineering industries that would prove valuable to Any Firm's client base.

▶ Gaps in Employment History (Assistant Curator)

Academically and personally, I have a Bachelor of Arts degree in Art History, have participated in several related seminars, and I have had occasion to visit many of the world's great museums. I am a frequent visitor to the Any Museum and a member of Friends of Any Museum, so I am familiar with your mission, target patronage, and educational and outreach efforts.

▶ Former Small Business Owner (Environmental Advocate)

As described on my resume, and revealed through the annual report also attached, I have a passion for environmental concerns and practical experiences in all of the above areas. For the past four years, I have been operating an entrepreneurial venture, Recycling

Renegades. I successfully acquired the first recycling permit in Cambridge, MA, for ferrous and nonferrous metal, aluminum, high-grade paper, and plastic. As owner and manager, I conducted research, developed pilot programs, formulated networks for voluntary recycling, picked up and processed materials, and distributed proceeds to community associations. While my motives were altruistic, my accomplishments proved profitable as well.

▶ Freelancer (Editor and Writer)

The attached resume details my projects to date, as well as my academic background, early experiences as an editorial assistant, and current status as a part-time English instructor. Whether editing or writing textbook materials, teacher workbooks, or ancillary activities and worksheets, I can tailor the content, tone and approach to a variety of purposes and audiences.

▶ Freelancer (Production Assistant)

Summarizing, personal and professional qualities I possess include:

- Three years as a freelance Production Assistant working on several commercial and documentary pieces.
- Skills and perspectives gained as chief assistant on Milk Carton Kids: An American Crisis, supporting preliminary research and writing, scheduling location shooting, and screening potential interview candidates.
- Breadth of administrative and logistical talents gained completing two public-service announcements for Miami Child Services, which included camera operation and heavy script and video editing.
- Patience, flexibility, creativity, and active listening skills required to thrive under the pressure of deadlines and working within the demands of pre-production, shooting and production stages.

▶ Military Background (Transportation Operator)

Key points on this document and those I would like to discuss during an interview include:

- Experience managing all phases of civilian and tactical Transportation Operations (vehicles from two-and-one-half-ton cargo trucks to ten-ton tractor trailers and petroleum tankers).
- Experience teaching courses and training troops about the total transportation cycle in the United States and abroad.
- Record of success contributing toward the efficient military operations and potential to do so at an in-house traffic, transportation, and distribution function or a commercial transportation depot.

▶ No Clear Career Path (Accounting)

To this program and your firm, I would bring the following:

- A Bachelor of Science degree, *cum laude*, in Finance.
- Four years of collections experience.
- Successful collecting of 90 percent of overdue accounts.
- Experience in accounts payable and accounts receivable.
- Knowledge of Excel, Lotus 1-2-3, Word, QuickBooks, and varied accounting applications.
- The competencies and commitment required to pass the CPA examination and adhere to strict professional and ethical standards.

▶ Overseas Employment History (Marketing Assistant)

Summarizing some of the points I would like to share via phone discussions and in-person interviews, I offer Any Corporation:

- Experience as an interpreter and translator working on international market research with the Marketing Department at the University of Paris, Sorbonne.
- Knowledge of concepts and terminology associated with marketing and advertising.
- Confidence and history of success as administrative assistant to professors and business executives.
- Trilingual fluency in English, French, and Italian, and strong proficiency in Spanish.

- Skills and perspectives gained completing a Bachelor of Arts degree in French, *summa cum laude*, from University of Rochester in Rochester New York.
- Communication and presentation skills gained tutoring individuals in foreign languages and English as a Second Language.
- Familiarity working and interacting with multilingual, multicultural individuals and groups.

▶ Recent Graduate (Assistant to Museum Director)

As my resume indicates, I recently participated in a program for art history majors at the Louvre. This involved studying European art and attending seminars on museum operations. Prior, I worked for two summers at the Metropolitan Museum of Art as a Museum Assistant at the information booth.

▶ Recent Graduate (English Teacher)

Supporting special education offerings, I learned of IEPs and district approaches to inclusion. I was proud to assist students with learning disabilities, as well as those who needed assistance with physical disabilities. I used lesson planning, instructional as well as tutorial talents gained in classrooms and other settings. Throughout my undergraduate years I participated in a volunteer literacy program, tutoring both youth and adults struggling with reading difficulties. The skills and perspectives gained as a student teacher and tutor will be foundations upon which I will build a successful teaching career.

▶ Recent Graduate (Legal Assistant)

Described in great detail on the attached resume, I have worked in a variety of legal settings throughout college. Currently, I am a volunteer for Temple's Student Legal Aid, supporting the efforts of law students helping undergraduates and community members with legal problems. I worked part time over the past three years as a peer probation mentor for the Allentown, PA, juvenile court. In addition to these experiences, last summer I served as a research assistant for the Chief County Clerk of Allentown, when I met Judge Malone.

▶ **Recent Graduate (Set Designer)**

As noted on my resume, I graduated recently from Clemson University with a Bachelor of Arts degree in Theater Arts and a concentration in Studio Art. Courses in modern drama, music and sound in theatre, set creation and design, intermediate painting, and woodworking all contributed to the skills I possess, and focused my aspirations toward Stage Design. As a an undergraduate, I designed and helped create props for numerous campus productions, including *The Tempest* and *Marco Polo Sings a Solo*, and I developed many storyboards and set design presentations.

Phrases for Closing Paragraphs

This is your chance to request an interview, reinforce your interest in the job, and quickly summarize why you're a great candidate. Whether you've been working for thirty years, just graduated from college, or never even went to college, your closing statement will generally convey the same thought—you are competent, your interest in the job is serious, you appreciate the company's consideration, and you look forward to future communication.

▶ **All Employment at One Company (Materials Manager)**

Past achievements within one organization prove my professional competencies and potential to succeed in new roles at Any Hospital. As your healthcare operations grow, since the acquisition of several local HMOs, I know that Materials Management issues will become crucial. Please, let's discuss how I might help link growth with efficiency.

▶ **Application for in-House Position (District Supervisor)**

I feel professionally and personally ready to handle the challenges of the District Supervisor position. During an interview I can confidently yet objectively share these qualifications with you and others involved in the selection process. I look forward to meeting with you to discuss my candidacy. Thank you for your consideration.

▶ Career Changer (Advertising Assistant)

I hope we will have the chance to discuss current or future opportunities during an interview. If no positions are available or anticipated, any referrals to other agencies would be welcomed.

▶ Career Changer (Marketing Executive)

I do hope that I will have the chance to soon present my qualifications and motivations in person. Please, do not hesitate to e-mail or call to arrange a meeting. And, I have asked some of my boating colleagues to contact you regarding their views of my potential.

▶ Career Changer (Product and Services Developer)

I would welcome your thoughts regarding where I might best contribute to Any Bank. I will call to confirm receipt of this note, to clarify next steps, and, I most sincerely hope, to arrange a brief meeting.

▶ Displaced Homemaker (Administrator)

If you are looking for someone with these skills, I hope you will give me the opportunity to speak with you. During a telephone conversation and, ideally, a meeting I can expand upon the above bullets and personalize my candidacy. A resume and cover letter can reveal a great deal, but in-person communication is, I believe, best.

▶ Fifty-Plus-Years-Old Job Candidate (Product Manager)

I would appreciate your consideration and look forward to speaking with you, with Sam Smith, or others you deem appropriate regarding how I might best contribute to Any Corporation, as you continue to work on the development of your new healthy snack line. I will call to discuss your thoughts regarding my candidacy.

▶ **Fired/Laid Off (Recruiter)**

Ideally, you and I could meet soon, whenever mutually convenient. I will call to confirm receipt of this fax and to discuss your reactions to my request for an interview. In advance, thank you for your consideration.

▶ **Former Small Business Owner (Environmental Advocate)**

I wish to utilize skills gained via this venture, and as an undergraduate environmental engineering major, at Any Environmental Agency. Will you be attending the environmental affairs conference in New York City? If we haven't connected by phone, e-mail, or in person prior, perhaps we can meet at the conference.

▶ **Freelancer (Editor and Writer)**

Could I speak to you about working on some of your projects as either Editor or Author? Attached is a piece written for an online newsletter as well as a brief note written by Kerry Williams, an editor at Textbook Company. I hope, these documents reveal the potential I possess to contribute to Any Publishing Company's efforts. Of course, I can provide additional writing samples and references, as needed.

▶ **Freelancer (Production Assistant)**

I've admired Any Production Company's work for some time and attended your screening of *Silent Victims* at the Miami Crime Awareness Convention last month. It would be wonderful if I could help on your next project, and future undertakings.

▶ **Gaps in Employment History (Assistant Curator)**

In addition to the targeted resume I have also provided a reference list of individuals familiar with my past experiences who can share views regarding my future potential. I would like to discuss full-time or part-time options. To date, whenever given the opportunity to work in an arts environment, I have succeeded. I hope I have that chance at Any Museum.

▶ Military Background (Transportation Operator)

Also, I am a trained professional, a graduate officer of the U.S. Army Transportation School, and I have completed my bachelor's degree. I would appreciate the opportunity to further describe my qualifications and the immediate and long-term contributions I could make to Any Corporation.

▶ Overseas Employment History (Marketing Assistant)

I will be in New York from February 14 through February 28 for a pre-relocation visit. Would it be possible to schedule an interview for that time? While I hope we will have had telephone and e-mail communications prior, it would be wonderful if we could meet during my upcoming visit. Of course, I am eligible to work in the United States and I anticipate paying all relocation expenses.

▶ Part-Time Employment History (Store Manager)

As my resume indicates, and as is the history of many who build successful careers, some of my Retail Management experience has been part time. I am now seeking a permanent position and the opportunity to build a career while I contribute to the growth of Any Retail Chain. Please allow me the opportunity to share how past experiences and accomplishments can predict future achievements via an interview.

▶ Recent Graduate (Assistant to Museum Director)

The eyes of a young visitor to your museum have grown into those of a diligent student, recent graduate, and hopeful candidate. While my heart still contains the enthusiasm and excitement I felt during early visits, my head is now is full of knowledge and career focus. Please grant me the opportunity to interview for and, someday, to become part of your staff. I will call to see if an in-person interview would be an appropriate next step.

► **Recent Graduate (English Teacher)**

Also attached are letters of recommendation and a favorite lesson plan. As you read these documents I hope you gain a sense of the teacher I wish to be. I know I can instill knowledge, inspire continued learning, and refine writing talents. I will call to confirm that I have completed all required steps and to inquire regarding the interview and selection process.

► **Recent Graduate (Legal Assistant)**

Prior to applying to law school in a few years, I wish to fine tune my knowledge of law and gain a greater sense of career focus and special interests. Ideally, I can do so at Any Firm. I will contact you within the week to further discuss the possibility of interviewing for this position.

► **Recent Graduate (Set Designer)**

Enclosed is a resume as well as some photographs of my work. Of course, I would like to show you my entire portfolio and discuss with you how I might contribute to Any Production Company's current and future projects. I have some great ideas for the sets of *Trivia Tunes* and *Videos after Dark* and hope to have the opportunity to discuss them with you.

► **Weak Educational Background (Parking Supervisor)**

With increased concerns about security has come increased focus on parking operations at facilities like Any Airport. I hope I have contacted you at a time when consideration can be given to a candidate who has proven by past experience that learning by doing is the best education. I would like to speak with you about current or future opportunities. Of course, references are available upon request. If you now utilize an outside vendor for parking operations, referrals to the proper person in that organization would be appreciated.

Chapter 7

25 Things Not to Say in Your Cover Letter

IT'S IMPORTANT TO POINT OUT that there are some things *not* to say in your cover letter. It may be true that the line between appropriate and inappropriate is often blurred in both casual and professional settings as people struggle to make themselves stand out from the crowd, but that doesn't mean you should adopt an "anything goes" attitude in an effort to get an interview. The point of this document is to help you get a job, so be careful not to discuss topics that could potentially detract from that goal. The following twenty-five phrases are examples of things not to say in your cover letter.

1. Don't tell your life story. "I was born in Wisconsin, one of three children. I did well in school. I was on the football team and editor of my school newspaper. I moved to Chicago to go to college and . . ." Keep your answer limited to the parts that will affect your suitability for the job.

2. Don't explain that you're gunning for a management job when you're aiming to interview for an entry-level position. "I want to run this place" is not an appropriate description of your long-term goals.

3. Don't say, "I plan to get my MBA as soon as possible," if that isn't relevant to the job. Avoid describing short-term goals that have nothing to do with the position you're interviewing for.

4. Don't highlight a general trait as your greatest strength. Saying, "I'm a hard worker who always get to work on time," leaves the reviewer of your cover letter wondering if you have any specific skills related to the job.

5. Don't overstate your enthusiasm for change. By saying, "I love change, and without it I get bored," will make companies wary of your commitment and get you flagged as someone who jumps from job to job every two years.

6. Don't focus on unimportant details. Saying, "My ideal work environment is an office with big windows and proximity to the train station," doesn't tell your potential employer what sort of work challenges you and what work pace best suits you.

7. Don't appear uninterested in your chosen field. "I decided to pursue a career in advertising because my dad's friend thought I'd be good at it," shows a lack of concern for your future, and it may cause the interviewer to doubt your decision-making abilities.

8. Don't take the focus off your strengths by emphasizing skills you lack. Telling someone, "I haven't worked in this field before, but I'm a fast learner" downplays any strengths you have, such as working well on a team or possessing good communication skills. Accentuate the positive as much as possible.

9. Don't be vague when listing your skills. If you're applying for a teaching position, you'll need to be much more specific than just saying "I love kids, and I'm a good teacher." What's special about the way you interact with children, and what makes you a good teacher?

10. Don't paint a picture of yourself as an iron-fisted ruler. If you're targeting a management position, avoid saying, "I'm strict, and in my office it's my way or the highway." Portray yourself as a hands-on manager who works alongside her employees.

11. Don't rely on your training or education alone to speak for the skills you possess. When describing your experience, don't say, "I graduated from Boston University with a degree in Mechanical Engineering." Instead, describe how and where you've applied your degree.

12. Don't leave out the details. Saying, "I'm good with patients and insurance" in your cover letter is not going to make you stand out against the candidate who says something like, "I dealt with insurance companies on a daily basis, and I found that if I learned how each one worked, it was a lot easier for the doctors in my practice to get paid and for patients to get reimbursed. I also worked at the reception desk at these jobs and was happy to be able to calm down anxious patients and hopefully offer some reassurance."

13. Don't forget to explain how you progressed in your job. By saying, "I started out as an assistant and was promoted to a senior position within one year," you don't give the reviewer much information about what you did in the meantime.

14. Don't confuse personal accomplishments with professional ones. While you may be tempted to boast, "My accomplishments include winning my softball team's biggest game of the season by hitting a grand slam," it's not something to mention in your cover letter.

15. Don't minimize the impact your work has had on your current company. Always highlight and focus on results in your cover letter. For example, "I wrote a manual explaining all bookkeeping department procedures in our company. New employees receive a copy of this manual, which helps them learn their job faster."

16. Don't fail to make the connection between your education and the position you're pursuing. Avoid saying, "Even though I have no experience managing media communications, I am eager to learn what the job entails." You must relate your background to the job. If it's a big stretch, reconsider your decision to apply.

17. Don't give the wrong impression of your interest in a particular company. "I'd love to work here because my best friend does" is not a good reason. If it's the only reason, again, rethink your decision to apply.

18. Don't badmouth your current boss. Never cite a disagreement between you and your boss or an inability to work together as a reason for pursuing a new job.

19. Don't discuss desired salary in your cover letter. Saying, "I must make at least $55,000" will be a major turn off.

20. Don't specify money as a motivating reason for pursuing a new job. When you say, "I am interested in earning a higher salary," your potential employer will wonder if you have any interest in the job or company.

21. Don't convey a sense of enthusiasm about using skills you don't currently possess. Someone with no prior research experience who says, "I am thrilled at the prospect of researching medical issues" will be flagged as a person requiring training or close supervision.

22. Don't display a lack of knowledge about your potential future employer. Instead of saying, "I am interested in learning more about your company," say, "I am interested in speaking with you further about this position." You won't be expected to know everything about the job from the posting alone.

23. Don't display a lack of knowledge about the industry you seek to join. If you're going to work for a book publisher, don't call the manuscripts *articles*. Know which buzz words will get your cover letter noticed, and use the language spoken by those already in the industry.

24. Don't say, "I'm looking for a nine-to-five job." It shows that you're not willing to put in extra time and effort if needed.

25. Don't say, "This Assistant position is clearly the next step I need to take in order to become a principal." You may think this statement shows ambition, but what it really says is that you don't care how you get the experience you need to advance to a higher position.

Chapter 8

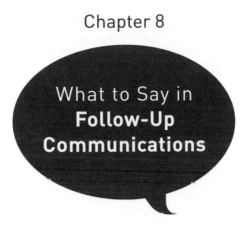

What to Say in
**Follow-Up
Communications**

THANK YOU NOTES, STATUS CHECKS, AND OTHER CORRESPON-
DENCE inspire continued consideration and enhance job search success.
E-mails, written notes, faxes, and voicemail follow-up efforts reinforce
your candidacy, resurrect consideration after rejection or lack of response,
and can transform network members into job search advocates.

This section provides a series of checklists that will help you follow up with your contacts at every stage in the job search process.
You'll find step-by-step instructions for writing thoughtful notes that
show your appreciation for interviews, referrals, references, and continued consideration, in addition to acceptance letters, resignation
letters, and decline letters.

After Telephone Conversation Before an Interview

✔ Thank your contact for the time he has taken to meet, speak, or
otherwise communicate with you about the position.

✔ Restate relevant experience, skills, and accomplishments that
will contribute to your success in the position.

✔ Express interest in meeting with your contact for an interview.

✔ Express gratitude for your contact's consideration of your
candidacy.

After a Job Interview

✔ Thank the interviewer for her time.

✔ Reiterate your interest in the position. It is acceptable to state outright that you would be thrilled to receive an offer.

✔ Briefly restate that your experience will be valuable in accomplishing the duties associated with the position.

✔ Notify your interviewer that you will check on the status of the decision-making process (if appropriate).

✔ Express your enthusiasm and end the letter by thanking your interviewer again for her time and consideration.

For a Good Reference

✔ Thank your reference for his willingness to offer support for your candidacy.

✔ Inform your reference of the outcome (hopefully positive!) of the interview.

✔ Extend an offer to return the favor if your reference ever needs your help.

✔ Thank your reference again for advocating on your behalf.

For a Letter of Recommendation

✔ Thank your contact for providing her recommendation.

✔ Notify your contact that her letter resulted in an offer being made, and that you've happily accepted it.

✔ Restate your gratitude and offer to help your contact in a similar manner should the situation arise.

For a Referral

✔ Announce your acceptance of the position for which you applied.

✔ Thank your contact for referring you for the position and putting you in touch with the appropriate person.

✔ Express your willingness to return the favor if the opportunity arises in the future.

✔ State your enthusiasm to begin your new job and thank your contact once again for his help.

After an Informational Interview

✔ Thank your interview for her time.

✔ Briefly state how the meeting influenced your pursuit of a particular position or career path. (For example, perhaps you will apply for acceptance into a specific educational program or contact a company about future employment.)

✔ Offer to keep your contact up to date on your progress.

✔ Inquire about any additional suggestions, referrals, or contact names that may assist you in the process.

✔ Thank your contact again for her time.

Resurrection Letter

✔ Mention your resume is currently under review, and provide the name of your contact at the company who indicated so.

✔ Direct recipient's attention to attached (if e-mailed) or enclosed (if mailed) resume and restate your continued interest.

✔ Briefly describe relevant experience related to the position and state your interest in arranging an interview.

✔ Thank recipient for her continued consideration.

Response to a Rejection

✔ Thank your contact for the giving you the opportunity to interview.

✔ Express gratitude for having been given the chance to meet him and learn more about the company.

✔ State your interest in future openings and, if applicable, freelance or contract-based assignments as well as special projects.

✔ Thank your contact again for his consideration.

Withdrawal from Consideration

✔ Remind your contact that you have submitted your resume and/or application for consideration.

✔ Notify contact of your reason for withdrawing your interest.

✔ Thank your contact for her time spent reviewing your application.

✔ Express a continued interest in the company and keep lines of communication open.

Rejection of an Offer

✔ Thank your contact for the offer of employment.

✔ Briefly explain reason for rejecting offer.

✔ Offer apologies for any inconvenience or issues that arise as a result of your rejection.

✔ Express sincere thanks for your contact's confidence in your abilities, and state that your interest in the position was sincere.

✔ Ask your contact to extend your gratitude to his colleagues for their time and consideration.

Acceptance Letter

✔ Acknowledge receipt of offer letter and state your acceptance.

✔ Express enthusiasm for the position.

✔ Confirm start date and resignation with current employer.

✔ Provide an e-mail address or phone number should contact be necessary prior to your start date.

✔ Reiterate your enthusiasm to join the company.

Address or Phone Number Change

✔ Notify your contact of the change in information.

✔ Direct attention to updated resume (whether attached or enclosed).

✔ State your interest in the position and your hopes to arrange an interview.

✔ Express gratitude for consideration of your candidacy.

Resignation Letter

✔ State, with regret, your resignation and effective date.

✔ Briefly describe your reason for resigning.

✔ Inquire about formal steps to take in order to complete any projects in progress.

✔ Inquire about necessary documentation from Human Resources.

✔ Thank current employer for the experience.

✔ Offer to be as involved in the transition process as possible.

✔ State your desire to continue a professional relationship with your employer.

✔ Express gratitude again for the opportunity to have worked there.

Part II

Resumes

Chapter 9

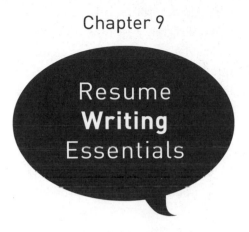

Resume
Writing
Essentials

THE PROCESS OF WRITING YOUR RESUME is not unlike the steps you follow to write a cover letter. You'll review samples, get ideas, identify your goals, make a first draft and revise it, and then distribute it. You may need to do some research to learn more about the industry you seek to enter so you know what to communicate on your resume, and on a larger scale you may need to review resume content requirements. In this section, you'll find some step-by-step advice that will help you stay on track.

The Seven Key Steps to Writing a Resume

Gaining focus and creating a strong, content-rich resume is easy when you have a plan to follow. These seven steps can guide you through the process:

▶ **Step One: Review Samples**
When looking at sample resumes, analyze them like a knowledgeable and focused job seeker excited about the task at hand. The goal is to identify the qualities you like.

The first thing employers and recruiters do when they want to fill a position is list the qualifications the job requires. They list these traits in order of priority according to which are essential, which are optimal, and which are merely desirable (or optional).

Sometimes job descriptions and postings include detailed qualification criteria, but more often these preferences are expressed vaguely.

As the job seeker, you are responsible for conveying your goals, objectives, and a clear sense of job purpose. The information on your resume should respond and relate to the qualifications listed in the job posting. You must create a powerful resume that mirrors your qualifications and follow that up with an interview that impresses the employers with your capability to perform the job.

▶ **Step Two: Consider Format, Content, and Order of Information**

Pick out your two or three favorite sample resumes. Examine them from top to bottom. Once you identify qualities of each you wish to adapt, consider some basic questions:

- What first impression will your resume generate? How is it formatted?
- What will appear first and most prominently on the page?
- How will your resume identify you? Will it include your e-mail address? Will it include your mailing address and all your phone numbers, including cell phone?
- Will you include an objective statement or a qualification summary?
- Will you present educational information before or after a qualification summary? Before or after experience?
- Will you order information about your work history, qualifications, and objectives with the most pertinent appearling earliest and most prominently at the top?
- Will you use as few lines as possible, reserving most of the page for critical content?
- Will you use columns, with dates on the left and descriptions on the right, or a block format?
- Will headlines be centered or left-justified?

Formatting Basics

The font you choose is the key to a well-formatted resume. Fonts should be traditional, easy-to-read, and common. You don't want to create a beautiful resume in some obscure font that will be replaced on your reviewer's computer by an automatic font substitution (probably destroying all your careful line spacing and other formatting work as well). The best fonts and point sizes for resumes are:

- Bookman Antiqua (9, 10, or 11 Point).
- Century Schoolbook (9, 10, or 11 Point).
- Garamond (10 or 11 Point).
- Palatino (8, 9, or 10 Point).
- Times (9 or 10 Point).
- Times New Roman (9, 10, or 11 Point).

For headlines, increase the font size two points at a time until the headline is emphasized but not disproportionate. You can highlight important elements with CAPITALIZATION, **bold face,** and *italics,* as well as with indentations, line spacing, and bullet points.

Identify Yourself

Letterhead is the best and easiest way to do this. You can design your own very simply. Your letterhead should include:

- Your name on the first line.
- Your full mailing address.
- The telephone number(s) where you can be reached during business hours.
- Your e-mail address.

Lose any cutesy or gimmicky e-mail moniker like Partyallnight@ or Muscleman@, and never use a current employer's e-mail address. You don't want your prospective employer to think (or know) you aren't giving 100 percent to your job while you're working.

Also, take the time to review your voicemail greetings on the phone numbers you include on your resume, both home and cell.

While you're in the job market, refrain from music, clever hellos, or other weird greetings.

Summarize Yourself

Some resumes use qualification or achievement summaries to present objectives and goals. Summaries follow or even replace objective statements. Sometimes these sections come at the end, providing the resume with a solid bottom line. Note that not all resumes include these elements; it's up to you to decide whether you need them.

Putting Your Experience in Order

The best resumes present the job seeker's most significant experiences first. Entries are grouped under headlines. They include undergraduate and graduate degrees, specialized training, and work history. Education can come at the top, as the first or second category, or you can present it last. Candidates with plenty of valuable on-the-job experience generally list that first, saving the bottom of the page for a summary of their education.

Academic achievements and honors can be presented in a bulleted list. To figure out what belongs on this list, think about courses, papers, and projects with special relevance to this field. You might also have pertinent extracurricular or community experience. In general, these activities should follow your education and employment entries.

Finally, it is important to note that your resume does *not* need to end with "References available upon request." That's a given.

▶ Step Three: Identify Your Objectives and Your Audience

What do you aim to achieve with your resume? Answer that question, and you will define your goals. You must also define, as best you can, who will be reading your resume. Your reviewers belong to the field. They use particular words, phrases, and other field-focused terminology when they talk about their work.

Your resume should clearly state your career objectives, but not necessarily with what was once called a *Career Objective*. Instead, your career objective should be conveyed by your content, clearly projecting your firmly focused qualifications as well as achievements.

▶ **Step Four: Inventory Your Qualifications and Achievements**

The best way to pick out your important achievements is to think in terms of the job or field you're aiming to enter. Free-form lists of random accomplishment are not as effective. You don't want to rely on your reviewer to figure out or analyze the significance of anything in your resume. It's your job to make your value clear.

Achievement summaries are the heart of any good resume. They should be enough to convince the reviewer of your commitment, your qualifications, and your obvious value. It's important not to skimp on the time or energy you put into summarizing your past accomplishments. To a potential employer, your past has everything to do with the future.

▶ **Step Five: Analyze Your Competencies and Capabilities**

Great resumes reflect past achievements and, via qualification summaries, project ahead to future roles and responsibilities. You are not limited to talking about what has been achieved. Instead, your resume is the perfect platform to express your confidence and competence to tackle the future.

▶ **Step Six: Draft and Critique Your Resume**

Your first draft should be inspired by the sample resumes you've reviewed and analyzed. They will probably influence your choice of content and the order of your information. Let them. Later on, you can go back and determine the best order of presentation and omit unnecessary entries.

As you put your first draft together, don't worry about keeping it to any particular length. It is better to start long and later edit it down. Write as spontaneously as you can. Don't rewrite as you go; there will be plenty of time for that when your draft is complete. Your finished resume should be concise. If after your best editing efforts it is still longer than one page, so be it! Employers do read two-page resumes, as long as they are well organized, with the most important information on the first page.

▶ **Step Seven: Distribute Your Resume**

Most of your resumes will probably go out via e-mail or be posted to the Internet, though you will still need a printed version as well. In either case, it's important to keep making a good first impression. Here's how you do it:

- Use a strong format, very simple graphics (as long as they contribute to your statement), and an attractive design.
- Use standard portrait orientation when printing your resume.
- Use bond or linen paper. White, ivory, natural, and off-white are your best color options. Use the same paper for your cover letters and other correspondence.

Your Resume Checklist

Here is an actual step-by-step review of what you must do to create or update your resume today. This list simplifies the actions already outlined and clarified previously. Have your laptop or desktop computer ready. You should soon be writing or typing, not just thinking. Without delay, you should be able to create or update your resume in less than a day.

✔ Identify at least two sample resumes to model. This should take no more than fifteen minutes.

✔ Reflect upon how and when these samples presented their information. Create a draft listing of headlines you might use in the order you want them to appear. This step should take about ten minutes.

✔ Concisely state your job-search goal as it will appear in a statement of objectives or as the headline of a qualification summary. This step should also take ten minutes.

✔ With this goal in mind, make a list of significant, related accomplishments. This should take about thirty minutes.

✔ Review significant, related accomplishments to link past accomplishments with future potential via a qualification summary. It is recommended that you actually draft your entire resume, including the objective, before you take on this task. No matter whether this section is presented first or last, writing this section should be your last, most important, and perhaps lengthiest task. This could take about an hour, but it can be done quicker.

✔ With model resumes in view, type a draft of your version. Don't think, just type. Later, you will complete self-critiquing and copyediting. This should take at most one hour.

✔ Conduct software-linked spell-checking and grammar reviews. Have someone else review for typos and format questions, then make revisions and complete the final version. While you should respect comments of colleagues and friends, remain confident that you are the best and ultimate judge regarding what should appear in your resume and how it should be presented.

✔ Draft and finalize your cover letter. Distribute your resume. The time it takes to complete this step will depend on whether you e-mail your resume or deliver it by hand.

Field Descriptions

Many industry publications compile long lists of criteria to help workers assess their career compatibility and evaluate their potential goals. The following list provides brief descriptions for a variety of fields. With this general idea of what comprises a field, you can more easily determine your particular focus and your qualifications for performing a particular function.

▶ Administration

The administrative field involves general office management as well as oversight of facilities and systems associated with day-to-day organizational activities. No matter their titles, many employees of this field work in administrative, customer service, or general office positions. On the other end of a wide continuum, those serving within these functions are also responsible for large operations and organizations. They generally supervise many individuals, projects, and resources. Job functions include office services, facilities, security, management, and project management roles.

▶ Architecture, Construction, and Engineering

This field is dominated by the principles and theories of science, engineering, mathematics, and design to solve and carry out initiatives within research, development, manufacturing, sales, construction, inspection, and maintenance.

▶ Arts and Media

This field includes the performing and fine arts; broadcast, print, and Internet media; and communication-oriented organizations. Settings include, but are not limited to, galleries, museums, radio and television stations, dot-com organizations, publishers, newspapers and magazines, public relations firms, and advertising agencies.

▶ Business

This sector includes almost any profit-driven activity. Most often, the business world is associated with large publicly or privately held companies that provide services or market products.

▶ Communications

The communications field involves writing, graphics, public relations, publicity, and promotions. It includes all activities associated with creating, distributing, and transmitting text and graphic information via varied print, video, audio, computer, and web-based media.

▶ Education

The education field includes private and public preschools, elementary schools, middle and secondary schools, colleges and universities, as well as tutorial and training operations.

▶ **Finance**

This field involves accounting, budgeting, treasury, auditing, and information systems activities. It includes collection, documentation, and analysis of financial data and the use of this data to make strategic decisions and share pertinent information with investors, regulators, and government entities. It also includes allocation and growth of capital required for annual operations as well as growth.

▶ **Government**

Government includes all local, state, federal, and multinational organizations that pass legislation, offer and regulate services, lobby, and promote specific programs and resources.

▶ **Health and Human Services**

Usually considered a member of the service sector, this field includes both individuals and facilities that offer medical, psychological, social, and related services. Practitioners can be private, government-affiliated, or have nonprofit status. Hospitals, clinics, residential treatment facilities, agencies, and special programs all fit within this field.

▶ **Hospitality**

This is a service sector that encompasses a broad variety of industries such as hotels, restaurants, casinos, travel, and tourism.

▶ **Human Resources**

This field involves recruiting, retention and staffing, compensation and benefits, training and development, as well as employee-relations efforts. It includes all hiring, career development, compensation, and personnel management activities.

▶ **Law**

The legal field includes services and systems associated with enforcement of laws, such as judicial, regulatory, corrections, investigation, and protection organizations. Employers include government and private agencies, law firms, and nonprofit entities, as well as courts and mediators.

▶ Marketing

Marketing involves new product development, product management, marketing analysis, research, product and sales support, advertising, promotions, and public relations, as well as customer services. These functions can take place in-house, in consumer and industrial product manufacturers, or at specialized consulting firms or agencies.

▶ Sales

The sales field involves direct sales, representative sales, distribution and arbitrage, and retail sales. It includes all activities associated with sales of raw materials used to create products or the sale of products directly to consumers. It can also involve sales of financial or other services.

▶ Science and Technology

The tech sector includes organizations and businesses associated with research, development, manufacturing, and marketing of new technologies. Activities can be purely research-and-development oriented, or they can be product or service oriented. Government, business, and education entities all fit within this specialized category.

▶ Technology and Operations

This field involves production, materials, traffic, and management of information systems. It includes overseeing or participating in the activities associated with producing tangible products and, with purchasing, receiving, storing raw material, components, or finished products. It is also associated with the allocation of human resources to specific assignments and with the operating, programming, or servicing of computers.

Chapter 10

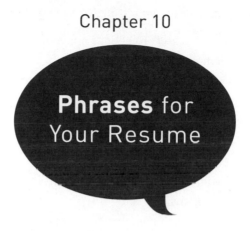

Phrases for
Your Resume

WHAT FOLLOWS IS A COLLECTION OF PHRASES grouped according
to common job titles. The phrases listed for each title describe job
duties and responsibilities. They're examples of actual phrases you
might use when describing your own work experience. The wording
here is intended to help you figure out how to phrase that experience.

Account Executive
- Marketed loan and financing programs to financial institutions
  and mortgage brokers.

Accountant
- Assisted with monthly closings and financial reporting.
- Worked directly with controller to prepare primary and second-
  ary public stock offerings
- Implemented Solomon general ledger accounting package.
- Installed and set up modules, developed procedures for new
  system, and trained staff.

Accountant, Senior
- Oversaw all accounting and payroll functions for a $20 million
  publicly held company that develops, manufactures, and markets proprietary X-ray systems.

- Assisted controller in preparing financial statements and SEC reports.
- Prepared budgets and projections and monthly budget-to-actual reports and distributed to managers.
- Reviewed work of staff accountant and approved journal transactions for data entry.
- Managed accounting duties of a venture-capital-funded start-up spin-off organization, including financial reporting and coordinating annual audit with external auditors.
- Interacted with systems and payroll services professionals regarding problems and solutions.
- Assisted with analyzing implications, making final decisions, and completion of consolidation of three European subsidiaries.

Accountant, Staff
- Monitored cash and accounts receivable for venture capital–funded software development firm.
- Assisted in general ledger close, including foreign currency translation of foreign subsidiaries.
- Trained new employees to administer the accounts-payable and order-entry functions
- Completed compilations, reviews, audits, and tax returns for individual and corporate clients.
- Created financial schedules and reports using Excel and Supercalc spreadsheet programs.
- Passed Audit, Law, and Theory portions of CPA exam at first sitting.

Accountant (Supervising), Senior
- Supervised, planned, and budgeted audit engagements.
- Oversaw and completed checks of audit reports, financial statements, and tax filings.
- Recruited, trained, supervised, and evaluated staff accountants.
- Gained experience from client assignments, including those in oil and gas, manufacturing, real estate, and nonprofit arenas. Proficient training use of spreadsheet packages.

- Served as liaison between Supervisor, Staff Accountants, and clients.
- Prepared financial statements, tax filings, and audit reports.

Accounting Analyst, Corporate
- Prepared and analyzed income statements, balance sheets, and earnings schedules for $9 billion corporation.
- Compiled 10k federal reserve, management, and analyst reports.
- Utilized trend reports to analyze balance sheet and income statement key ratios.

Accounting Assistant
- Compiled daily reports for magazine and advertising revenues.
- Completed Accounts Receivable and Payable efforts.

Accounting Intern
- Supported efforts of Relationship Managers, servicing depositors with accounts in excess of $500,000.
- Completed compilations, reviews, audits, and tax returns for individual and corporate clients.
- Created financial schedules and reports using Excel spreadsheet programs.
- Supported transactions and addressed inquiries, developed reports, and assisted colleagues and customers.

Accounting Manager
- Completed SEC Reporting and Disclosure forms.
- Managed general ledger closing and maintenance.
- Supervised and reviewed all accounting and finance areas.
- Administrated 401(K) pension plan. Implemented accounting, payroll, and manufacturing software.
- Reported directly to CFO, providing financial data and analytical reports to maximize profits and support managerial decisions.

- Hired, trained, evaluated, and supervised accounting, bookkeeping, and analyst professionals.
- Involved with corporate management in areas of acquisition and corporate development.

Accounting Technician

- Maintained and reported on financial records and created financial statements associated with money market mutual fund for sixty corporate clients.
- Balanced Trial Balance and generated journal entries.
- Maintained, compared, and reconciled the fund on three computer systems.
- Assisted system analysts in preparation and implementation of new computer system.

Administrative Assistant

- Provided administrative support for new business development group; assisted CFO with special projects.
- Ensured smooth workflow; facilitated effectiveness of fourteen sales consultants.
- Directed incoming calls; initiated new client application process; maintained applicant record database.
- Aided in streamlining application process.
- Assisted in design and implementation of computer automation system.

Administrative Assistant to the President and Chief Executive Officer

- Prioritized daily activities of CEO.
- Set up and maintained tickler system.
- Composed and edited correspondence for President.
- Assisted CEO with sensitive customer and employee relationships.
- Recorded and distributed Management Committee minutes.
- Maintained and distributed monthly department reports.

Administrative Assistant to the Chief Executive Officer

- Coordinated and prioritized daily activities of Board Chairman.
- Performed administrative functions in support of CEO.
- Required an in-depth knowledge of the bank, financial community, investors, and customers.
- Assisted with preparation for Board of Directors and Shareholder meetings.
- Recorded and distributed minutes of Board, Shareholder, and Executive Committee meetings.
- Maintained CEO's travel and appointment schedule, using computerized scheduling system.

Administrator, Central Personnel

- Coordinated statewide reclassification study.
- Organized questionnaires and individual interviews.
- Evaluated, analyzed, and rewrote job descriptions; prepared study package for senior management approval.
- Established related managerial files.
- Dealt with diverse personnel-related projects.

Advertising Account Supervisor and Media Coordinator

- Trained, guided, and directed staff of five while monitoring ad placement system.
- Assisted in creation of advertising campaigns and acted as liaison between client, agency, and media vendors, including selection, budget, and advertisement placement.

Advertising Media Planner, Senior

- Directed all phases of media planning services for national accounts, primarily based in eastern region.
- Planned media and placement for five of the firm's largest clients, with annual media budgets ranging from $1 million to $7 million, and total media budgets in excess of $15 million.
- Oversaw efforts of two Media Coordinators, a Media Assistant, and two support professionals.

- Created Excel and Access systems to track media plans and purchases, client quarterly sales, and profits.
- Regularly interacted with account services colleagues and clients to address queries, determine commitment to existing plans, and redirect plans as needed.

Advertising and Public Relations Internship

- Conducted market research, wrote press releases, produced traffic reports, worked media events, and assisted with advertising production.

Architect

- Assisted with development and testing of Computer-Aided Design and Database software.
- Provided demonstration and technical support for pre- and post-sales activity.
- Acted as subject matter expert for future software enhancements and requirements.
- Served in leadership roles for various joint studies teaming with IBM and other major corporations in the evaluation of CDB software for architecture.
- Participated in conceptual design, design development and construction documentation of architecture and landscape design.
- Created exploration, analytical, and presentation models materially and on computers for residential and commercial projects.
- Fabricated sculptural wood and bronze detail elements installed in varied projects.

Art Assistant, Advertising

- Produced paste-ups and mechanicals for full-service advertising agency.
- Operated Photostat camera and coordinated logistics for photo shoots.
- Brainstormed with creative team.

Art Instructor, Secondary
- Developed new and updated existing curriculum regularly for Studio Art, Art History, and Art Appreciation courses.
- Focused Studio Art projects on composition, color, and conceptual problem solving, requiring completion of projects using varied media, including charcoal, pen and ink, acrylics, and airbrush.
- Inventoried, ordered, and controlled budget of approximately $10,000 annually.
- Implemented curriculum with classes for gifted art students, including a district-wide art competition and scholarship in 1993.

Art Instructor, Elementary
- Visited school sites on a regular basis implementing a creativity-focused curriculum.
- Teamed with teachers to incorporate art projects and related lessons into existing units.

Assistant to the Director of Public Relations
- Assisted in promotion and publicity of special events.
- Developed press kits and releases to initiate, maintain, and maximize media relations.
- Compiled easy-to-access and update computerized publicity files using FileMaker Pro.
- Researched prospective consumer markets using Internet and direct-contact techniques.

Audit Trainee
- Conducted audits to complete Federal and State regulatory documentation associated with the FDIC.
- Assessed efficacy of policies and procedures related to fiscal, regulatory, and customer service standards.
- Gained knowledge of operating procedures associated with departments including Personal Banking, Small Business Banking, and Home Equity Loans.

Auditing Analyst

- Prepared contract proposals and illustrative cost calculations.
- Constructed Actuarial Valuation and analyzed actuarial gains and losses.
- Independently generated regular reports for forty individual clients and oversaw development of reports for sixty corporate clients.
- Determined the minimum and maximum contribution allowable by law for the IRS.
- Assured accuracy of comprehensive financial information database.

Auditor (Internal), Senior

- Conducted operational and financial audits of manufacturing subsidiaries.
- Designed and implemented audit programs to test the efficiency of all aspects of accounting controls.
- Recommended changes and improvements to corporate and divisional management.
- Trained and supervised staff auditors in all aspects of the audit engagement.

Bank Branch Manager/Commercial Business Development Officer

- Co-managed District Officer Call Program to retain, expand, and track commercial customer base.
- Instituted Branch Neighborhood Equity Call Program, which enhanced sales of Home Equity and first and second mortgage products 33 percent over a six-month period.
- Designed and managed District Product Development Program, which included development of H.E.L.O.C., Home Equity Loans, residential mortgage products (Two-Year Fixed ARM, Five-Year Fixed ARM), Business Installment Loan (BIL), and marketing collateral.
- Served as one of two Chicago-Area Sales Trainers, supervising professional sales training program for twenty-three branch network, which included Train-the-Trainer, market identification and definition, needs analysis, program development, implementation, results assessment, and follow-up responsibilities.

Bank Branch Manager/IRA Specialist

- Designed brochures for IRA Marketing Program and instituted model for customer focus groups.
- Co-designed and managed new IRA Marketing strategies through Customer/Client Focus Groups.
- Managed overall loan operations of third largest branch, with transactions averaging over $10 million per year.

Bank Branch Manager/Mortgage Development Specialist

- Developed Branch Neighborhood Equity Call Program to introduce and expand Home Equity Programs resulting in a 16 percent increase in Lines and Loans in first month.
- Designed and managed Branch Product Development and Customer Information and Sales incentives.

Bank Teller

- Processed account transactions; reconciled and deposited daily funds.
- Informed customers of bank products, referred public to designated personnel, provided account status data, and handled busy phone.
- Oriented, trained, supervised, and delegated tasks for new hires.
- Assisted with planning and implementing extended-hours customer service strategies.

Barback

- Handled customer service and cash intake.
- Assisted with liquor inventory.
- Performed security services.

Bartender and Bar Manager

- Served patrons, purchased wine, alcohol, beer, and mixes.

Bookkeeper

- Supervised general ledger through trial balance, as well as A/P, payroll, and payroll tax returns for construction and home improvement firm with annual revenues in excess of $2 million.

- Converted bookkeeping procedures from written documents to in-house computer system.
- Coordinated department's workflow, supervising A/R and A/P Clerks.

Bookkeeper, Senior
- Oversaw bookkeeping for mortgage and home equity loan firm, specializing in addressing first home purchases, debt consolidation, and educational payment needs of clients from diverse financial backgrounds.
- Generated and presented general ledger and investors' monthly reports for firm that generated over $10 million in mortgage and loan portfolios annually.
- Oversaw A/R and A/P staff to ensure accuracy of accounts.
- Monitored efforts of third-party payroll services checking accuracy of scheduled payments.
- Managed multiple accounts for major investor and real estate developer with commercial and residential properties in several states.
- Interacted effectively with all finance-savvy senior managers specifically reporting to CFO.
- Supported annual auditing and tax efforts of CPA firm.

Brand Manager and Director of Marketing Operations for Technical Imaging
- Spearheaded implementation of corporate objectives within the Technical Imaging Division.
- Conceived and energized all marketing strategies and provided feedback on program performance and recommendations to corporate senior managers.
- Directed and supervised staff of ten with responsibilities for generating $250 million in sales with a $150 million margin for core products.
- Prepared and effectively controlled a $7 million marketing expense and a $4 million advertising budget.

- Created first end-user direct-mail strategy generating a 30 percent response rate and selling 400,000 units in first year.
- Mounted trade show exhibitions including designing booths, collateral materials, and advertisements. Secured $200,000 in pre-booked sales within a month of trade show presentations for four new products.

Budget Analyst
- Balanced $1.3 billion budget using internally developed and regularly revised software.
- Reconciled accounts on ISA/ABC system to other financial systems.
- Assisted management in budget preparation.
- Conducted training classes on the financial system for upper-level management.
- Prepared comparison of expense to budget reports for executives on demand and on weekly, monthly, and quarterly basis.
- Submitted accounts and IRS filing for the Political Action Committee.
- Generated financial analysis and reporting projects using Focus Report Writing and Excel, including macro programming, and MS Word.
- Contributed annually to budget development and strategic planning processes.

Busboy
- Set and cleared about twenty tables per evening of large dining room.
- Trained new bus people.

Campaign Assistant
- Supervised chapter campaign duties.
- Assisted the Executive Director with administrative responsibilities, such as personnel and budget.

Case Manager
- Served within counseling and referral roles for at-risk students and their families.

- Coordinated outreach, intake, and referrals for those with financial, educational, and medical issues.
- Maintained detailed case records and statistics for reports distributed to district and state officials.

Case Worker
- Assessed client needs, developed treatment plans, and managed cases.
- Communicated with court officials.
- Served as child advocate for court proceedings.

Case Worker, Director (Case Management Services and Legal Advocate)
- Provided counseling and referral services for residents of shelter for abused women and their children.
- Trained and interacted regularly with twenty-four-hour hotline volunteers, supporting telephone crisis counseling and authorizing admission of residents on an emergency basis and for long-term transition periods.
- Conducted individual and group orientations, took case histories, and facilitated counseling sessions.
- Assisted women completing temporary restraining orders and served as liaison with legal counsel.
- Provided expert testimony during domestic violence legal cases and reported outcomes to staff.
- Assisted with public relations and fundraising and regularly contributed to grant writing activities.

Chief of Campus Police, Assistant
- Assisted with personnel, budget, and procedural oversights associated with a department of twenty full-time and twenty part-time security professionals.
- Recruited, trained, and reviewed performance of professional and administrative personnel.
- Patrolled on foot and via automobile, using strong observational and interaction skills.

- Upheld laws and codes of the State of Maryland and Johns Hopkins University.
- Cooperated with law enforcement agencies, regularly interacting with Deputy Sheriff.
- Conducted community outreach and educational efforts, focusing on alcohol use and abuse, safe dating, and property protection.
- Served on Student Life Committees and assisted with judicial investigations.

Civil Litigation Specialist/Office Manager

- Managed office and staff of three secretaries, ensuring smooth operation of firm with three attorneys and billings in excess of $1.5 million and awards of over $10 million annually.
- Interviewed clients; prepared files and discovery; handled multiple cases.
- Requested and reviewed medical documentation.
- Negotiated and settled cases with defense attorney and insurance companies.
- Attend mediations and conciliations.
- Prepared clients for depositions and trials.
- Controlled and maintained law office accounts utilizing accounting and billing software.
- Regularly attended seminars on personal injury law.

Clinic Therapist (Orthopedic In- and Outpatient)

- Developed treatment plans for chronic-pain and cardiac patients.
- Presented regular in-service on hip and knee prostheses.

Computer Systems Analyst

- Completed database management, systems analysis and design, workstation maintenance and repair, and LAN management tasks.

- Reduced process time and purchasing errors by developing an online program that allowed the purchasing department to track the status of all purchasing invoices.
- Developed purchase order program for that improved data entry speed and reduced data entry errors.

Coordinator, Special Events
- Created and Coordinated Special Events and Promotions within $425,000 marketing budget.
- Selected and wrote event advertising, promotional materials, and publicity copy.
- Handled charity fundraising, corporate image positioning, and community outreach efforts.

Counseling and Mental Health Services Intern
- Counseled undergraduate and graduate students with personal, academic, and career issues.
- Addressed psychological and developmental needs of multi-cultural and diverse 3,600 undergraduates and 1,000 graduate students.
- Assessed and diagnosed clients on the basis of presenting problem, history, and rating on Personality Assessment Inventory (PAI).
- Participated in two hours of individual supervision and one hour of group supervision per week.
- Served as a liaison between Counseling Center and University Health Services through involvement in the development of Feel Fit in February speakers series and outreach program designed to meet the health needs of student populations.

Counseling Psychologist
- Facilitated individual and group counseling for clients diagnosed with varied neurotic, psychotic, developmental, and behavioral disorders.
- Collaborated with health-service professionals to development treatment plans for emotionally disturbed adolescents.

- Assisted clients in developing survival skills to aid transition from residential to independent living.
- Coordinated service networks for academic, psychological, and social assistance.

Counselor
- Served as assessment, recruitment, and referral specialist.
- Traveled to community sites and executed presentations to recruit prospective parents for minority children.
- Conducted testing and home studies of prospective parents to determine eligibility.
- Followed up for evaluation purposes three months, six months, one year, and two years post-adoption.
- Served as referral source to private and public mental health services as needed.

Counselor, International Primary School
- Administered psychological and educational testing for students ranging from pre-kindergarten to fifth grades.
- Counseled students, families, and teachers.
- Designed remedial and therapeutic plans.
- Led group activities for self-image enhancement and behavior modification.
- Worked with teachers on preventive strategies for social and disciplinary problems.

Counselor, School
- Counseled students individually and in groups; designed specific counseling programs to meet needs.
- Responded effectively to various on-campus crises via crisis intervention strategies.
- Coordinated and oversaw IEP meetings and specific meetings designed to help high-risk students become more successful in school.
- Consulted daily with teachers and parents regarding student performance.

- Teamed with psychologist presenting information for special education students to parents and teachers.
- Facilitator of workshops, presentations, and programs for students, teachers, and staff.

Counselor (School), Intern

- Counseled students on personal, educational, and career issues.
- Developed and implemented guidance services in a multicultural setting; included social skills groups, divorce groups, and disability awareness program.
- Conducted individual and group counseling for students
- Worked with the "Latinos Unidos" club to improve cultural awareness.
- Developed and implemented preschool curriculum to enhance language skills of developmentally delayed students.
- Coordinated with parents on designing an educational plan to facilitate the development of their children.

Dental Assistant

- Assisted dentist in prophylactic procedures: provided necessary tools, sterilized equipment, comforted patients.
- Provided secretarial assistance.

Dental Hygienist

- Provided prophylaxis treatment, teeth cleaning, oral hygiene education, and periodontal scaling.
- Administered Novocain prior to painful procedures.

Dental Hygienist, Surgical Dental Assistant, and Assistant Office Manager

- Provided state-of-the-art individualized prophylaxis treatment to adult and adolescent patients.
- Administered teeth cleaning, gum massage, oral hygiene education, and periodontal scaling procedures and supervised interns undertaking similar procedures.
- Scheduled patients for appointments for surgical procedures and provided pre-surgical preparation.

- Recorded temperature and blood pressure, inserted intravenous units, and administered sedatives.
- Provided postoperative care in person and via telephone follow up. Recorded vital signs every ten minutes until patients were conscious; established patient comfort; provided necessary information to patients regarding new medications and possible side effects.
- Handled accounts payable and receivable and health insurance transactions.

Dental Clinic Director and Clinical Instructor
- Supervised clinic with rotating groups of dental students and support personnel.
- Evaluated student performance via videotape voice-overs and written reports.
- Annually analyzed financial viability of clinic, instituted regularly revised plans to increase profitability, and managed business related activities.

Dental Trainee/Extern
- Served in rudimentary observation and support roles before advancing to Dental Assistant.
- Sterilized instruments, processed X-rays, scheduled appointments, maintained patient relations.

Dentist
- Provided comprehensive dental care and trained staff members.
- Developed marketing plan, established and allocated marketing budget, and oversaw business operations of practice composed of one dentist, one hygienist, and one support professional.

Dentist (General Practice, Owner)
- Purchased large dental practice through a leveraged buy-out.
- Determined and successfully implemented long-term growth strategies.

- Supervised a staff consisting of two other dentists and six support personnel.
- Provided comprehensive care for over 2,000 patients.
- Lead the office in steadily increasing production and revenues.
- Updated practice and computerized equipment.
- Presently facilitating transition of practice to new owner.

Editor, Senior

- Evaluated general trade reference titles and assess profit potential, acquire titles, and negotiate contracts.
- Oversaw publication, from development and editing to production, publicity, and marketing.
- Served as in-house editor for internal and external newsletters and web documentation.

Editor/Writer

- Edited and wrote large proposals for government contracts.
- Designed format and coordinated production.
- Organized and maintained up-to-date books through several revision cycles.
- Interpreted client requirements and determined applicability of proposal responses.

Engineering Technician

- Prototyped and tested new PC products, drawing schematics and expediting parts for these new PC products. Designed and coded multi-user database management software for engineering use.
- Expedited the parts for over twenty-five telecommunications terminal prototypes. Built, troubleshot, and transferred those prototypes to various departments for testing.

Finance Assistant, Commercial

- Prepared daily client loan advances and payment activity.
- Maintained client loan/collateral statements.

- Assisted with preparation of departmental reports and loan agreements.

Guidance Counselor and English as a Second Language Instructor
- Counseled students and families for clientele ranging from pre-kindergarten to twelfth grade.
- Administered psychological and educational testing.
- Designed complete record keeping system for all students.
- Implemented behavior modification programs.
- Administered achievement, vocational, and college prep tests.
- Made policy on admissions and discipline.
- Worked with teachers on individual educational and behavioral programs.
- Taught English as a Second Language to students in third–sixth grade.

Human Resources, Director of
- Oversaw hiring, training, and all personnel responsibilities for insurance broker with 400 employees.
- Determined technology and procedures related to maintaining and updating personnel files, ensuring compliance with federal and state regulations pertaining to benefits and wages.
- Supervised grievance adjudication.
- Performed claim payment internal audits.
- Coordinated activity with reinsurance carriers.

Human Resources and Staff Development, Director of
- Developed and implemented overall human resource policies.
- Provided leadership in the areas of personnel, payroll, labor relations, training, and affirmative action for operations with over 2,000 employees.
- Administer personnel and payroll procedures, policies and systems to meet management and employee needs.
- Consulted with Chairman, Executive Board, managerial staff, and supervisors to ensure policy compliance with applicable statutes, rules, and regulations.

- Advanced agency Affirmative Action Plan.
- Determined appropriate grievance procedures required to resolve labor disputes.
- Acted as liaison for regulatory agencies: EOHS, OER, DPA, State Office of A.A., and PERA.
- Maintained staff training program.
- Interfaced with legal staff when addressing discipline and grievances.

Investigator/Case Manager (Human Services)

- Conducted assessments and developed treatment plans for family caseload.
- Maintained documentation of contracts and provided crisis intervention and family therapy.
- Served as advocate for clients in court and with community agencies.

Laboratory Technician

- Produced and processed blood components.
- Labeled and released for transfusion and manufacture.
- Performed viral immunology testing and irradiation of blood products.

LAN Coordinator

- Analyzed, developed, and maintained application software for multisite engineering LAN.
- Provided training and user support for all applications to LAN users.
- Maintained departmental PC workstations including software installation and upgrades.
- Reduced data entry errors and process time by developing an online program allowing program manager to submit model number information.
- Replaced time-consuming daily review board meetings by developing a program which allowed engineers to review and approve model and component changes online.

Legal Intern

- Researched and drafted motions on criminal law and procedural issues. Interviewed clients at New Mexico correctional institutions.
- Argued bail motions in several state district courts.
- Negotiated plea and bail agreements for defendants accused of misdemeanors. Attended criminal trials and depositions.

Legal Secretary/Legal Assistant

- Greeted clients, maintained files, and completed administrative tasks.
- Prepared documents for legal proceedings involving real estate transactions.
- Entered client information into Excel- and Access-driven computer system.

Librarian

- Provided excellent patron services when covering circulation and reference desks.
- Gave instructional guidance to patrons, including use of computerized and manual index tools and catalogs.
- Focused interactions on empowering and instructing patrons while creating positive relationships.
- Addressed reference questions by demonstrating proper Internet and printed resources.
- Planned and presented regular community education programs.
- Recorded incoming periodicals and journals on computerized system and strip resources for security.
- Compiled statistics on door count, circulation, photocopies, and reference activities.
- Served on Acquisition Committee and provide quarterly and annual recommendations to Budget Committee.

Librarian/Audio Visual Coordinator

- Supervised comprehensive secondary school library, overseeing volunteer, professional, and student staffs.

- Established annual educational plans and regularly supported instructional efforts of teachers.
- Completed daily patron services and operations efforts and supervised student study periods.
- Interacted with Budget Committee to establish and monitor annual budgets.
- Ordered publications as well as software, and maintained audio-visual equipment.

Management Consultant
- Provided marketing, behavior, and research counsel for advertising, public relations, and marketing consulting firm.
- Participated in internal and external strategic planning for *Fortune* 500 firms, government agencies, nonprofits, and health-care providers.

Market Research Associate
- Managed behaviorally based research projects including proposal writing; methodology, instrument, and sample development; field coordination; data coding, analysis, and report writing.
- Included customer and employee studies, communication audits, market analysis, name/logo testing, constituency relations, positioning, and consumer studies.
- Completed projects for insurance providers, hospitals, and private practices.

Market Research Consultant
- Established firm, conducted client outreach, recruited three associates, and oversaw all operations activities.
- Built consumer behavior models using multivariate techniques, including regression and discriminate analysis, and cluster analysis.
- Analyzed data from national survey to identify purchase intents and patterns for business-to-consumer direct marketers.

- Presented information to senior management of client organizations.
- Specialized in entrepreneurial start-up activities, business plan development, and venture capital solicitation.

Market and Strategic Management Research Consultant

- Conducted large-scale quantitative research projects based in customer satisfaction measurement and total quality implementation, including design, coordination, statistical analysis, and report generation.
- Specialized in business-to-business services, e-commerce, and health care.

Marketing Assistant

- Cold-called high school and college students and parents, marketing college and graduate school entrance exam preparation courses.
- Yielded 35 percent attendance at seminars and simulations used to market services.

Marketing Representative, Senior

- Managed assigned territory including prospecting new distribution sources, rehabilitating nonperforming agencies, and terminating relationships.
- Served in lead role for all insured sales presentations by conducting strategy negotiations, making presentations, and facilitating actual presentation.

Marketing, Vice President of

- Identified target markets, constructed complex questionnaires, conducted telephone interviews, compiled and analyzed data for research activities associated with entrepreneurial start-up.
- Conducted focus groups to identify market segments and penetration.
- Wrote and presented report to management including strategic recommendations.

- Addressed all marketing research needs.
- Gathered data to develop comprehensive business plan and marketing reports.

Nanny
- Provided live-in child care for two boys, currently ages two and four.
- Provided environmental enrichment and personal care.
- Supervised play, transported children to preschool and other activities, and assisted with meals.
- Reinforced parental rules and values.
- Accompanied family on short and long trips and vacations.

Nurse Practitioner
- Provided gynecologic, obstetric, and primary care in collaboration with physicians in private practice.
- Evaluated and managed acute and chronic gynecologic and obstetric problems, including: abdominopelvic pain, genitourinary problems, infections, breast concerns, endocrine-related problems, osteoporosis, and postoperative and pregnancy complications.
- Evaluated and managed wide array of primary care problems including EENT, allergic conditions, dermatological problems, infectious diseases, chest pain, and respiratory, gastrointestinal, and musculoskeletal problems.
- Performed annual and employment exams and prenatal and postpartum care.
- Counseled and prescribed for cholesterol and weight management, contraception, menopause, osteoporosis, and mood disorders.
- Developed health education handouts and presented staff in-service training.
- Performed periodic Quality Assurance review for onsite laboratory.
- Acted as preceptor for Nurse Practitioner and Physician Assistant students.

Nurse Practitioner, Senior

- Evaluated and managed health problems including: infectious diseases, allergic conditions, dermatological problems, respiratory, gastrointestinal, genitourinary, endocrine, and musculoskeletal problems, traumatic injuries, and occupational health issues.
- Provided routine and preventive care, employment and sports physical exams.
- Initiated gynecologic services for Eastman School of Music.
- Made health education presentations, acted as preceptor, and served on Training and HIV Task Force.
- Coordinated University Health Services Library used by nurses, nursing students, and patients.

Pastry Chef, Assistant

- Worked with Executive Pastry Chef, monitoring baking, mixing, and finishing of cakes, pastries, and a full range of bakery products on an as-needed basis.
- Completed special orders for banquets, catered functions, and hotel restaurant.

Pastry Chef and Bakery Manager

- Plan and prepare desserts on a daily basis for restaurant patrons.
- Oversee all operations of retail bakery and prepare desserts and breads for catered functions.
- Prepared an extensive assortment of desserts, rotating on a weekly basis, including cakes, cookies, cobblers, puddings, tarts, special-order desserts, and wedding cakes.
- Created breakfast pastries and breads for lunch specials.
- Planned and executed monthly menu which included six desserts, two sorbets, two ice cream dishes, and two fresh breads daily for lunch and dinner.
- Ordered all bakery and dairy supplies, and prepared desserts for retail store and special orders.

Patrolman
- Performed all standard policing functions, earning excellent ratings annually.
- Interacted and communicated with town officials regarding proactive and reactive efforts.

Physical Therapy Aid
- Assisted with ultrasound, muscle stimulation, massage, and interferential treatments.
- Served as translator using Spanish language skills with selected patients.

Production Assistant
- Booked main guests and panelists for weekly topical talk show.
- Generated and researched story ideas.
- Conducted video research.
- Edited teasers for show.
- Organized production details for studio tapings.
- Coordinated publicity ads in local newspapers.

Production Intern
- Assisted producers of live, daily sports interview and call-in show.
- Researched and generated story ideas.
- Pre-interviewed guests.
- Covered shoots and wrote promos.
- Produced five segments.

Professor
- Taught undergraduates Criminal Law, Criminal Procedures, Crime in America, and Business Law.
- Stimulated class involvement through use of case studies, mock trials, and law-school simulation.
- Served as Freshman Advisor to diverse students and Faculty Advisor to pre-law majors on an annual basis.

Professor, Assistant

- Taught undergraduate courses in Business Administration and Law, including: Criminal Law, Crime in America; Courts and Criminal Law; Criminal Procedures; Crime in America; and the Courts.
- Taught First Year Law students Criminal Procedures and Juvenile Procedures.

Programmer Analyst/Senior Programmer

- Supervised Junior Programmers on varied System Projects.
- Actively participated in projects involving e-commerce, CRM, BI or ERP functions.
- Developed, maintained, and supported Sales Illustration Systems in "C."
- Wrote "Illustration Software Installation" routine in INSTALIT software.
- Designed file transfer process for Mainframe to PC using NDM software. Hands-on experience with PC hardware, Windows, IBM, Novell Software, Emulation Software (Rumba, Extra, etc.), Dial-In Software (SimPC, XTalk, etc.) and have understanding of LAN technologies.
- Developed an Executive Information System on the mainframe using COBOL 2.
- Designed and implemented system enhancements and new products.

Promotional Assistant

- Implemented promotional campaigns, wrote copy, and designed advertisements. Enhanced attendance via creative competitions and corporate sponsored give-aways.

Public Relations Manager

- Served as consultant to seven state chapters regarding campaign problems and activities.
- Organized regional campaign meetings; spoke at several campaign conferences.

- Reviewed legislation and brought specific bills to the attention of the proper committee or individual.
- Staffed the Legislative Advisory Committee and followed through on specific bills.
- Developed fundraising programs.
- Conducted the previous two annual campaigns for the newly merged Central Chapter.

Publicist

- Personally support media relations, campaign development, and implementation efforts associated with professional athletes, education, and not-for-profit clients.
- Interact with clients regularly to address needs and fine-tune annually updated strategic media plans.
- Draft, edit, and finalize news releases, speeches, and press packets.
- Develop and maintain relationships with regional and national print and broadcast media, supporting efforts to maximize desired coverage.
- Serve as client spokesperson and as press conference coordinator.

Publicity Assistant

- Publicized new books and authors.
- Assisted with television, radio, and print media tours and individual appearances.
- Created and implemented author questionnaire to maximize publicity generated through professional contacts.
- Wrote press releases and designed press packets.
- Responded to review copy requests.

Real Estate Loan Officer

- Originated real estate loans, developed marketing plan to expand business in Santa Clara County.

- Conducted cold calls, created individualized mortgage broker packets.
- Completed individual and group presentations designed to generate loan business.
- Implemented first-ever real estate expo promotional event.

Real Estate Sales Associate (Residential and Commercial)
- Served in comprehensive sales as well as mortgage and lease-advisory capacities for residential and commercial clients for one of the Bay Area's largest branch offices.
- Prospected new buyers and sellers via monthly seminars, direct-mail, and e-mail campaigns, appearances on radio programs, and print and television ads.
- Regularly exceeded sales goals, twice receiving national Gold Jacket recognition for top 10 percent production, three times receiving $100 million Club recognition for annual sales and leases, and annually receiving Top Producer recognition for regional and state sales figures.
- Licensed in residential and commercial sales, property management, and financing and leasing.

Real Estate Territory Manager (Regional)
- Recruited to open and develop Bay Area for multiline commercial accounts.
- Generated territory volume of $4 million from $250,000.

Recruiting Manager (Executive Recruiting)
- Reviewed and revised annual college recruiting strategies and yield targets with VPs of Human Resources, Merchandising, and Operations.
- Developed, proposed, and monitored annual college recruiting budgets of approximately $75,000.
- Regularly reviewed and established target school listings, contacts, and recruiting dates.

- Trained college team liaisons and leaders to make effective campus recruitment presentations.
- Organized senior executive involvement in Career Days second interview processes.
- Facilitated College Recruiting Team discussions regarding Management Development Program offers.
- Recruited for, hired, and oversaw fifteen Summer Interns and ten Academic-Year Interns annually.
- Assisted training staff with planning educational and social activities associated with initial portions of a ten-week program that blends classroom instruction with career networking and skills training.

Rehabilitation Therapist (Cardiac)
- Acted as program coordinator for exercise regimen and provided treatments using ultrasound, electric stimulation, massage therapy, and stretching/strengthening exercises.
- Coordinated aquadynamics program for chronic-pain patients.

Rehabilitation Therapist (Pediatric)
- Coordinated treatment of amputee children and children with congenital birth defects.
- Created Alive with Pride program now functional at thirty national hospitals.
- Developed child-oriented play program and trained teachers via elementary school seminars.

Restaurant Manager
- Oversaw operations of 250-seat facility averaging over $10,000 daily sales, offering American cuisine luncheon and dinner service to store patrons.
- Scheduled, motivated, and supervised staff of twenty-five full-time and part-time servers per shift.
- Monitored daily and monthly receipts and expenditures.
- Communicated with store and corporate management regarding sales targets and profit strategies.

Restaurant Manager, Assistant

* Oversaw operations of 175-seat facility averaging over $3,000 daily food sales and $3,000 wine and alcohol sales, offering luncheon, dinner, and after-dinner service.
* Supervised staff of thirty employees per shift, controlled inventory, deposited cash, maintained physical plant, and completed daily and weekly reports for after-hours club catering to elite patrons.
* Monitored food costs, effectively communicated with chef and prep staff regarding costs.
* Prepared and submitted weekly, monthly, and quarterly reports to owners.
* With chef, planned weekly menus.

Retail Buyer (Apparel Department), Junior

* Developed sales volume from $5.5 million to $7.5 million.
* Consistently achieved net operating profit of 50 percent, highest in company.
* Implemented promotional strategies and developed key classifications directly responsible for volume increase.
* Developed electronic and direct communication networks supplying product knowledge to sales staff and impacting strategic planning of vendor programs.
* Instituted e-mail communication strategies and status-tracking efforts.
* Chosen as Merchant of the Year 2008, 2009, and 2010.

Retail Buyer, Assistant

* Acted as liaison with vendors and warehouse to assure timely merchandise delivery of men's coordinates, coats, swimwear, and activewear.
* Interpreted, analyzed, and responded to OTB, selling reports, and seasonal plans.

Retail Sales Manager (Divisional)

* Handled furniture, electronics, and basement store with $5.6 million in sales for the year 2008.

- During mall expansion, held store sales volume within plan by achieving 12 percent increase.
- Priorities included constant evaluation of stock levels and content, goal setting, development of key personnel, and achieving a high motivational level.

Sales Account Executive (Advertising)
- Sold time and production support to potential clients.
- Assisted with establishment of all media and production plans, proposals, and budgets submitted to potential and existing clients.
- Implemented existing local, regional, and national strategies and media sales programs.
- Increased sales and production revenues.

Sales Account Executive (Advertising), Senior
- Established and maintained national corporate accounts as well as regional and local accounts.
- Interacted with national sales, regularly identifying and leveraging new packages based on demographics and ratings.
- Utilized production experience to establish and grow strategy targeting regional and local revenues, primarily generated from independently owned retailers and service providers.
- Developed relationships with regional ad agencies, specifically media planners, to establish client-focused team approach.
- Accounted for over $2 million in new clients revenues over four-year period, and average annual revenues of $500,000.
- Initiated and developed marketing strategies and target grid for the second-ranked TV station in fifth-largest market for effective sales programs/promotions.

Sales Account Executive, Dealer
- Oversaw completion of relationship building, bidding, delivery, and all sales efforts required to market products and services through dealer locations.

- Initiated cooperative sales strategy with reseller business owners.
- Designed marketing promotions and directed reseller's sales efforts into business and education accounts.
- Grew sales by 400 percent to $20 million.
- Oversaw training and completed performance reviews of ten to fifteen Sales Representatives.

Sales Account Manager, National

- Developed and implemented national sales strategy for computer and peripheral manufacturer, consultant, and support-service provider.
- Initiated, built, and nurtured relationships with several *Fortune* 500 corporations including Ackler Industrial, The Carnulton Group, Hanlon and Associates, and Polamin Company.
- Oversaw resale accounts as well as direct-user accounts. Involved identification and analysis of potential business applications within target accounts and cultivation of key business relationships with senior management to facilitate sales.
- Grew profits 200 percent over five years to $15 million amidst decreasing unit pricing, increasing sales goals, and enhanced competition.
- Completed all five years in the top 12 percent of the National Account Channel as Golden Star Award winner.
- Created new revenue streams resulting in an estimated $30 million in sales and $40 million in new services for the company.
- Regularly reported sales results and status of strategies to senior marketing executives and CEO.

Sales Representative (Corporate Chain)

- Provided administrative and technical sales support to corporate chain account locations, including Power Electronics, Computer Corral, and Circonne Computer.
- Regularly called upon accounts to maximize knowledge of retail personnel, address concerns, and promote in-store visibility.

- Developed marketing promotions and trained store personnel.
- Tracked individual store sales and profit data to determine efficient coverage schedule and recognize particular achievements.

Secretary (Departmental)

- Answered phones, scheduled appointments, greeted patients and visitors, and prepared and filed charts.
- Typed and printed invoices and requisitions.
- Supervised inventory and general office organization.
- Served as liaison between physicians, staff, and patients.

Secretary to Executive Vice-President and Senior Loan Officer

- Managed Secretarial Staff supporting commercial loan officers.
- Coordinated staff meetings and presentations to Board of Directors.
- Prepared monthly departmental and divisional reports for distribution.
- Updated and maintained Policy and Procedure Manual on a timely basis.

Secretary to the Senior Vice Present Commercial Division

- Set up Commercial Loans on System.
- Prepared monthly reports for Board of Directors.
- Updated financial statements.
- Maintained appraisal files.
- Coordinated loan renewals.

Security, Head of

- Managed all aspects of security for hotels and adjoining properties.
- Hired, scheduled, supervised, and evaluated personnel.
- Provided all policing functions, with emphasis on defusing potentially violent situations.
- Cooperated extensively with Baltimore and Bethesda Police Departments.

Social Worker
- Provided services for clients and families with medical, psychological, housing, and financial needs.
- Supervised agency volunteers and graduate student interns.
- Worked collaboratively with various community agencies to provide needed serves.
- Conducted in-service training to staff and those from other agencies.

Social Worker, Clinical
- Diagnosed, evaluated, and treated children, adolescents, adults, and families living within the guidelines of Care and Protection Petitions.
- Interacted with legal, medical, and psychological professionals.
- Provided individualized social work services for children and adolescents, including pregnant teens, foster-home residents, and those meeting court-mandated criteria.
- Maintained accurate and thorough documentation via case records.

Social Worker (District)
- Provide direct social work services to elementary, middle, and high school students and families.
- As member of interdisciplinary team, establish, implement, and monitor effectiveness of Independent Educational Programs.
- Regularly communicate with parents, teachers, and special-education professionals regarding individual students.
- Conduct group discussions with students and parents pertaining to developmental, behavioral, and medical issues.

Store Manager
- Manage Spinner's largest-volume store, with sales of approximately $30,000 per week.
- Handle all merchandising, inventory control, ordering, cash control, and maintenance.

- Oversee store opening and closing procedures.
- Direct sales floor activities, assist customers, and address customer concerns.
- Input data to prepare daily sales reports and regularly use weekly and monthly data to develop sales and promotional strategies.
- Hire, train, and coordinate a staff of twenty-six.
- Work with Spinner corporate colleagues as well as record company professionals to develop local marketing and advertising strategies, supplementing national campaigns.
- Inspire sales staff to develop and implement special promotions and events.
- Won two merchandising display contests.
- Received the Super Spinner Sales Award for exceeding sales goals

Store Manager, Assistant
- Promoted from trainee to Assistant Manager within twelve months.
- Conceptualized and implemented employee training and effectiveness program.
- Hired, trained, and supervised staff of six serving customers of specialty men's clothing store.
- Provided exceptional customer services to high-end consumers, regularly including direct e-mail and phone contact, and relationship building.
- Tallied daily receipts and made bank deposits.
- Opened and closed store, handled customer service issues, and oversaw cash control.
- Maintained inventory levels, monitored merchandise, provided feedback to owner/buyer regarding trends and need for reorders.

Student Clinician (Speech Pathology)
- Diagnosed, then planned and administered therapy to children with apraxia, language delay, hearing impairment, and articulation disorders.

- Used Visual Phonics and American Sign Language with hearing-impaired child client.
- Diagnosed, then administered therapy to adult displaying motor speech disorders and aphasia.
- Established home programs to effectively train and motivate parents, spouses, and others.
- Wrote case summaries documenting clinical goals, approaches, and achievements.

Student Teacher (Third Grade)

- Independently established and presented lesson and unit plans.
- Created specific interdisciplinary Reading and Work unit, focusing on reading skills for varied jobs, and including visiting career field representatives.

Systems Engineer

- Coauthored software test plan for computer prototypes.
- Researched, wrote, and edited test procedures.
- Developed computer engineering test tools.
- Wrote database application to track and generate reports on problems found during development.
- Organized preproduction testing of prototypes.
- Analyzed requirements for new processes to improve product testing.
- Created software that automated work-related processes, such as generating status- and engineering-change request reports.

Systems Manager

- Researched, wrote, and edited proposal used to identify needs and fund networks and desktop configurations composed of eight personal computers and two printers
- Supervises three Technology and Systems Consultants for office with thirty full-time employees.
- Planned and oversaw completion of special project teams related to existing and future technology needs and potential purchases.

- Regularly conducted software- and hardware-related trouble-shooting and audit activities.
- Interacted with product vendors and customer service and technology support professionals.
- Designed 24/7 backup and retrieval system for accounting databases and word-processing data.

Systems Programmer
- Initiated start-up and implemented operations.
- Designed and managed implementation of a network providing the legal community with a direct line to Supreme Court cases.
- Developed a system that catalogued entire library's inventory.
- Used Cs to create a registration system for a university registrar.

Teacher
- Taught infant, preschool, and after-school programs.
- Planned curriculum, organized activities, communicated with parents and staff regarding children's growth and development.
- Enhanced skills development through interactive play and song.
- Responded to annual increase in students and move to new facility.
- Worked with owner on goals and assisted with annual licensing documentation and visitation.

Teacher, Substitute
- Instructed academic lessons to K–12 population; lesson development and classroom management.
- Worked with developmentally challenged students.

Teacher, Summer School (English)
- Planned and implemented lessons focusing on literature, grammar, writing, and research.
- Addressed remedial needs of students.

Teaching Assistant (Biochemistry Laboratory)
- Assisted students in biochemistry laboratory.

- Worked with professors to prepare materials for use in the laboratory and graded quizzes and laboratory reports.
- Created web page allowing students access to test results.

Teacher (Voice and Piano)
- Instructed approximately seventy voice, piano, and composition students.
- Presented six recitals annually, working with students to select and prepare performance pieces.
- Regularly used video and electronic piano computer system to provide audio and visual feedback.
- Guided students through application process for admissions and auditions for music programs and professional performance and composition.

Telemarketing Professional
- Cold-called residential and commercial consumers, assessing domestic and international calling needs, and then recommending and marketing long-distance programs.
- Consistently achieved at least 125 percent of sales goals.
- Landed largest commercial accounts during 2008–2009 and 2009–2010 Fiscal Years.

Television and Radio Station Producer (Campus Cable)
- Wrote hard news, feature stories, scheduled/interviewed guests.
- Responsible for researching materials for mini-documentary.
- Scheduled and interviewed quests for round-table discussions.
- Wrote and edited scripts and edited master tape.
- Researched materials and packaged tapes for production.
- Performed as camera technician, stage manager, and teleprompter operator.

Travel Consultant
- Arranged individual and group travel, regularly yielding monthly billings in excess of $10,000.

- Promoted agency via weekly visits to senior residences as well as college campuses.
- Regularly attended training sessions related to airline offerings and reservation systems updates.
- Coordinated air ticketing requests and tour departures using APOLLO and SABRE systems.
- Served as agency specialized for cruise industry.
- Regularly attended sessions hosted by cruise and air carriers, educating regarding options and plans.
- Tracked international and domestic fares, sharing data with colleagues daily.
- Issued tickets and final itineraries for air and cruise customers.
- Maintained and filed pertinent materials and assisted with updating of website.
- Assisted with projects associated with marketing of Disney World, Disneyland, and Disney Cruises.
- Prepared detailed financial reports and assisted senior management with development of strategic goals.

Tutor and Advisor (Summer Enrichment Program)
- Advised, tutored, and taught specialized courses to selected group of high school students.
- Planned and implemented ten-week Study Skills, SAT Preparation, and Writing Skills seminars, focusing on at-risk students with the potential to succeed in college.
- Created assignments-based "Reality Academy," an ideal high school.

Underwriter (Insurance)
- Analyzed all personal lines of business to determine acceptability and to control, restrict, or decline, according to company guidelines.
- Supervised all personal lines of business for Arizona and New Mexico.

- Kept current with changing policies, rates, and procedures, explaining coverage, rules, forms, and decisions to agents, staff, and insured.

Veterinarian's Assistant (Surgical)
- Assisted clinicians and students treating patients, and provided room pre- and postoperative care.

Veterinarian's Assistant (Surgical), Senior
- Perform pre- and postoperative care and emergency care.
- Monitor ventilation and vital statistics of premature and critically ill animals.
- Collect and ship blood samples, perform intravenous and arterial catheterization, intubation of endotracheal and nasogastric tubes.
- Organize labs for and oversee veterinary students and clinical instruction sessions.

Veterinary Animal Technician/Research Assistant
- Directed hygienic procedures on 300 animals, including surgery and necropsies.
- Conducted research on pet food products and analyzed studies on nutrition, zinc, urine, feces, fluid therapy, medication, breeding, and artificial insemination.
- Collaborated in testing new vaccine for feline leukemia, submitting reports for FDA approval.
- Supervised and scheduled twenty center and union employees in conducting research.

Veterinary Assistant
- Assisted with daily diagnosis and treatment, and served as ICU specialist, completing oral, IV, IM, SQ, fluid therapy-, radiology-, hematology-, immunology-, chemotherapy-related tasks.
- Administered, assisted, and maintained anesthesia during surgery.

Waiter, Head
- Managed, opened, and closed high-volume four-star restaurant.
- Hired, trained, scheduled, and supervised waitstaff.
- Led weekly quality assurance and menu discussion sessions.
- Oversaw special catering events held onsite and at residences of patrons.
- Provided efficient service to full bar, serving area, and catered affairs.
- Addressed concerns and special requests.
- Reconciled gratuity intake in accordance with tax regulations.

Witness Advocate
- Interviewed victims and witnesses, prepared documents, and organized information for court appearances.
- Assisted attorneys during trials, taking notes and facilitating access to evidentiary documents.

Writer (Technical) and Senior Project Administrator
- Research data and accurately describe the installation, removal, erection, and maintenance of all military hardware.
- Outline wiring diagrams, draw part breakdowns for illustrators, draft and finalize all descriptions associated with use of and training to use military hardware.
- Serve as overall program lead for specific projects in A-3, EA-3, and EP-3E programs.
- Work on IPB, MIM, and IFMM for all maintenance levels.
- Transform various source materials, including engineering drawings and wiring diagrams into user targeted–written and disc-driven documentation and illustrations.
- Served as project lead, including editing, layout, and corrections.

Chapter 11

25 Things Not to Say in Your Resume

The real estate on your resume is valuable, and you'll be neither the first nor last person to wish you had more space on the page. With that in mind, make sure the experience you've listed actually belongs there. Anything that's too vague, overly personal, irrelevant, or simply untrue should be taken off. The following list reviews twenty-five things you shouldn't say in your resume. Read them all, and if necessary, revise.

1. Don't say, "I know how to go online, and I can use a PC" when listing technical skills. Mention specific software programs, operating systems, and industry-specific applications if appropriate for your goals.

2. Don't include, "I bought my first house" in your list of accomplishments. It is an accomplishment, but it doesn't communicate any strengths to the reviewer.

3. Don't describe your objective as being, "To secure a developer position within commuting distance of my house." True or not, it says nothing of what you can bring to the company.

4. Don't lie about your responsibilities. Saying you, "Edited manuscripts submitted by authors" is very different than saying you "Logged in manuscript submissions from authors." All it takes is one reference check to get the truth.

5. Don't list affiliations that have nothing to do with your job or the industry in which you work. Including that you are the "Founding member of the Thirsty Thursdays Happy Hour Club" will not win you points, in most cases.

6. Don't get bogged down in the details. If you progressed to a more senior level position in the same company, don't list the same duties under your newer title, even if you continued to perform many of them.

7. Don't list every job you've ever had since you started working as a teenager. Only list your most recent professional (and volunteer) experience as it relates to the job for which you're applying.

8. Don't overlook volunteer experience. "Work Experience" doesn't have to be the only headline used or experience cited and described in your resume.

9. Don't include salary requirements in your objective statement. Stating that your goal is "To earn a six-figure salary" will tell your potential employers you're only interested in money.

10. Don't include a long list of extracurricular activities or hobbies unrelated to the job or field you're trying to get into.

11. Don't say, "References available upon request." This is a given and therefore unnecessary to say on your resume.

12. Don't include, "GPA: 2.8; 2.9 in major." Your GPA should only be listed if it is 3.0 or above.

13. Don't include street addresses and zip codes when identifying the companies where you've worked. It will take up extra space unnecessarily.

14. Don't include failed projects in your list of work-related accomplishments. Less is more in this situation.

15. Don't include your age in your contact information.

16. Don't clutter your resume with redundant phrases, (e.g., saying you have a "proven track record of success.")

17. Don't include a list of college courses on your resume if you're not a recent graduate. At some point, your on-the-job experience will outweigh your coursework.

18. Don't point out that you were fired from a job. Listing it on your resume without first having the opportunity to explain the circumstances will diminish your chances of getting an interview.

19. Don't provide any information about your religious affiliation (or lack thereof). Listing a leadership role in your church, for example, is something you should avoid doing, unless it is directly related to your goal.

20. Don't mention any political affiliations, either. The person reviewing your resume might not share your views, so it's best to keep this information to yourself. Stay focused on what pertains to the job and your experience.

21. Don't fabricate relationships that don't exist. Networking is important; however, there's a difference between knowing *of* someone and actually knowing them. Your connections will be checked, so don't provide misleading information.

22. Don't use other people's achievements to make yourself look good. For example, avoid phrases such as, "Played a direct role in helping marketing intern get promoted to marketing assistant by providing mentoring and leadership support." Such a statement does not highlight your promotion, and it's vague.

23. Don't mention personal relationships anywhere on your resume. It's no one's business whether you're married or divorced. The same goes for sexual orientation.

24. Don't provide information about any crimes you've committed. Regardless of how the circumstances affected your employment, don't include it on your resume.

25. Don't provide inappropriate contact information. Consider e-mail addresses and telephone numbers for your current job off limits. Provide only personal contact information, and make sure your e-mail address is something professional that identifies who you are. For example, an e-mail address along the lines of firstname_lastname@example.com will be regarded much more seriously than iluv2party@example.com.

Chapter 12

Buzz Words
and **Action**
Verbs for Your
Resume

BUZZ WORDS ARE A VITAL TOOL for anyone hoping to craft a targeted, effective resume and land his dream job. Using industry-specific buzz words will make your resume stand out to the hiring managers and human resource professionals reviewing them. This section contains a list of buzz words organized by industry followed by a list of regularly used action verbs.

Accounting and Finance

Accounting and finance buzz words highlight experience with accounting, budgeting, treasury, auditing, and information systems activities. This includes collection, documentation, and analysis of financial data and the use of this data to make strategic decisions and share pertinent information with investors, regulators, and government entities. It also includes allocation of capital required for annual operations as well as growth.

► Resume Buzz Words

1099 Tax Information
A/P
A/R
Absorbing Cost
Abusive Tax Shelter
Accommodative Monetary Policy
Account Aggregation
Accounting
Accounting Software
Accounting Systems
Accounts
Accounts Payable
Accounts Receivable
Accredited Investor
Acid Test
Acquisitions
Actual Reports
Actuarial Department
Actuarial Valuation Report
Adjusted Gross Income
Administrative Leadership
ADP System
Advances
Affiliate
Affinity Investment Scheme
Allotment Needs
Alternative Investment Market
Analysis of Financial Data
Analytical Services
Annual Budget Process
Annual Budgets
Annual Capital Budgets
Annual Operations
Annuity
Appropriation of Money
Asset Management
Asset Reconciliation
Asset Responsibility
Assets
Audit Papers
Audit Requests
Audit Schedules
Auditing
Auditors
Audits
Automated Transmission Process
Balance of Trade
Balance Sheets
Bank Balances
Bank Reconciliations
Bank Training Program
Bar Charts
Bear Market
Bellwether Stock
Benefits Reports
Bids
Big Five
Big Three
Bill Payment
Billing Errors
Billing Systems
Black-Scholes Model
Blue Chip Stock
Board of Directors

Bond and Corporate Financial Services
Bond and Equity Transactions
Bond Market Association
Bonds
Bookkeeping
Boston Stock Exchange
Branch Office
Bridge Financing
Brokerage Firm
Brokerage License
Brokerage Services
Brokers
Budget
Budget Account
Budget and Investigated Variances
Budget Control
Budget Projections
Budgeting
Bull Market
Bureau of Economic Research (BEA)
Bureau of Labor Statistics (BLS)
Burn Basket Execution
Business Administration
Business Cycle
Business Development
Business Experience
Business Model
Business Plan
C.O.B.R.A.
Capital
Capital Budget
Capital Expenditure
Capital Gain
Capital Growth
Capital Surplus Statement
Cash
Cash Account
Cash Availability
Cash Disbursement
Cash Earnings
Cash Flow
Cash Management
CDs
Check Cashing Center
Check Disbursement
Check Verification
Checkbook Maintenance
Check-Cashing Center
Checks
Chicago Stock Exchange
Cincinnati Stock Exchange
Claim Liabilities
Claims Processing
Client Relations
Client's Asset Base
Close the Books
Closet Index
Coding of Receipts
Collections
Commerce Department
Commercial Credit Unions
Commercial Lending
Commercial Loan Operations
Commissions

Commodities
Commodity Futures
Commodity Options
Composite Index
Composite Table
Composite Yield
Compound Interest
Computer Models
Computer Systems
Consulting
Consumer Confidence Index (CCI)
Consumer Credit
Contract Negotiation
Contract Proposals
Contractors
Contracts
Conversion Parity
Convertible Debt
Coordinated Payments
Corporate and Municipal Securities
Corporate Banking Services
Corporate Clients
Corporate Finance
Corporate Financial Data
Corporate Financial Reporting
Corporate Lenders
Corporate Securities
Corporation Account
Cost Estimators
Cost of Living Adjustment (COLA)
Credit Analysis
Credit Balance
Credit Bureau
Credit Reporting
Credit Terms
Currency
Custody Services
Customer Agreement
Customer Inquiries
Customer Relations
Customized Credit Solutions
Customized Investment Portfolios
Data Processing
Database Management
Day Trader
Debt
Debt Consolidation Services
Debt Underwriting
Decimal Pricing
Deferred Compensation Retirement Plan
Department of Commerce
Deposit Accounts
Derivatives
Derivatives and Asset Management
Devaluation
Development of a Mission
Direct Deposits
Director Labor and Standard Costs
Disbursement and Tracking of Loans
Disclosure Forms
Discount Brokerage
Discretionary Income
Discretionary Investment Management
Disposable Income
Divestiture
Dividend Credit
Dividend Receivables

Dividend Reinvestment Plan
Dividend/Interest Payments
Documentation
Dollar Bond
Donated Stock
Dow Jones Composite Average
Dow Theory
Due Diligence
Dynamic Pricing
Earned Surplus
Earnings Reports
Earnings Schedules
Earnings Season
Economic Indicators
Economics
EDP
Efficient Market Theory (EMT)
Emerging Markets
Employee Benefits Reports
Employer-Employee Relationships
Enforcement Policies
Equity
Equity Funds
Equity Ratio
e-Reporting
Escrow
Escrow Deposit
Estate Planning
Eurobonds
European Union (EU)
Exchange Rate
Excise Tax Laws and Regulations
Expenditures
Expense Recording
Expense Reports
Expenses
Federal/State/Unemployment Taxes
Filing Procedures
Finance
Financial Accounting
Financial Advisory Services
Financial Analysis
Financial Expertise
Financial Modeling
Financial Plan
Financial Reporting
Financial Statements
Financial Strategies
Financial Systems
Financial Trend Analysis
First and Junior Trust Deed Loans
Fixed Assets
Fixed Income Securities
Fixed-Income Sales and Trading
Fleet Financing
Flexible Funding Alternatives
Focus Sessions
Forecasts
Foreign Currency
Foreign Exchange
Foreign Markets
Fraud Account Functions
Fund Coding
Fund Custody Services
Fund Expenses
Fund/Sponsor Investments
Future Sales and Trading

GAAP and SSAP Formats
GCAS Productivity
General Ledger
Global Fund Services
Global Macroeconomics
Global Markets
Global Trade Services
Government Entities
HMO Rates
Home Loans
Homeowners
Illustrative Cost Calculations
Income Statements
Income-Related Statements
Inequities
Information Systems
Institutional Equities
Insurance and Financial Services
Insurance Products
Integrated Financial Solutions
Internal Control Procedures
Internal/External Reporting
International Banking Services
International Bond Funds
International Economics
International Index Assets
Investment Banking
Investor Relations
Investor Services
Investors
Invoices
IRA
IRS Filing
IRS Service Policies
ISA/ABS Systems
Issuance of Policies
Journal Entries
Journal Transactions
Key Ratios
Leasing Companies
Legal and Credit Files
Lending
Liabilities
License Agreements
Lien Mortgage Loans
Line Management
Listed Companies
Loan Documents
Loan Payments
Lotus
Management Information Systems
Management Services
Managerial Accounting
Manual Worksheet System
Manually Issued Policies
Market Averages
Market Awareness
Market Indicators
Market Invoices
Marketing
Markets
Merchant Investment Banking
Mergers and Acquisitions
Middle- and Upper-Income Markets
Money Management
Money Market Account
Money Market Instruments

Month-End Journal
Monthly Closing
Monthly Financial Statements
Monthly Forecasts
Monthly Manufacturing Accounting Report
Mortgage Loans
Mortgages
Municipal Securities
Mutual Funds
NASD Regulations
NASDAQ
National/International Markets
New Benefits
New York Stock Exchange
Online Investments
Operating Budget
Operational Support
Options
Originating (Brokering and Funding)
Outstanding Payable Balance
Outstanding Tax Obligations
Overdrafts
Overdue Accounts
Partnerships
Past Due Interest
Payable Vouchers
Payroll
Payroll Coverage
Payroll Functions
Payroll Records
Personnel
Petty Cash
Planning Refinement
Portfolios
Premium-Based Workers' Compensation
Pricing Policies
Primary and Secondary Public Stock Offerings
Principal Auditor
Private Client Services
Private Companies
Probabilities
Problem Resolutions Skills
Production Costing
Profit Plans
Profit Sharing
Profitability
Pro Forma Statements
Property and Casualty Carrier
Public Companies
Public Finance
Public Relations
Purchase Orders
Purchasing
Quantitative Analysis
Quarterly/Monthly Reports
Real Estate and Mortgage Loans
Real Estate Transactions
Receipts
Record Transactions
Recordkeeping Services
Regulators
Regulatory Bodies
Remit Payments
Reports
Repurchase Agreements
Residential Loan Applications
Retail Banking

Retirement Accounts
Retirement Management
Retirement Programs
Retirement Services
Retrospective Refund Liabilities
Revenue Collection
Royalties Computation
Sales
Schedules
SEC Reporting
Secured Business Lending
Secured Loan Programs
Securities
Securities Lending Services
Securities Services
Securities Trading
Security Discrepancies
Self-Insurance Program
Selling
Shareholder Account Activities
Shareholder Inquiries
Shares
Single Country Funds
Single-Family Residences
Spending Behavior
Spreadsheets
State Insurance Regulations and Legislation
Statistics
Stock Brokerage Licensure
Stock Market Investments
Stock Research
Stocks
Strategic Decisions
Strategic Plans
Tax and Insurance Escrow

Tax and Regulatory Requirements
Tax Filings
Tax Forms
Tax Liabilities
Tax Returns
Tax Shelters
Taxable Fixed Income
Tax-Deferred Investments
Tax-Exempt Assets
Telephone Collections
"Tiered" Interview Techniques
Trade Capture Settlement
Trade Management Development
Trade Settlements
Transaction Management
Transfers
Travel and Entertainment Reconciliations
Travelers Checks
Treasury
Treasury Bills
Trend Reports
Trial Balance
Trust and Banking Markets
Trust Departments
Unbillable/Uncollectible Business
Underwriting
Underwriting Philosophy
Underwriting Results
Valuation
Variable Annuity Products
Vendor Identification Files
Vendor Payments
Weekly Cash Requirements
Wire Transfers
Workers' Compensation

Administrative

These buzz words are for applicants looking for general management and office positions. They reflect an involvement and familiarity with general office management as well as oversight of facilities and systems associated with day-to-day organizational activities. Important skills include administrative, project management, customer service, and light labor.

▶ Resume Buzz Words

Account Records Maintenance
Account Transactions
Accounts Payable
Accounts Receivable
Ad Placement
Adding Machines
Administrative Policies and Procedures
Administrative Support Services

Advertising
Agendas
Analysis
Appraisal Files
Archives
Articulate/Expressive Speaker
Associates Degree
Association Membership

Bank Services
Banking Processes
Billing
Billing Systems
Bills of Lading
Bookkeeping
Branch Audits
Budget Requirements
Business Administration
Business Forms
Business Letters
Busy Phone Work
Calculators
Certified Mail
Clerical Functions
Clerical Skills
Client Files
Client Relations
Client/Customer Correspondence
Coding
Commercial Loan Files
Company Literature
Computer and Software Applications
Computer Operation
Computer Skills
Conferences
Confidential Records
Contract Bids
Consultant
Correspondence
Courier Services
Credit Checks
Customer Inquiries
Customer Relations
Customer Service
Daily Activities
Daily Deadlines
Daily Deliveries
Daily Fund Deposits
Daily Office Functions
Daily Reporting
Data Entry
Data Gathering
Data Processing
Database Management
Departmental and Divisional Reports
Design Composition
Detail Oriented
Dictaphone
Direct Mail
Dispatch
Documentation
Donor Relations
Editing
e-Mail
Employee Appraisals
Equipment Maintenance
Event Planning
Expense Accounts
Expense Reports
Express Mail
Facilities Management
Fax Messages
Federal Express
File Coding
File Maintenance
Filing Systems

Financial Management
Financial Statements
Forms
General Accounting Procedures
Human Resources
Inbound and Outbound Mail
Incoming Calls
Incoming Mail
Information Trafficking
Inquiry Resolution
Insurance Claims and Payments
Inter-Building Correspondence
Interviews
Inventory
Inventory Analysis
Inventory Control
Inventory Discrepancies
Inventory Systems
Invoicing
Logistics
Mail Processing
Marketing Forecast Reports
Mass Mailings
Material Coordination
Meeting Minutes
Meeting Planning
Meetings
Member Appointments
Membership
Merchandising
Monthly Charges
Monthly Payroll
Monthly Reports
Multiline Phones
Multiple Projects
Newsletter
Office Equipment
Office Management and Operations
Office Procedures
Office Reports
Online Database
Organization Policies and Procedures
Packing Slips
Payable Invoices
Periodical Production
Personnel Functions
Personnel Management
Personnel Records
Petty Cash
Phone Requests
Photo-Typesetting
Physical Inventory
Plan Meetings
Positive Attitude
Presentations
Press Releases
Problem Identification and Resolution
Problem Solving
Procedural Enhancement
Procedure Manual
Procedures
Processing
Product Displays
Production Schedules
Promotions/Contests
Proofreading
Public Inquiries

Public Relations
Purchase Orders
Questions and Complaints
Reconciliation
Record Keeping
Reference Library
Registered Mail
Relocation Policy
Report Generation
Report Writing
Reports
Research
Rules/Regulations
Sales Reports
Sales Support
Schedule Hours
Schedule Management
Secretarial Staff
Seminars
Shipping/Receiving
Shorthand
Site Visits
Special Events
Special Projects
Speed Writing
Spreadsheets
Staff Meetings
Staffing Needs
Statement Transcription

Statistical Typing
Statistics
Stenography
Strict Deadlines
Supervisory Skills
Survey Data
Switchboard
Systems Enhancement
Tax Returns
Telephone Inquiries
Telex
Time Records
Time Sheets
Trade Shows
Training Skills
Transcription
Travel Arrangements
Travel Calendar
Travel Vouchers
Troubleshooting
Typing
UPS
Vendor Relations
Word Processing
Words Per Minute (WPM)
Workers' Compensation
Workflow
Writing Skills

Aerospace

Positions in this field might be in manufacturing, commercial or military aviation, or research. Aerospace industry buzz words display experience with manufacturing, engineering, and maintenance of commercial, military, and business aircraft; helicopters; aircraft engines; missiles; spacecrafts; and materials, related components, and equipment. This includes scientific research; hands-on work repairing and constructing aircraft equipment and parts; guaranteeing customer safety through quality assurance testing; and producing reliable, high-quality products.

▶ Resume Buzz Words

ABS Resins
Acquisition Management
Activity Reports
Actuators
Adapter Cards
Advanced Combat Systems
Advanced Fighter Aircraft
Advanced Technology Products
Aerospace Defense Products
Aerospace Ordnance Devices

Aerospace Systems
Aerospace Telemetry
Air Defense Technologies
Air Force Material Command
Air Traffic Control
Air/Coastal Defense Radar Systems
Aircraft
Aircraft Avionics
Aircraft Components
Aircraft Engines

Aircraft Fuel Systems
Aircraft Fuselages
Aircraft Maintenance
Aircraft Modification
Aircraft Refueling
Altitude
Analysis Reports
Appliances
Audio Accessories
Automation
Aviation Communications Products
Avionic Display Systems
Avionic Mechanisms
B-2 Spirit Stealth Bomber
Boeing 747
Braking Control Systems
Broadcasting
Cabin Interior Products
Cabin Video Systems
Capital Services
Casting Foundry
Circuit Breakers
Circuits
Combat Systems
Command/Control Systems
Commercial Aircraft
Commercial Aircraft Parts
Commercial Jet Transports
Commercial Pumping Systems
Computer Bus Structures
Computer Peripheral
Computer Systems Development
Computer-Based Information
Control Equipment
Control Systems
Control Valves
Controls
Corporate Aircraft
Coupling Equipment
Data Communications Hardware Products
Data Interchange Services
Database Systems Support
Defense Industry
Defense Systems
Design Activities
Displacement and Pressure Transducers
Distribution of Electricity
Ducting Systems
Dynamic Hydraulic and Mechanical Testing
Dynamic Testing
Edge-Lighted Plastic Panels
Electric Motors
Electrical Components
Electrical Distribution
Electrical Modules
Electrical Supply Houses
Electromagnetic Parts
Electromechanical Locks
Electronic Components
Electronic Firing Systems
Electronic Industrial Automation Products
Electronic Systems
Electronics
Electro-Optics
Emergency Rescue Equipment
Energy Extraction Applications
Engine Components

Engine Instrumentation
Engine Parameters
Engines
Environmental Testing
Ethernet
Evaluation Reports
Executive Aircraft
Explosive Devices
External Commercial and Industrial Customers
F/A-18
Filters
Filtration Equipment
Fire Detection/Protection Systems
Flight Controls
Flight Simulators
Flight Test Data
Fluid Power Systems
Freight Air Carriers
Fuel
Fuel Pumps
Fusing Devices
General Aviation Aircraft
Global Support
Ground Support Services
Heavy Equipment
Helicopters
High-Security
High-Technology Ferrous
Hydraulic
Igniter Assemblies
Industrial Applications
Industrial Automation and Control
Industrial Gas Turbine Engines
Industrial Lighting Products
Industrial Machinery
Industrial Use
Inertial Navigation and Guidance
Information Systems Management
Inter-Computer Network Communications
Interior Aircraft Equipment
Jet Aircraft Engine Parts
Jet Engines
Laminates
Large Commercial Aircraft
Laser Firing Systems
Latching Devices
Light Machining
Liquid Propellant
Local Area Network
Logistics
Logistic Support Analyses
Major Aircraft Manufacturers
Manufacturing Methods
Manufacturing Support Services
Marine Systems
Measuring Methods
Mechanical Separation Devices
Medical Supplies
Medical Systems and Equipment
Microcircuits
Microelectronics
Microprocessor-Based Electronic Sequencers
Military Aircraft
Military Missiles
Military Planes
Missile Systems
Missiles

Molecular Biology Research Items
Nacelle Systems and Components
Navigation Control Systems
Navigational Instruments
Network Topologies
Networking Products
Nonferrous Castings
Operations Research
Optical Equipment
Optical Pick-Offs
Orbiting Satellites
Ordnance-Related Products
Panel Meters
Passenger Air Carriers
Passenger Control Units
Passenger Video Entertainment Systems
Performance Polymers
Plastics
Pneumatic Component Parts
Policies
Positioning Instruments
Power Cartridges
Power Systems
Precision Fastening Systems
Precision Measuring Scales
Precision Patterned Glass and Metal Products
Pressure Regulators
Pressure Transducers
Procedures
Processes
Product Development
Programming Experience
Pumps
Quality Assurance
Quality Control
Radar Equipment
Radio and Television Transmitters for Aircraft
Remote Network Access Communications
Repair Services
Replacement Parts
Resistors
Rocket Engines
Rotary and Linear Optical Incremental
    Encoders
Satellite Guidance Systems
Satellite-Based Communications Systems
Scientific Applications

Sensors
Service Accessories
Servovalves
Shared Services
Sheetmetal
Silicones
Simulation-Based Devices
Simulator-Related Training Services
Small-Launch Vehicles
Software Systems
Solid Rocket Motors
Sophisticated Aerospace Equipment
Sounding Rockets
Space
Space and Communications
Space and Aviation Systems
Space and Missile Systems Center (SMC)
Space Applications
Space Systems Architecture
Space Vehicles
Specialty Insurance
Speed
Strategic Missile Systems
Strategic Weapon Systems
Superabrasives
Systems Analysis
Systems Engineering
Systems Management
Tactical Air Defense Systems
Tactical Missile Systems
Tactical Weapon Systems
Technical Guidance
Technical Products
Testing
Token Ring
Training Devices
Training Services
Transmission
Transportation Systems Products
Troubleshooting
Turbine Engines
Valves
Vibration (Random/Sine) Testing
Waterjet Propulsion Systems
Weapon Systems
Wiring Systems

Apparel, Fashion, and Textiles

Buzz words in this industry highlight experience with clothing design, export, and sales; knowledge of current style or style characteristics; or the manufacturing, weaving, and knitting of fabric, yarn, or cloth. This includes work with curtains, drapery, shoes, and sportswear; skill with nonwoven fabrics, textile goods and finishing, and yarn and thread mills; or the buying, handling, shipping, receiving, and selling of such goods.

▶ Resume Buzz Words

Absorbency
Accent
Accessories
Acetate
Apparel
Apparel Design Arena
Apparel-Manufacturing Company
Apprenticeship
Artwork
Assortment
Automotive Distribution
Bandages
Baseball Caps
Bedroom Ensembles
Belts
Block and Slopers Development
Blouses
Brand Names
Brands
Bridal Gowns
Care Labels
Carpet
Casual Wear
Catalog Sales
Chain Stores
Chamois Flannel
Children's Sleepwear
Cloth Labels
Clothes
Clothing Manufacturers
Coats
Color
Comforters
Commission
Complete Line
Consumer Markets
Convert Fabric
Core Products
Cotton
Cotton-Blend Fibers
Curtains
Daywear
Denim
Department Store Merchandise
Design Concepts
Designer Jeans
Designer Lines
Designs
Detail
Die-Casting
Direct Marketing
Distribution Centers
Diversified Line
Divisions
Draperies
Dress Shirts
Dresses
Dye-Printing Process
Dyeing
Elastic Knitting
Export
Extensive Range
Eye Glasses

Fabrics
Fashion Apparel Products
Fibers
Filament
Finished Home Products
Footwear
Formalwear
Furnishings
General Merchandise Stores
Global Retailer
Goods
Grade Rules
Half Sizes
Hand-Knitting Yarn
High-Quality Fabric
High-End Velvet
High-Spec Industrial Applications
Home Fashion Products
Home Furnishings
Import
Independent Textile Converter
Industrial Distribution
Industrial Hosiery
Industrial Markets
Industrial Processes
Industrial Uniforms
Interior Furnishings
Intimate Apparel
Inventory
Jackets
Jeans
Jersey Fabrics
Junior Sizes
Knit
Knit Healthcare Products
Knitted Fabrics
Knitted Fleece
Knitted Textile Fabrics
Labels
Laces
Leather Apparel
Leisure Shirts
Leisurewear
Licensed Labels
Licences
Licensing
Loungewear
Luggage
Lycra and Rubber Products
Mail Order Catalogs
Major Discounters
Manmade Fibers
Manufacturers
Manufacturing Plants
Marketing
Markets
Mass Merchants
Mass Volume Retailers
Material
Measurement Charts
Medical Products
Men's Apparel
Merchandise

Metal and Coil Slide Fasteners
Micro-Safe Fiber
Misses' Sizes
Narrow Elastic Fibers
National and Regional Chains
Nationally Distributed
Natural and Synthetic Fibers
Neckwear
Nonwovens
Novelties
Nylon Fibers
Nylon Travelers
Outerwear Line
Packaging Products
Pants
Paper Making Machines
Patternmaking
Patterns
Petite
Petite Dresses
Pillows
Plaids
Plastic Injection Moldings
Polyurethane-Coated Fabrics
Principal Buyers
Printed Fabrics
Printed Items
Private Label Sleepwear
Private Labels
Private Retail
Private-Label Designer
Processing Wool
Processing
Producing Pattern
Product Development
Production
Products
Purses
Quality Control
Retail Outlets
Retail Sales Prices
Retail Units
Retailers
Robes
Rug Kits
Sale
Sales Category
Samples
Scarves
Sewing Thread
Sheets
Shirts
Shoes
Skirts
Slacks
Special Machinery Spools
Special Occasion Dresses
Specialty Fabrics
Specialty Markets
Specialty Stores
Specialty Weaves
Spinning Cotton
Sportswear
Sportswear Items
Spun Yarns
Stores
Stretch Panties

Styles
Suits
Support Facilities
Synthetic
Synthetic Filament Polyester
Synthetic Thread
Tailored Men's Clothing
Tapes
Textile Outerwear
Textile Products
Textile Products Manufacturing
Textile Wholesaler
Textile Yarns
Textiles
Textured Nylon
Texturing
Towels
Trading
Trimmings
T-Shirts
Twisting
Undergarments
Uniform Shirts
Uniforms
Upholstery
Value-Priced Apparel
Variety
Warp Knit Fabrics
Washable Service Apparel
Watches
Wear
Weaving
Weekend Casual Sportswear
Wide-Warp Knit
Winding
Window Treatments
Women's Apparel
Women's Sheer Hosiery
Woodturnings
Woolen Coats
Worldwide
Woven
Woven Finished Fabrics
Woven Greige Fabrics
Woven Synthetics
Woven Velvets
Wrinkle-Free Cotton Fabrics
Yarns
Young Ladies'
Young Men's Apparel
Youth Market

Architecture, Construction, and Engineering

In these fields, effective buzz words highlight one's experience with applying scientific and mathematical principles to the design, layout, and construction of machines, structures, buildings, and systems. This includes planning the physical composure of a bridge, house, or monument; graphically conceptualizing the mathematical dynamics of huge land structures; and physically preparing, assembling, or renovating pre-existing architecture.

► Resume Buzz Words

Accident Reconstruction
Accident Statistical Data Analysis
Aggregates
Air Conditioning Systems
Airfield Lighting Power Distribution
Airfields
Airports
Architectural Planning
Architectural/Engineering Services
Asphalt Felt–Based Linoleum
Asphalt Paving
Aviation
Banks
Biomechanics
Brick Masonry
Bridge Inspection
Bridges
Budget Development
Builders
Building Entrances
Building Materials
Building Plans
Building Products
Building Restoration
Buildings
Business Support Services
Cabinets
Carpet Base
Chemicals
Civic Centers
Civil Disciplines
Civil Engineering
Coal
Coal Production
Code Compliance
Commercial Architecture
Commercial Construction
Commercial Industries
Commercial Services
Compressor/Vacuum Pump Products
Computer Aided Design (CAD)
Conceptual Design
Concrete Repair

Condominiums
Construction
Construction and Renovation Projects
Construction Base
Construction Drawings
Construction Forensic Services
Construction Maintenance
Construction Management
Construction Management Firm
Construction Management Services
Construction Services
Construction Site
Construction Support
Construction/Structural Engineering
Consulting Services
Contract Documents
Contract Drawings Development
Contractor Submittals
Contractors
Cost Control
Cost Estimates
Cost Estimation
Crushing Operation
Curtainwall Systems
Defense Industry
Design
Design and Construction Phases
Design Calculations
Design Drawings
Design Reports
Design Tasks
Document Review
Doors
Drafting Team
Drainage
Drainage and Flood Control
Drawing Review
Earthwork Volume
Educational Facilities
Electrical Construction
Electrical Subcontracting
Electricity
Electronic Security System Projects

Energy
Energy Industry
Energy Management
Engineering
Engineering Consulting
Engineering Design
Environmental Assessments
Environmental Consulting
Environmental Engineering
Environmental Studies
Equipment Management
Equipment Rental Sales and Service
Estimates
Extensive Variety
Exterior Finishing Materials
Fabricated Products
Facilities and Transportation
Facings
Feasibility Studies
Federal Programs
Field Crews
Field Engineering and Inspection
Field Experience
Field Reports
Field Responsibilities
Financing Operations
Fire/Life Safety Design
Fittings
Floor Adhesives
Flooring
Flooring Products
Frame Parts
General Contracting Firm
General Contractor
Geotechnical Investigation
Geotechnical Services
Global Services
Government Bases
Graphics
Hard Floor Coverings
Hazardous Waste Assessment and Remediation
Heating and Air Conditioning Equipment
Heating Systems
Heavy Construction
Heavy Industrial Construction
Heavy Rail
Heavy-Civil Contractor
Highway Capacity
Highway Contractor
Highways
Homebuilders
Hospitality Projects
Hotels
Industrial Complexes
Industrial Facilities
Infrastructure Systems
Interior Design Services
Job Site Management Team
Labor Units
Laboratories
Land Planning
Lateral and Axial Pile Analyses Programs
Lav-Tops
Layout
Leading Mortgage Finance Company
Lighting Control and Monitoring System
Lighting Products

Loss-Control Services
Maintenance Services
Major Bridges
Major Cargo Airports
Management Consulting
Manufacturing Industry
Marine Facilities
Marine Investigations
Material Take-Off
Materials and Product Testing
Mechanical Contracting
Mechanical Design Drawings
Mechanical Estimates
Mechanical Subcontracting
Metal Fabrication Services
Metal Siding
Metals
Minerals
Monitor Panels
Multidisciplinary Approach
Multifaceted Construction Firm
Multifamily Apartment Complexes
Nonresidential Architectural Building Products
Nuclear Fuel
Occupancies
Office Buildings
Operating Groups
Operation and Construction Management
    Services
Pavement
Petrochemical Industry
Petroleum Refining
Pharmaceuticals and Biotechnologies
    Industries
Piping Pricing
Piping Takeoffs
Planning
Plumbing
Plumbing Supplies
Policyholders
Pollution Control
Polymers
Power Distribution
Precast Concrete
Prevention of Accidents and Failures
Private Sectors
Probable Risk Assessment
Procurement
Procurement Management
Professional Services Organization
Programming
Project Conception
Project Planning
Project Team
Properties
Protection of Traffic Plan Development
Public Facilities
Public Sectors
Public Works
Pulp
Quality Control
Quantity Estimates
Quantity Takeoff Calculations
Railroads
Railway Signal Engineering Designs
Range Hoods
Ready-Mixed Concrete

Real Estate Agencies
Refrigeration Contractor
Related Mobile Home Products
Relevant Codes
Remediation Services
Remote Site Camps
Renovation
Research Laboratories
Residential
Residential Building Maintenance Services
Restoration
Risk Prevention/Mitigation
Road/Highway
Roof Domes
Roof Vents
Roofing
Safeguard the Environment
Semiconductor
Sheet Metal Fabrication
Siding
Single-Family Homes
Slope Stability Modeling Programs
Solar Energy Components
Solid Waste
Spatial and Statistical Analysis
Specialists
Specialty Construction Services
Specialty Sheets of Foam
Specifications
Sports Facilities
Sprinkler and Irrigation Products
Steel Industry
Storefronts
Streets
Structural Concrete Construction
Structural Engineering
Structural Projects

Stucco
Subcontractors
Suppliers
Surety Claim Services
Surveying
System Safety and Reliability
Task Areas
Technical Consulting
Technical Presentations of Proposals
Tenant Improvements
Tile
Toplights
Total Engineering
Traffic
Traffic Signal Design and Maintenance
Training
Transition Strip Accessories
Transportation
Transportation Markets
Transportation Model Network Coding
Transportation Related
Tunnels
Value Management
Valves
Ventilation
Warning and Labeling Issues
Waste Management
Wastewater Collection
Wastewater Reuse
Wastewater Treatment
Water Management
Water Resources
Water Treatment and Distribution
Water/Wastewater Services
Waterfront Facility
Wide-Ranging Climates
Window Framing

Arts, Entertainment, Sports, and Recreation

These buzz words are just some of those from the often glamorous worlds of entertainment, sports, and arts; each individual field within these industries will have many more specific terms that might be used to demonstrate your knowledge and experience. Arts-resume buzz words display experience with production or arrangement of sounds, colors, forms, movements, or other visual elements. Entertainment-industry buzz words exhibit experience-producing performances or shows to amuse, please, or divert an audience's attention. Entertainment buzz words also display experience working for studios, networks, production companies, record companies, and radio stations. Sports and recreation buzz words highlight experience with both competitive and relaxing activities such as games and matches.

▶ Resume Buzz Words

360-Degree Theater Systems
Action/Adventure Films
Actor Management
Amusement Park
Ancient Art
Animation
Arcade
Art Department
Art Media
Awards Shows
Background
Ballets
Banquet Facilities
Botanic Gardens
Broadcasting
Broadway Theaters
Cable Television Networks
Casinos
CD Manufacturing and Distribution Facility
CD-audio and CD-ROM Mastering and
    Replication
Children's Cartoons
Circus
Coaching Staff
Comedic Theater
Comedy Films
Concerts
Concession Facilities
Conservation and Curatorial Departments
Contracted Artists
Convention and Meeting Facility
Dance
Digital Effects
Digital Images
Director Management
Discovery Labs
Documentary
Editing, Design, Sound, and Related Services
Education Services
Educational and Research Programs
Entertainment
Entertainment Production Company
Event Television
Exercise Programs
Exhibition Halls
Family Audiences
Fashion
Feature-Length Motion Pictures
Fellowships
Film Development
Film Distribution Company
Film-to-Tape and Tape-to-Film Transfer
Finishing
First-Run Syndication
Fitness and Aerobic Classes
Fitness Center
Foreign Television Networks
Free Television
Fulfillment Services
Full-Service Health and Fitness Club
Giant Screen
Guest Hotel Facilities
Hair
Harness Racing Facility

Hiking Trails
Historic Artifacts
Historical Interpretation
History Museum
Home Video
Horseracing Tracks
Independent Multimedia Manufacturing
Integrated Merchandising
Intellectual Property Rights
Interactive Games
Interactive Media
Internships
Laser Disc Licensees and Distributors
Laser Video Disc Recording
Layout
Lectures
Leisure and Entertainment Company
Libraries
Licensing
Live Animals
Live Entertainment
Low-Budget Theatrical Motion Pictures
Made-for-TV Movies
Magazines
Makeup
Manuscripts
Media Company
Meets
Merchandising
Miniseries
Modern Art
Motion Picture Business
Motion Picture Film Processing
Motion Pictures
Museums
Music Production
National and International Tours
National Basketball Association (NBA)
National Football League (NFL)
National Hockey League (NHL)
Major League Baseball (MLB)
Nature Center
Newspapers
Nonprofit Art Gallery
Nonprofit Arts Showcase
Nonprofit Cultural Organization
Nonprofit Performing Arts Theater
Off-Broadway
Off-Line and Online Video Editing
On-Broadway
Online Services
Opera
Opera House
Orchestra
Outdoor Activity Programs
Packaging
Paddle Boats
Parks
Pay Television
Performing Arts Facility
Personal Training
Photo Finishing
Pipeline
Political Satire

Popular and Classical Records
Portable Simulator
Practice
Preservation of Buildings and Ships
Production Planning
Professional Hockey
Professional Resident Theater Company
Professional Sports Teams
Prospecting
Publications and Reproductions
Publishing
Puppetry
Recreation Program
Regional Cable Television Sports Networks
Research Library
Revisualization Sequences
Rights to Films
Roller Skating Rink
Satellite Transmission Uplinking Services
Schedules
Set Dressing
Shakespearean Productions
Sitcoms
Snack Bar
Special Effects
Special Interest Programming
Special Productions
Sports Highlights
Stakes Races

State-of-the-Art Theaters
Student Art Exhibitions
Studio Facilities and Technology
Syndicates
Talent and Literary Agency
Talk Shows
Tanning
Television Programs
Theatrical Exhibitions
Theatrical Performances
Toy Design
Type Design
Uniforms
Vaudeville
Venues
Video and Film Duplication
Video Post-Production Services
Video Theater
Videocassette and Audiocassette Duplication
Virtual Reality Theater Systems
Visual Arts Museum
Warehousing
Water Theme Park
Websites
Weights
Women's National Basketball Association
   (WNBA)
Women Viewers

Automotive

Buzz words for the automotive industry highlight experience in repair shops and with producing automotive equipment and knowledge of auto sales and services.

▶ Resume Buzz Words

Accessories
Air Conditioners
Air Filters
Air Injection
Airbag Electronics
Airbags
Alignment
Alloy Wheels
All Wheel Drive
Aluminum Bodies
Antilock Braking Systems (ABS)
Antilock Brakes
Assemblies
Assembly Services
Auctions
Auto Body Parts
Auto Reconditioning
Automatic
Automobile Doorframes
Automobile Parts
Automotive
Automotive Aftermarket
Automotive Design

Automotive Electronic Controls
Automotive Electronics
Automotive Glass
Automotive Occupant Restraint Systems
Automotive Parts
Automotive Regulators
Automotive Roll Form Products
Automotive Seating Systems and Components
Automotive Service
Automotive Starting Systems
Automotive-Original Equipment
Axles
Ball Bearings
Bimodal Vehicles
Blow Moldings
Body Stampings
Book Value
Brake Linings
Brake Pads
Brakes
Brazed Assemblies
Bus Specialty
Bushings

Caliper
Camping Trailers
Car Stereos
Cars
Certified Automotive Parts Supplier
Chassis
Chemicals
Child and Infant Seats
Climate-Control Systems
Clutch
Clutch Plates
Coatings
Coils
Combined Markets
Combustion Chamber
Commercial Vehicles
Compressor
Connecting Rod
Continuous-Strand Fiberglass
Contract Manufacturing Services Solutions
Conversion Facility
Conversion Van
Convertible Systems
Coolant
Coolant Systems Pressure Gauges
Custom Vehicles
Custom-Designed
Customers
Customizes
Cylinder Head
Cylindrical
Dealers
Decorative Laminates
Delivery Vehicles
Design
Development
Diesel Engines
Differential
Displays
Distributor
Domestic
Door Systems
Driveshaft
Drivetrain Components and Systems
Dry Freight Vans
Electric Automotive Switches
Electric Motors
Electrical
Electrical Automotive Equipment
Electrical Power Distribution Equipment
Electronic Controls
Electroplating
Engine Components
Engine Mounts
Engine Parts
Engineering Services
Exhaust
Exhaust Systems
Exterior Automobile Mirrors
Exterior Enhancement Programs
Extruded Plastic Materials
Fabricated Glass
Factory Equipment
Fifth Wheels
Financing
Flat Glass Products
Flat Tire
Flatbed Trailers

Floor Consoles
Fluid Connectors
Fluid Power
Fluid Systems Components
Four Wheel Drive
Frames
Franchised Auto Dealerships
Franchised Automotive Service Locations
Front Wheel Drive
Fuel Filters
Fuel Injection
Fuel Injectors
Fuel Pumps
Fuel Systems
Fuel-Carrying Systems
Fuel-Handling Products
Full-Line Vehicle Manufacturers
Full-Size Vans
Fully Loaded
Gaskets
Generating Systems
Halogen Headlamp
Headlights
Heaters
Heavy Truck Chassis
Heavy Trucks
Heavy Vehicle Systems
Heavy-Duty Trucks
Hoses
Hydraulic Power Units
Hydraulic Products
Hydraulic Pumps
Ignition Systems
Import
Independent Supplier
Independent Suspension
Industrial Products
Inflatable Restraints
Information Technology
Injection Moldings
Inspections
Instrument Clusters
Instrument Panel Components
Interior Automotive Products
Interior Trim
Iron Castings
Latch Assemblies
Light Truck Seating Systems and Components
Light Trucks
Light Vehicle Aftermarket
Light Vehicle Systems
Lighting Products
Lighting Systems
Limited Slip Differential
Maintenance
Manual
Manufactured Goods
Mass Transit
Metal Automobile Components
Metal Stampings
Midrange Diesel Engines
Midsize/Luxury Car Group
Mini Motor Homes
Minivans
Miscellaneous Automobile Parts
Molded Materials
Molded Plastics
Motor Coaches

Motorhomes
Motors Insurance
Octane Reading
Off-Road Machinery
Oil Caps
Oil Changes
Oil Filters
Options
Original Equipment Manufacturers (OEM)
Overdrive
Overhead System Components
Oxygen Sensors
Park Models
Parts
Passenger Cars
Pickup Truck Bedliners
Pickup Trucks
Pinion Steering Gears
Pistons
Piston Rings
Plastic Fasteners and Clips
Plastic Injection Molding
Plastic Interior Items
Plastic Products
Pneumatic Products
Power Rack
Power Units
Powertrain
Powertrain Components
Powertrain Systems
Precision Parts
Precision Stamping
Product Design
Production Facilities
Push Rod
Quarter Panel
Radiator Pumps
Radiator Valves
Radiators
Recreational Vehicle Manufacturers
Recreational Vehicles
Refined Motor Cars
Refrigerated Trailers
Related Components
Rental
Replacement Parts
Replacement Parts Distribution
Research and Development (R&D)
Residual
Resins
Resonator
Ride-Control Products
RV
Safety Restraint Products
Sale
Sales/Service Groups
Sales-Automotive Aftermarket
Sealing
Seals
Seat Belts
Seats
Sectors
Sedans
Sensors
Service Centers
Service Operations
Sleeve Bearings
Small Car Group

Specialized Applications
Specialized Fibers
Specialized Truck Bodies
Spoilers
Sport-Utility Vehicles (SUV)
Standard Transmission
Steering Linkage
Strut
Sun Visors
Sunroofs
Supplies
Suspension
Suspension Ball Joints
Suspension Parts
Suspension Systems
Tail Lamps
Tapered Roller Bearings
Test Drive
Testing
Thrust Washers
Tier One Supplier
Tier Two Supplier
Timing
Tinted Glass Products
Tires
Tool Building Services
Tooling Applications
Torque
Traction Control
Tractors
Trailer Hitches
Transmission Bands
Transmission Parts
Transportation Manufacturing Firm
Travel Trailers
Trimming
Truck Bodies
Truck Campers
Truck Doorframes
Truck Drivetrain Systems
Truck Group
Trucks
Tune Up
Turbocharger
Universal Joint
Upscale Model
Used Cars
Valve Train
Valves
Van Bodies
Van Campers
Vehicle Development Groups
Vehicle Leasing
Vehicle Parts
Vehicle Transport Services
Vehicular Lighting Products
Vibration Control Parts and Systems
Washers
Welded Assemblies
Wheel Base
Wheels
Wholesale Distribution
Wholesale Value
Windows
Worldwide Markets

Biotechnology and Pharmaceuticals

The buzz words in these industries are often highly technical, and exhibit a science background. Resumes may demonstrate experience with cellular biology, vaccine research, prescription drugs, over-the-counter medicines, chemical compounds used in pharmaceuticals, and tools used to diagnose diseases. Relevant experience includes synthesizing new drugs, testing of drugs, determination of dosages and delivery forms (such as liquid or tablets), calculating cost-effectiveness of a proposed drug, and selling/marketing of pharmaceuticals.

▶ Resume Buzz Words

Advanced Cellular and Molecular Biology
Agricultural Biotechnology
Allergies
Analytical Tools
Anemia
Antibodies
Antiviral
Aqueous-Based Synthetic Solutions
Aseptic Processing Design
Assay (ELISA) Test Kits
Autoimmune
Bioinformatics
Biomedical Research
Biopharmaceutical Development
Biopharmaceutical Fermentation
Biosciences
Biostatistics
Biotechnology
Blood Management Systems
Blood Tests
Bone Marrow Transplantation
Breakthrough Drug
Calibration Programs
Cancer Research
Cardiovascular Disease
Cell Biology
Cell Lines
Cell-Based Functional Secondary and Tertiary
    Assays
Centrifuges
Chemical Manufacturing
Chemotherapeutic Pharmaceuticals
Clean Room Certification
Clinical Laboratories
Clinical Laboratory Services
Clinical Trials
Clinics
Cohort Studies
Compliance
Compound Screening
Computer Validation
Computerized System Validation
Contract Research Organization (CRO)

Contract Sales Organization (CSO)
Critical Care Products
Cultured Primary Cells
Data Analysis
Data Processing Software
Data Sets
Dermatology
Detection and Measurement Equipment
Development and Consulting
Diabetes
Diagnostic Analysis
Diagnostic Imaging
Diagnostic Medical Devices
Diagnostic Tests
Dialysis Centers
Direct-to-Consumer (DTC) Marketing
DNA Synthesizers
Donor Center
Dosing
Double-Blind
Drug Delivery Systems and Technologies
Drug Discovery
Drug Optimization Programs
Drug Strategies
Education
Electrophoresis Systems
Engineering Sciences
Environmental Monitoring Programs
Environmental Testing
Enzymatically Dissolved Hair Samples
Enzyme-Linked Immunosorbent
Epidemiological Issues
Epidemiological Research
Epidural Anesthesia
Ethical Pharmaceuticals
FDA Approval
FDA Compliance Strategies
Formulary
Gas Chromatography/Mass Spectrometry
Gene Therapies
General Chemical Systems
Generic Drug
Genetics

Genomics
Gerontological Studies
GMP Audits
Good Manufacturing Practices (GMP)
Government and Private Industry Research
Grant Proposals
Growth Deficiency Treatment
Health and State Policy
Healthcare Policy
Health Inequalities and Disparities
Health Insurance
Hematology
Hormones
Human Genetic Information
Human Therapeutics
Humanized and Human Monoclonal Antibodies
IC50/ED50 Values
Immunoassays
Immunodiagnostic Products
Immunological Reagents
Immunology
Impact Research Programs
In Vitro
In Vivo
Industrial Microbiology
Infectious Diseases
Intravenous Systems and Solutions
Inventory Management
Investigational New Drug (IND) Application
IQ, OQ, and PQ Protocols
IV Accessories
Laboratories
Large-Scale Surveys
Life Science Systems
Life Sciences
Longitudinal Analysis
Manufacturing Regulations
Measurement and Analysis of Physiologic Data
Medical Affairs
Medical Conditions
Medical Immunodiagnostic Test Kits
Metabolic Diseases
Metabolism
Metabolites
Multidisciplinary Research
Natural Growth Conditions
New Drug Application (NDA)
Observational Studies
Ophthalmic Pharmaceuticals
Ophthalmology

Organ Preservation Solutions
Organ Transplantation
Over-the-Counter (OTC) Drugs
Patented Drugs
Patient Care
Patient-Specific Intravenous Drugs
Pharmaceutical Companies
Pharmaceutical Devices
Pharmaceutical Discovery
Pharmaceutical Products
Pharmaceuticals
Pharmacy Services
Phase I
Phase II
Phase III
Pipeline
Placebo-Controlled Protocol
Plasma Exchange
Preclinical Stage Programs
Public Health Research
Quality Control/Quality Assurance (QC/QA)
Quantitative Analysis
Reagents
Recombinant DNA
Regulatory Affairs
Regulatory Issues
Reproductive Disorders
Research and Clinical Applications
Research Methodologies
Retrospective Studies
Robotic Workstations
Scientific Instruments
Side Effects
Social Determinants of Illness
Social Research
Specialty Chemical Systems
Sterilization Processes
Surveillance
Testing for Acute and Chronic Human Illnesses
Therapeutic Systems
Thyroid Disorders
Tissue and Organ Replacement
Treatment for Life-Threatening Diseases
U.S. Food and Drug Administration (FDA)
Urine Tests
Urology/Gynecology Studies
Vaccines
Validation
Veterinary Applications

Communications

Industry buzz words in the area of communications highlight writing, graphics, public relations, publicity, and promotions skills and experience. This includes activities associated with creating, distributing, and transmitting text and graphic information via varied print, video, audio, computer, and web-based media. Some of the buzz words listed concerning editing and writing would also be useful for those applying for positions in publishing.

▶ Resume Buzz Words

Acquisition of Titles
Administrative Skills
Advertising
Annual Fact Book
Antenna Designs and Measurements
Art and Production Elements
Arts and Entertainment
Articles
Assignments
Asynchronous Transfer Mode (ATM)
Audio Production
Authors
Automatic Call Distributors
Automation Solutions
Backlist
Blemishes
Book Production
Booklets
Broadcasting Operations
Business Presentations
Cable Television
Call Center Management
Call Centers
Camera Operation
Campaign Letters
Casting Contracts
Catalogs
CDs
Cellular Phones
Circulation Records
Classified Advertisings
Collaboration
Columns
Commercials
Communications Intelligence Collection
Communications Management
Communications Service Provider
Communications Systems
Computer-Telephony Integration Solutions
Consumer Markets
Content
Content Development
Contributing Writers
Copyedit
Corporate Imaging
Cover Story
Creative Writing
Darkroom Procedures
Data Communications Equipment
Data Communications Services
Data Management
Data Services
Data Systems
Deadlines
Design
Desktop Publishing
Digital Music Service
Direct Mail
DSL Products
Editing
Editorial Changes
Editorial Committee
Editorial Direction
Educational Programs

Electronic Telecommunications Test Equipment
e-Mail Systems
Facsimile Systems
Fact Checking
Federal Agencies
Fiber-Optics
Films
Formatting
Frame Relay
Freelance Projects
Fundraising
Galleys
General Interest Topics
General Trade Reference Titles
Government Network Solutions
Grammar
Grant Proposals
HDTV
Healthcare Communications Systems
High-Bit-Rate Digital Subscriber Line (HDSL)
High-Speed Data
Historical Articles
Independent Telephone Operating Companies
In-Depth Features
Industrial Films
Institutional
Integrated Microwave Antenna Subassemblies
Interconnect Carriers
International Newsletter
Internet
Internet Access
Internet Equipment
Interview
LAN Internetworking
Layout
Ledger
Lighting and Broadcasting System
List Building
Local and National Affiliates
Locator Systems
Low-Radar Cross-Section
Manuscripts
Marketing
Marketing Proposals
Media Lists
Media Relations
Media Tours
Medical Journal
Monograph
Monthly Newspaper
Multimedia Group
Negotiated Contracts
Network and Data Services
Network Architectures
Network Operations
Network-Affiliated
News
News Briefs
News Casting
Newscasts
Newsletters
News Media
Newspapers
On-Air

Order Filling
Page Maker
Pamphlets
Paste-Up/Mechanicals
People Skills
Periodical Publishing
Planning and Forecasting Packages
Poetry
Press Kits
Press Releases
Printers
Private Communications Networks
Private Network Managers
Problem Analysis
Production
Production Details
Program Hosting
Promotions
Proofread
Props
Prototype
Public Carrier Providers
Public Relations
Public Service Announcements
Publication
Publication Process
Publicity
Publicity Files
Publishing Process
Radio Broadcasting
Record Maintenance
Recruitment Experience
References
Reporting Software
Reports
Reproduction
Research Findings
Research Papers
Research Papers and Reports
Residential Local and Long Distance Telephone
  Services
Review
Satellites
Schedules
Scholars
Scripts

Signal Reconnaissance Equipment
Skin
Social and Political Issues
Specialized Publications
Speeches
Stage Design
Standards and Procedures
Story Development
Story Ideas
Style Criteria
Subscribers
Subscription Orders
Subscriptions
Surface Flaws
Surveys
Switched Multimegabit Data Service
Tape Recording
Technical/Engineering
Telecommunications Signals
Telephone Equipment
Telephone Systems
TelePrompter
Television
Television Commercials
Text
Textbooks
Touchtone Telephone
Trade Magazines
Trade Newspaper
Trends
Updates
Video and Voice Applications
Videoconferencing
Voice Messaging
Voice Systems
Voicemail
Voice-Processing
Volunteer
Wardrobe Arrangements
Wide Area Network (WAN)
Wireless Access Network
Wireless Service Plans
Word Process
Work Flow Systems
Writing

Computers and Mathematics

For positions in the computer industry, buzz words are highly technical and change fairly rapidly. Effective buzz words highlight experience with defining, analyzing, and resolving business problems and
utilizing knowledge of computer systems to examine problems and
design solutions. Important skills and experience include planning
new computer systems or devising ways to apply existing systems to
operations that are still done manually.

Resumes for positions in mathematics should spotlight activities ranging from the creation of new theories and techniques to the translation of economic, scientific, engineering, and managerial problems into mathematical terms.

▶ Resume Buzz Words

Accounts Payable
Accounts Receivable
Administrative Tasks
Algorithms
Alternative Concept Development
Applications
Architecture
Architecture Requirements and Capabilities
Backup and Multiplatform Connectivity Systems
Batch System
Billing Systems
Bookkeeping
Bugs
Business Problems
Business Re-Engineering
C++
Client Database
Client Support Services
Client/Server Technology
CMS-2
COBOL Programming
Coding
Communications Technology
Computer Information Systems
Computer Interface Circuitry
Computer Program Requirements
Computer Programming Languages
Computer Reselling
Computer Science
Computer Software
Computer Systems
Conversion Products
Customer Needs
Customer Requirements
Customer Service System Consulting
Data Acquisition
Data Communication Systems
Data Communications
Data Entry
Data Migration
Data Processing
Data System Design and Implementation
Database Management
Database Repair/Troubleshooting
Database Systems
Deadlines
Design and Implementation
Developmental Math
Device Driver
Differential Equations
Digital Audio and Video Tools
Disk System
Documentation
DOD Telecommunications Technology, Architecture, Policy and Standards

DOS Batch Files
Drivers
Dynamical Systems Analysis
Electronic Components
Engineering Projects
Engineering Solutions
Failure and Analysis Reports
Fault Tolerant Signal Generation Software
File Structure
Financial Reporting Systems
Fixed Storage Space
Flowcharts
Hardware Products
Host Users
Information Architecture
Instructions and Guidelines
Integration
Internet Sales Systems
IT Planning
LAN Management
Large-Scale Networking Environments
Logical/Manageable Components
Mainframe Production Environment
Management and Technology Consulting
Manufacturing Efficiency
Manufacturing Test Systems
Membership Records
Memory Upgrades
Microcomputer
Mini Computers
MIS
Monitor Networks
Multiuser Database
Multivariable Calculus
Network-Based Applications
Network Configuration
Network Installation
Network Interface Cards
Network Management
Network Tools
Networking Solutions
Noncompliant Issues
Online Message System
Open Systems
Open Systems Migration
Operating Efficiencies
Operating Systems
Operational Procedures
Optical Disks
Parallel Architectures
PC Products
PC Software
Performance Standards
Peripheral Manufacturers
Preproduction Testing

Process Control
Process Time
Product Demos
Product Presentations
Products and Components
Programming Skills
Project Cost Effectiveness
Prototype
Real-Time Computer Programs
Real-Time Embedded Software Design
Real-Time Interactive Visual Communications
Real-Time Simulation
Record Compilation
Reliability
Reporting Systems
SAS Programming
Server Machines
SGI Workstation
Shared Storage Systems
Software
Software Design
Software Development
Software Guide
Software Implementation
Software Testing
Software Upgrades
Source Code
Specifications
Statistical Knowledge
Strategic Planning
Subassemblies
System and Subsystem Interface
System Design Engineering
System Enhancements

System Safety
System Testing
Systems Configuration
Systems Engineering
Systems Test and Integration
T1 Connection
Technical Directions
Technical Notes
Technical Reports
Technical Solutions
Technology Integration
Terminal Servers
Test Data
Test Networks
Test Plan
Test Procedures
Test Software/Hardware
Troubleshooting
Uninterrupted Transmissions
UNIX Market
User Manuals
Utilities
Video Communications
Video Images
Visual Basic
Visual Programming Languages
Voice Communications
VxWorks
Warehouse Development Tools
Whitepapers
Windows
Workstation Configuration
Workstation Maintenance
Workstations

Education and Library Sciences

Education buzz words display a familiarity with child development, kindergarten and elementary school education (including math, language, science, and social studies), private and public preschools, elementary schools, middle and secondary schools, colleges and universities, as well as tutorial operations. Library science buzz words highlight experience related to the collection and cataloging of library materials and direct information programs for the public.

▶ Resume Buzz Words

Absent
Academic Development
Academic Schedule
Accountability
Accreditation
Administrative Problems
Advertising
Aesthetics
After-School Programs

Age Appropriate
ALA Filing Rules
Alertness and Coordination
Algebra I & II
Algorithm
Alumni Relations
Appreciation
Art
Artistic Skills

Audiovisual
Authentic Assessment
Author
AV Equipment
Balanced Development of Children
Balanced Reading
Basic Academic Skills
Behavioral Problems
Behavioral Strategies
Bibliographic Data
Bibliographies
Block Scheduling
Books
Bookstore Operations
Brain-Based Learning
Budget Planning
Building Self-Esteem
Bus Stops
Business Math
Card Catalog
Cataloging
Certification
Chair Meetings
Charter Schools
Child Development
Child-Centered Teaching
Chronically/Terminally Ill Children
Circulation Desk
Class Trips
Classroom Safety
Classroom Supervision
Classrooms
Coach
Cognitive Development
Cognitive Skills
Collaboration Skills
Collaborative Projects
College Archives
College-Level Courses
Committees
Computer Curriculum
Computer Lab
Computers for Classroom Management
Consensus
Content Areas
Copyright Policies
Course Descriptions
Crafts Instruction
Creative Expression
Creativity
Critical Thinking
Cultural and Recreational Activities
Curricula Methods
Curriculum
Curriculum Development
Curriculum Plans
Daily Lesson Plans
Daily Operations
Day Camp
Debater
Decode
Department of Education
Department of Social Services (DSS)
Department of Youth Services (DYS)
Departmental Text
Detention
Development of Initiative and Self-Reliance

Dexterity
Direct Mail
Direction
Disabled Students
Discovery Learning
Donor Gifts
Drilling
Education
Education Expeditions
Education Institutions
Education Plans
Education Reform
Education Reinforcement
Educational and Psychological Testing
Educational and Recreational Activities
Educational Committees
Educational Requirements
Elementary Education
Elementary School
Emotional Methods
Emotionally Disturbed Class
English
Environmental Simulation
Evaluation
Exercises
Faculty and Staff Counsel
Food Service Management
Fundraising
Geometry
Grades 9–12
Grades K–8
Grades/Marks
Group Counseling
Group Presentation
Group Study
Guidance Counselor
Half-Time
Handbook
Handicaps
High School
Higher-Order Thinking
History
Honors
Index Tools
Indexes
Individual IEP's
Individual Lesson Plans
Individualized Treatment/Education Plans
Infant Care
Intellectual Methods
Interpreter/Translator
Journals
Junior High
Language
Language Arts
Language/Learning Disabilities
Leadership Training
Learning Aids
Learning Disability Class
Learning Through Play
Lectures/Seminars
Letter Sounds
Library Services
Life and Career Skills
Lifelong Learning
Literacy and Numeracy Skills
Mass Media Communications

Mathematics
Media Releases
Microfiche
Microfilm
Monograph Collection
Montessori Method
Multicultural Populations
Multiculturalism
Multioffice Communication
Multiple Intelligences
Museum Trips
Music Lessons
Negotiator
New Book Orders
Newsprint Publications
NLM Classification System
Nonprofit Service Organization
Numerical Ability
Observation Skills
One-to-One Instruction
Onsite Visitation
Oral Language Skills
Orientation Programs
Outcome-Based Education
Outings
Parent Involvement Committee
Parent Relations
Parent Teacher Association (PTA)
Parent-Teacher Conferences
Peer Tutoring
Performance Standards
Personal Care and Play
Phonics
Photo Indexing
Photocopy
Photocopy Policies
Physical Development
Physical Skills
Physical Therapy
Portfolio Assessment
Positive Behavior Modification Techniques
Pre-Calculus
Preparation
Preschool/Daycare Setting
Press Releases
Private School
Procedures
Program Coordination
Progress Reports
Project Approach
PTSA
Public Relations
Public School
Public Service
Public Speaking
Publishing
Pupil-Led Play
Reading
Reconstitution
Recreational Activities
Recruiting
Reference and Search Files
Reference Questions
Reference Services
Religion
Remedial Math
Remedial Reading

Research
Residence Halls
Retrospective Conversion
Role Model
Rote Learning
SAT Preparation
Scholarships
School Administration
School Board
School Policies
School Year
Science
Secondary School
Secretary of Education
Severe Emotional Disabilities Classroom
Sign Language
Social Studies
Special Education
Speech Pathology
Spelling
Staff Meetings
State Standards
State-Certified
Statistics
Student Accomplishments
Student Activities
Student Affairs Calendar
Student Assessment
Student Athletes
Student Evaluation
Student Groups
Student Performance
Student Relations
Substitute
Success-Oriented Group
Summer School
Superintendent
Superintendent of Public Instruction
Systems
Tardy
Teacher Dues
Teacher Evaluation
Teacher Recruitment
Teacher Union
Teacher-in-Service Training
Teaching Aids
Teaching Methods
Teaching Skills
Teaching to the Test
Teaching/Training
Terminals
Textbooks
Therapeutic Group Services
Traditional Teaching Mode
Training
Trigonometry
Troubleshooting Skills
University
University Students
Vocational Counseling
Vocational Interest
Voucher
Weekly Meetings
Whole Child Development
Whole Language
Workshops
Writing

Engineering

Buzz words from the various fields of engineering demonstrate experience with the theories and principles of science and mathematics and with designing machinery, products, systems, and processes for efficient and economical performance. This includes designing industrial machinery and equipment for manufacturing goods, defense systems, and weapons for the armed forces. Other important skills and experience include planning and supervising the construction of buildings, highways, and rapid transit systems; and designing and developing consumer products and systems for control and automation of manufacturing, business, and management processes.

▶ Resume Buzz Words

3D Modeling
Acoustic Testing
Aerodynamics
Allocation
Analog Electronics
Architecture Enhancements
Assembly Design
Assembly Modification
Bid and Cost Plus Work
Bid Sheets
Bidder Lists
Board of Safety Standards
Buildings
C Programming
C4 Navigation and Intelligence
Cable Products
Capital Equipment
Ceramic Capacitors
Chemical Engineering
Chemistry
Circuitry
Civil Engineering
Commercial Projects
Competitive Analysis
Complex Electromechanical Systems
Component Evaluation
Components and Assemblies
Compression Tests
Computer Product Design
Computer Programming
Computer Software Packages
Computer-Based Transducers and Loud-
    speaker System Measurement
Conceptualization
Conflicts Resolution
Consistency and Compatibility
Construction Coordination
Construction Estimates
Construction Industries

Contract Engineering
Cost Reduction
Customized Security
Data Collection and Analysis
Data Performance Characteristics
Design and Construction of RF Equipment
Design Methodologies
Design Verification Testing
Detailed Models
Development Environment
Digital Electronics
Documentation
Dynamic Systems
Economical Solution
Efficiency Control
Electrical Analysis
Electrical Design
Electrical Engineering
Electronic Design
Electronic Equipment
Electrostatic Discharge
Emissions Testing
Engineering Estimates
Engineering Field Supervision
Engineering Management
Environmental Engineering
Environmental Problems
Environmental Regulations
Environmental Testing
Fabrication Methodologies
Facilities
Facilities Engineering
Facilities Inspections
Flow Patterns
Fluid Compression
Fluid Mechanics
Fluid Systems
Functionality
Geological Formations

Global Marketing
Government Markets
Hardware Evaluation
High-Density Surface Mount Printed Circuit/
    Wiring Board (PWB)
High-Speed Applications
High-Temperature Environments
Hydraulic Systems
Hydrologic Surveys
Industrial Engineering
Industrial Projects
Information-Based Systems
Injection Molding Design
Integrated Systems
Interdisciplinary Requirements
Internal Controls
Justification Studies
Land Surveying Services
Line Balancing
Load Monitors
Logical Performance Characteristics
Logistics
Maintenance Documentation
Management Processes
Manufacturing
Manufacturing Problem Resolution
Manufacturing Processes
Marine Engineering
Master Specifications
Mathematical Models
Mechanical and Control Systems
Mechanical Design
Mechanical Design Integrity
Mechanical Engineering
Mechanism Design
Microscopic Analysis
Mission-Critical Programs
Motion Control
Mounting
Networked Systems
Networking Functionality
New Product Development Environment
OEM
Operations Manual
Part Tolerance
Parts Modeling
Performance Characteristics
Petroleum Accumulation
Petroleum Generation
Petroleum Migration
Phase Separation
Physical Performance Characteristics
Planning
Polishing
Powder and Bulk Solids Handling
Power Supply Test
Preproduction Engineering Prototypes
Preventive Maintenance Programs
Process and Procedure Development
Process and Project Documentation
Process Control
Process Development
Process Improvements
Process Methods
Process Sheets
Product Development
Productivity

Professional Consulting
Programmable Logic
Project Cost
Project Engineering
Project Management
Project Specifications
Project Start-Up
Prototypes
PWB Fabrication
Qualitative Analysis
Quality Assurance
Quality Assurance Tests
Quality Control
Quantitative Analysis
Radiation Monitoring Equipment
Radiological Controls
Reactor Design
Reactor Maintenance
Reconnaissance
Regulatory Compliance
Regulatory Requirements
Reliability and Quality Assurance
Reliability Life Testing
Research and Development (R&D)
Safety Regulations
Scheduling
Scientific Discovery
Sheet Metal Design
Space Platforms
Space Systems and Electronics
Specifications
Statistical Analysis
Statistical Process Controls
Stress Analysis
Structural Design
Subsystems
Surveillance
Susceptibility Testing
System Analysis
System Baselines
System Characterization and Test
System Dynamics
Systems Analysis
Systems Dynamics
Systems Maintenance
Technical Guidelines
Technical Guides
Technical Support
Technical Writing
Tensile Tests
Test Planning and Field Operations
Test Plans
Test Processes
Test Specimens
Testability and Verifiability of Requirements
Testing Policies
Testing Standards
Theories
Thermodynamics
Thermoforming Design
Timing Violations
Tooling
Top-Level System Architecture
Vendor and Partner Technology Relationships
Weight and Distribution Properties
Worst-Case Scenarios
Written Specifications

Executive and Managerial

Executive and managerial positions exist in all types of businesses. Executive buzz words should highlight experience ranging from general supervisory duties to running an entire company. Relevant skills include management of individual departments within a larger corporate structure, motivating workers to achieve their goals as rapidly and economically as possibly, budgeting and directing projects, and evaluating company processes and methods to determine cost-effective plans.

▶ Resume Buzz Words

Account Management
Account Retention
Accounting
Accounts Payable
Accounts Receivable
Administration
Administrative Detail
Advertising
Allocation
Annual Sales
Appointment Generation
Asset Base
Asset Management
Auditing
Audits
Banking Objectives
Banking Operations
Banking Transactions
Benefit Eligibility
Benefits Coordination
Bookkeeping
Branch Consolidation
Branch Management
Budget
Budget Development
Budget Planning
Budgeting
Budgets
Business Contacts
Business Development
Business Software
Business Strategies
Capability
Cash Administration
Cash Disbursement
Cash Flow
Certified Public Accountant (CPA)
Check Processing
Claim Errors
Claims
Claims Adjustments
Claims Processing
Client Base
Client Relations

Cold Calling
Commercial Balances
Commercial Financing Enterprise
Commercial Loans
Commercial Paper Transactions
Commercial Real Estate
Commissions
Communications
Company Programs
Compatible
Competitive Analysis
Complaint Activity
Compliance
Consultation
Consulting
Contingency
Contract Management
Contractual Agreements
Contractual Modifications
Corporate Clients
Corporate Mission
Corporate Planning
Corporate Returns
Corporate Strategy
Correspondences
Cost Reports
Credit Lines
Custom and Importing Regulations
Customer Education
Customer Relations
Customer Service
Data Processing
Database
Database Management
Day-to-Day Operations
Direct Mail
Direct Response Agencies
Domestic Letters of Credit
Efficient Operations
Employee Morale
Employee Training
Equipment
Evaluation
Expense Control

Expenses
Facilities
Facility Coordination
Fiduciary Income
Finance
Financial Controls
Financial Management
Financial Reports
Financial Statements
Financial Transactions
Franchise Management
General Ledgers
Hardware
High-Dollar Contracts
Hiring
Import/Export Shipments
Incremental
Individual Returns
Insurance
International Letters of Credit
Inventory
Inventory Control
Invoices
Lead Development
Leasing
Lending
Logistics
Long Term Goals
Loss Prevention
Maintenance
Major Accounts
Management
Manpower
Marketing
Marketing Activities
Markets
Merchandising
Mobility
Motivation
Negotiation
New Business Development
New Products
Objectives
Operational Objectives
Operations
Outside Sales and Support Staff
P&L Management
Payables
Payroll
Personnel Management
Personnel Relations

Policies and Procedures
Product Awareness
Profit Loss
Profit Margin
Progressive Organization
Projection
Promotions
Property Management
Prospects
Provider/Client Communication
Public Relations
Purchasing Process
Purchasing Systems
Quality Control
Receivables
Records
Referrals
Regulatory Requirements
Relationship Management
Reorganization
Reports
Restaurants
Retail Banking
Retail Sales
Revenue
Revenue Development
Sales Experience
Sales Expertise
Sales Objectives
Sales Presentations
Sales Support
Sales Techniques
Scenarios
Scheduling
Service Contracts
Service Operations
Small Business
Staff Supervision
Statistics
Store Operations
Supervision
Supervisory Experience
Tax Issues
Team Management
Technical Support
Third-Generation
Time-Phase
Training
Transitional
Troubleshooting
Yearly Transactions

Food and Beverages/Agriculture

Industry buzz words for these fields highlight experience with growing, processing, packaging, shipping, receiving, storing, preparing, and selling consumable products. This includes farming; transport and delivery of products between farms, processing plants, and vendors; scientific research and development of products to ensure quality and safety of foods; and export and sale, both foreign and domestic.

▶ Resume Buzz Words

Advanced Breeding
Advertising Claims
Agricultural
Agricultural Chemicals
Agricultural Commodities
Agricultural Products
Agricultural Trade Association
Animal Feed Ingredients
Animal Oils
Baby Food
Baked Products
Baking Breads
Basic Ingredients
Beef
Beer
Beer Brands
Beer, Wine, and Spirits Distributor
Beverage Vending Company
Beverages
Biotechniques
Bottled Water
Bottling Facility
Brands
Brewing
Business Efforts
Cabernet Sauvignon
Cakes
Canned Beans
Canned Fruits and Vegetables
Canned Meat Products
Canola
Cans
Cash Advances
Cattle Feeding Procedures
Cereals
Cheese
Chemical Dispensing Equipment
Citrus Growing and Processing Firm
Coin-Operated Vending Machines
Commercial Soups
Commodities
Commodity Trading
Competitive Prices
Competitively Priced
Condiments
Confections
Consumers
Convenience Food
Cookies
Cooking Oil
Corn
Corn Refining Process
Corrugating
Costing
Cotton
Cottonseed Flour Products
Creative Solutions
Crop Areas
Crop Growth
Crop Insurance
Crop Nutrients
Culinary Background
Dairy Dessert Products
Dairy Products

Define Problems
Dehydrator
Dessert Products
Diet Soft Drinks
Dips
Distribution
Diversified
Diversified Livestock Company
Doughnuts
Drinking Water
Dry Bulk Warehousing
Edible and Industrial Plant Oils
Eggnog
Erythritol
Ethanol
Farm
Farm Products
Farmers
Farming
Feed
Feed Ingredient Trading
Feedlot
Fermentation Lab
Fermentation Products
Fermentor Systems
Fertilizers
Financial Markets Division (FMD)
Flavoring Products
Food and Consumer Products
Food and Cosmetic Product Regulations
Food and Seed Industries
Food Industry
Food Processing Businesses
Food Production
Food Products
Food Safety
Food Safety Systems
Food Service Disposables
Food Service Experience
Formulas
Freight Management
Fresh and Frozen Fish Products
Frozen Foods
Frozen Meats
Frozen Potato Products
Fruits
Fuel
Functional Foods Markets
Genetic Engineering
Genetically Engineered Plants
Government Regulations
Grain Merchandising
Grain-Based Foods
Grains
Greenhouse
Groceries
Growers
Ham
Handling
Harvesting
Herbs
High-Fructose Corn Syrup
High-Quality
Horticulture

Hybrids
Ice Cream Manufacturer
Imports
Incremental Break Boxes
Industrial-Grade Starches
Ingredients
Institutions
Inventory Management
Irrigation
Juices
Ketchup
Labels
Lamb
Livestock Marketing
Livestock Production
Livestock Quality
Local Vineyards
Luncheon Meats
Major Producer
Major Trader
Malt Beverages
Manufacturer
Manufacturing
Margarine
Market
Market Conditions
Meat Products
Merchandising
Military Markets
Milk
Minerals
Mines
Nationally Distributed Food Products
Natural Ingredients
Nonagricultural
Nutritional Products
Oilseeds
Order Placement
Order Selection
Packaged Food Companies
Packaging
Pasta Products
Pasta Sauces
Pest Control
Pet Food
Pharmaceutical
Phosphates
Pickles
Pinot Noir
Plant Breeding
Plant Products
Planting
Pork
Portion Control
Potash
Premium Line
Premium White and Red Varietal Table Wines
Premium Wines
Prepared Feeds
Processed Consumables
Procurement
Product Specifications
Protein Powders
Proteins
Public Stockyards
Pudding
Purchasing

Quality Control
Quality Raw Materials
Quick-Service Restaurants
Raising Livestock
Ready-To-Eat Cereals
Recognized Brand Names
Reconditioning
Refrigerated
Rent
Repackaging
Replenishment
Restaurants
Retail Locations
Rice
Risk Management
Rolls
Salad Dressings
Salt Products
Sauces
Sauvignon Blanc
Seafood
Seasoning Blends
Seasoning Mixes
Seasonings
Seed
Seed Varieties
Smoked Salmon Ravioli
Snack Foods
Soft Drinks
Sour Cream
Soy Flour
Soy Isolates
Soy Milk
Soy Protein
Soybeans
Spaghetti Sauces
Specialty Food Company
Specialty Food Items
Specialty Ingredient
Spices
Sports Beverages
Starches
Sterility Control
Storing
Strain Management
Sweeteners
Temperature Controlled
Tomato Sauces
Tomato-Based Products
Transporting
Tryptophan
TVP
Veal
Vegetable Oil Refinement
Vegetable Oils
Vegetable Products
Vegetables
Vendors
Vitamin C
Vitamin E
Vitamins
Wheat
Wholesale Food Distributors
Wholesale Outlets
Wholesaler
Yogurt

Government

For those interested in positions in politics and government, buzz words highlight experience in executive, legislative, judicial, or general government agencies as well as with public agencies, such as firefighting, military, police work, or the United States Postal Service. This includes researching and evaluating military materials; cleaning, maintenance, and general service for public works; participating in political campaigns by networking, fundraising, or organizing; and working to control narcotic and dangerous drug use through prevention and law enforcement. It also includes mail pickup and delivery experience, public relations and press work, and public outreach activities.

▶ Resume Buzz Words

Administration
Administrative Offices
Administrative Services
Advanced Development Programs
Agency
Agency Management
Agricultural Production
Agriculture
Air and Water Pollution
Air Quality
Annex Building
Area-Wide Governmental Organization
Assistance Services
Bank Holding Companies
Borrowing Transactions
Briefing Reports
Broadly Based Exploratory Programs
Building Activities
Bureau
Business Administration
Business Interests
Business Relationship
Central Headquarters
Central Management Agencies
Chamber of Commerce
Citizens
City Council Offices
City Departments
City Highways
City Manager
City Transportation Department
Classification Compliance Audits
Coastal Waters
Committee
Community Service Jobs
Complete Range of Mail Pickup and Delivery
  Services
Computerized Procurement Systems
Constitutional Officer

Consumer Rights
Consumers and Businesses
Control Audits
Coordinating Food Protection Programs
Debate
Debt Management
Defense Contract Management
Democratic Party
Department of Industrial Accidents
Department of Labor and Workforce
  Development
Dependents
Developing Countries
Diplomatic Capabilities
Disaster Management
Disaster Prevention
District Court
Domestic Disputes
Econometrics
Economic and Educational Support
Economic Conditions
Economic Development
Economic Growth
Economy
Education
Educational Issues
Educational Programs
Elections
Emergency Situations
Energy
Enforcement
Engineering
Environmental Protection
Environmental Quality
Environmental Sciences
Environmental Studies
Exchange Rate Management
Executive Branch
Export Counseling

Federal Bank
Federal Benefits
Federal Campaigning Activities
Federal Environmental Laws
Federal Government
Federal Government Agency
Federal Labor-Management Relations
Federal Planning
Federal Records
Federal Reserve Notes
Federal Space Exploration Program
Field Locations
Field Offices
Finance
Financial Institutions
Fire Prevention
Fish and Wildlife
Food Protection Program
Food Stamps
Foreign Intelligence
Functional Divisions
Funding
General Services
Generating Electricity
Government Assistance
Government Offices
Government Organization
Government Program Applications
Government Registration Activities
Governmental Organization
Government-Owned Facilities
Government-Run
Governor
Grant
Guidelines
Health and Human Services Facility
Highway Maintenance
Human Health Protection
Impact of Trade
Import
Inadequate Housing
Income Distribution
Income Tax Returns
Independent Auditor
Information Services
Information Technology
In-House Research
Institutional Issues
International Agency
International Aid
International Companies
International Lending Agency
International Trade
Issuance of Licenses
Job Market
Job Placement
Jobseekers
Justice
Labor Unions
Land Use
Law
Law Enforcement Services
Legal Cases
Legal Determinations
Legal Services
Legislative Branch
Legislative Requests

Legislators
Lending to Third World Nations
Local Businesses
Local Government Agency
Local Office
Long-Term Economic Growth
Macroeconomics
Maintenance and Improvement
Mandate
Manufacturing Quotas
Mayor's Office
Medicaid Services
Medical Devices
Medical Emergencies
Medico-Public Health Laboratory
Metro
Metropolitan Development
Missions
Monetary Policy
Monetary Theory
Multidisciplinary Support
National Cemeteries
National Headquarters
National Health Programs
National Law Enforcement Agency
National Parks
Nationwide Healthcare Programs
Natural Resources
Nature and Wildlife Preservation
Naval Warfare Centers
Navy Needs
Nonprofit
Nuclear Materials
Nuclear Power
Objective Trade Expertise
Operations
Organization Analysis
Passport Acceptance
Patent
Patrols
Physical Sciences
Police Department
Policies
Political and Legislative Support Functions
Political Economy
Productivity of Natural Resources
Public Buildings
Public Expenditure
Public Finance
Public Order
Public Use
Public Works
Purify City Water
Quality Health Care
Quality of the Environment
Radiation Emitting Products
Recreation Areas
Rectifying Disputes
Recycling Services
Reducing Manufacturing Costs
Regional Offices
Regional Planning Agency
Regional Problems
Regional Training Institutes
Regulation of Companies
Regulatory Agency
Regulatory Commission

Renewable Energy
Repair Services
Republican Party
Roads and Highways
Safe Living Conditions
Sale of Consumer Products
Securities Market
Security Documents
Security Products
Seminars
Senior Services
Significant Economic Changes
Small Business
Snow Plowing
Space Systems Technology
Special Investigations
Standards
State Entities
State Government
State Parks and Reservations
State Representation
State Tax Information
State-Run Agencies and Universities

Statewide Financial and Compliance Audits
Statistical Material
Statistical Methodologies
Statutory Filings
Street Repairs
Tax Forms
Tax Publications
Trade Actions
Trade Association
Trade Seminars
Traffic Congestion
Transportation Planning
U.S. Industries
U.S. Paper Currency
U.S. Policy
Urban Development
Utility Companies
Volunteers
Water Supply
Welfare Office
Work Force Conditions
Workers' Compensation Claims

Health and Medical

Buzz words from the vital health and medical fields demonstrate experience with illness, working toward achieving and maintaining healthy lifestyles, and helping to address and resolve related issues, such as insurance and medical claim forms. This includes working directly with patients and their families in dealing with health problems; assisting patients by providing medical advice regarding prescriptions, insurance claim forms, and related issues; and researching medical treatments and techniques.

▶ Resume Buzz Words

Acute and Chronic Patients
Agency Staff
AIDS
Ambulatory Services
Anatomy/Physiology
Anesthesia Operations
Angioplasty
Appointments
Behavioral Programs
Biochemistry
Blood Chemistry
Blood Draws
Bone Fractures
Budget Preparation
Budget Responsibilities
Burn Patients
Business Management Activities
Calisthenics
Cardiac Anatomy

Cardiac Catheterization
Cardiac Patients
Case Management
Childbirth
Chronic Pain
Chronically Ill
Clerical Support
Client Eligibility
Clinical Cardiology
Clinical Instruction
Clinical Operations
Communication Disorders
Community Hospitals
Comprehensive Care
Computer Literacy
Conduct Disorders
Conferences and Lectures
CPR
Crisis Intervention

Crowns
Daycare Centers
DEA Regulations
Dental Impressions
Dental Laboratory
Dental Materials
Dentures
Department Budgets
Departmental Meetings
Diet Aides
Dietetic Technicians
Discharge Planning
Disease Research
Drills
Drug and Alcohol Abuse
Drug Delivery
Echocardiography
Educational Counseling
Educational Videos
EKG
Electric Stimulation
Emergency Care
Emergency Medical Procedures
Emergency Services
Emergency Treatment
Exercise Classes
Family Conferences
Filing Systems
First Aid
Follow-Up Medical Treatments
Formal Education Programs
Front Desk Procedures
Gastroenterology
Government-Funded Food Programs
Grinders
Health/Recreation Clubs
Heimlich Methods of Resuscitation
Hematology and Serology Testing
Historic Research
HMO's
Home Care
Home Care Agencies
Home Health Agencies
Hospital Policies
Hospital, State, and Federal Guidelines
Human Services
ICU
Individualized Treatments
Infusion Therapy Services
Inhalation Therapy
Injured Patients
Inlays
In-Patient and Outpatient Care
In-Service Consultation
Instrument Set-Ups
Insurance Companies
Intensive Aerobics
Intravenous Therapy
IV Antibiotic Therapy
Lab Procedures
Lab Results
Laboratory Operations
Lathes
Manic Depression
Massage Therapy
Medical Equipment
Medical Management
Medical Photography

Medical Records
Medical Research
Methodology
Metropolitan Hospitals
Modalities
Motivational Skills
MRI Department
Multidisciplined Practice
New Medications
Nursing Home Placement
Nursing Practice Standards
Nursing Services
Nutrients
Nutrition
Nutritional Care Plans
Order Entry
Outpatient
Parenteral and Enteral Nutrition
Pathology
Patient Care
Patient Charts
Patient Records
Patient Relations
Patient Services
Patients
Pediatric Patients
Pediatric/Emergency Medicine
Personality Disorders
Pet Food Products
Pet Nutrition
Pharmaceutical Companies
Pharmaceuticals
Pharmacology
Pharmacology and Behavioral Modification
    Methods
Physical and Psychosocial Needs
Physical Standards
Physical Therapy Standards
Policy and Procedures Development
Polishers
Post-Op Care
Postoperative Care
Preliminary Diagnoses
Preoperative Care
Prescription Reimbursement Claims
Prescriptions
Primary Nursing Care
Private Practice
Psychiatric Care
Psychology
Psycho-Social Assessments
QA Monitoring
Qualitative Research
Quality Assurance
Quantitative Research
Radiology
Referring Physicians
Respiratory Therapy
Service Related Incidents
Severely Ill Patients
Side Effects
Skilled Nursing Assessment
Social Services
Specialized Nursing and Medical Care
Staffing Issues
State-Funded Programs
Statistical Reports
Strength and Stamina

Stretching
Stretching/Strengthening Exercises
Strokes
Substance Abuse
Surgical Procedures
Teaching
Therapy
Tracheotomy Care
Ultrasound
Unit Doses

Urinalysis
Ventilators
Veterinary Medicine
Vital Signs
Word Processing
Work-Related Injuries
Workshops
X-Ray Department
X-Ray Procedures
Yoga

Hotels and Restaurants

In these service industries, buzz words reflect experience and familiarity with restaurant management, food services, banquets and conventions, guest/customer service, and promotions. Other valuable skills include culinary, business/accounting, interpersonal communication, and facilities management. Many of these buzz words would also apply for many positions in the travel industry.

▶ Resume Buzz Words

ACF (CEC) Certification
ACF Apprenticeship
Administrative
Amusement Facilities
Audio Equipment
Bakeries
Bakery and Confectionery
Banquet Activities
Banquet Equipment
Banquet/Meeting Facilities
Bar Set-Up and Breakdown
Beauty Culture
Bookkeeping
Budgeted Food Costs
Buffet and Restaurant Displays
Buffing Wheel
Burnishing Machine Tumble
Cafes
Cash Control
Cash Handling Procedures
Casual-Dining Restaurants
Catering
China, Glass and Silver Service Inventory
Cleanliness
Cleanup of All Banquet Functions
Cocktails
Company Standards
Conference Center
Cookery Craft
Coolers/Storerooms
Country Clubs
Culinary Arts
Culinary Management

Culinary School
Cultural Centers
Customer Satisfaction
Daily Quality Checks
Deluxe Hotels
Dinnerware
Dishwashing Machine
DJs
Drive-Thru Restaurants
Eating Venues
Employee Relations
Ethnic Cuisine
Excess Production
Exclusive Health Clubs
Family-Oriented Restaurants
Fast-Food Restaurants
Federal, State, Local Safety and Health
    Regulations
Fine Dining
Floor and Capacity Charts
Flow of Guests
Food and Facilities Management Services
    Company
Food and/or Beverage Orders
Food Preparation and Presentation
Food Preservation
Food Production Management
Food Retailing
Food Service Companies
Food Service Facilities
Food Service Handlers Certification
Foreign Hotel Institutions
Franchises

Fresh Products
Front Office Operation
Glassware
Global Sales
Groundskeeping
Guest Occupancy
Guest Services
HACCP Standards
Health Department Rules
Hiring
Home Science
Hospitality Management
Hotel Accounting
Hotel Management
Hotel Standards
Housekeeping
Ingredients
Integrated Facilities Management
International Hospitality
Inventory and Food Costs
JCAHO Knowledge
Kitchen
Leisure and Tourism
Leisure Attractions
Licensed House Management
Liquor and Wines
Live Entertainment
Luxury Hotel
Management Experience
Meat Blocks
Meeting Rooms
Menu
Menu Development
Menu Planning for Various Disease States
Nightclub Promotions
Nutritional Requirements
Nutritional Screening and Assessment
Online Reservations
Organizational Functions
Orientation
Outsourcing Solutions
Personality
Pizzeria

Plant Operations and Maintenance
Plating and Presentation
Portion Sizes
Pots, Pans, and Trays
Presentation
Pre-Shift and Regularly Scheduled Meetings
Prices
Problem-Solving Capabilities
Promotions
Proper Food Handling
Public Recreation Facilities
Quality Standards
Reception
Recruiting Efforts
Refrigerators
Reservation
Resorts
Restaurants
Roadside Lodges
Room Set-Ups
Safety Procedures
Sales Figures
Sanitation Practices
Scheduling
Server Stations
Special Packages and Promotions
Spoilage
Squirrel POS System
Staff Development
Staffing
Tables
Techniques and Standards
TIPS Certification
Tourism
Training
Trash and Garbage Removal
Travel
Vendor and Distributor Relations
Vocational Training
Weddings
Weekly and Monthly Inventories
Worktables

Human Resources

Human resources buzz words display experience recruiting, interviewing, and hiring employees according to their qualifications and suitability to the organization. Additional responsibilities often include encouraging a productive company culture by effectively utilizing employee skills and fostering job satisfaction; handling employee health and pension plans; and maintaining and articulating knowledge of government regulations regarding labor and employee benefit regulations.

▶ Resume Buzz Words

Accounts Payable System
Accounts Receivable System
Ad Management
ADA
Administration
Affirmative Action
Background Checks
Behavioral Sciences
Benchmarking
Benefit Checks
Benefit Consulting
Benefits
Benefits Administration
Blended Learning Solutions
Business Results
Business Value
Candidate Pool
Candidate Screening
Career Counseling
Career Development
Career Fairs
Claim Adjudication
Client Management
Coached Learning Solutions
Coaching
College Programs
Compensation and Payroll Functions
Compensation Consulting
Compensation Data
Compensation System
Competencies
Confidential Personnel Records
Consultative Skills
Content Assessment
Contract Negotiations
Contracts
Corporate Communication
Corporate Learning
Corporate Performance
Corporate Philosophy
Creation of Reports and Correspondences
Current Trends
Customer Service
Delivery Assessment
Departmental Contacts
Departmental Expenditures
Development Initiatives
Direct Mail
EEO/AA Compliance
e-Learning
Electronic Learning Solutions
Employee Counseling
Employee Effectiveness
Employee Records
Employee Relations
Employee Relationship Management Solution
Employee Status Forms
Employees
Employment
Entitlement
Evaluation Process
Executive Bonus Plan
Executive Search Companies
Exempt Positions

Federal and State Laws
General Ledger
Global Leadership Attributes
Grievance Interviews
Grievance Procedures
Gross Sales Reconciliation
Hard-Core Unemployed
Health Care and Group Benefits
HRIS Technologies
HRMS Products/Solutions
Human Capital Strategy
Induction Programs
Industry Trends
Insurance Payments
Integrated Development Approach
Internal and External Resources
Internal Staffing
Interview Process
Invoice Processing
Job Descriptions
Job Requirements
Key Business Outcomes
Key Competencies and Deliverables
Labor Disputes
Labor Management
Labor Relations
Leader Effectiveness
Leadership Assessment Tools
Leadership Development Programs
Leadership Responsibilities
Maintenance Bills
Management
Management Techniques
Maternity Leave
Measurement
Meetings
Mentor
Merit Budget Recommendations
Methodologies
Modularized Learning Solutions
Needs Analysis
Networking Activities
Non-Exempt Positions
Office Interviews
Office Supply Maintenance
Open Enrollments
Open Positions
Organizational Development
Organizational Learning
Organizational Objectives
Outplacement Services
Payroll Database
Payroll Transmissions
Pension/Health and Welfare Reports
People Development
Performance Development
Performance Management
Performance Measurement and Rewards
Permanent Personnel Actions
Permanent Positions
Personnel
Personnel Policies
Placement
Portfolio assessment

Position Analysis
Potential Candidates
Pre-Screening
Pricing Information
Private Sector
Productivity
Professional Associations
Professional Development
Professional Staffing Costs
Program Delivery
Progressive Human Processes
Prospective Employees
Qualified Professionals
Real-Time Information
Recruiting Resources
Recruitment
Recruitment Sources
Reference Checks
Referrals
Regulations
Regulatory Agencies: EOHS, OER, DPA, PERA
Reinsurance Carrier
Request For Proposals (RFP)
Resume Preparation
Retirement Consulting
Return on Investment (ROI)
Salaried Jobs
Salary Administration
Salary Reviews
Salary Surveys

Self-Directed Learning Solutions
Skills Testing
Staffing
Statistical Records
Strategic Human Resource Planning
Team Development
Team Performance
Team-Based Environment
Telemarketing
Temporary Assignments
Termination
Time and Labor Solutions
Training
Tutoring
Unclaimed Wages
Unemployed Youth
Unemployment Insurance
Unions
Unskilled
Vacation Schedules
Vendor Selection
Visitors
Wages
Web-Based Enterprise Applications
Website Job Postings
Workers' Compensation
Workflow
Workplace Laws
Workplace Stress

Insurance

For the insurance industry, appropriate buzz words highlight experience with contracts, claims, personal injury, workers' compensation, and assets. This includes knowledge of different areas of insurance, such as fire, theft, automotive, property, business, health, and disability. Familiarity with premiums, appraisals, policies, financial planning services, and insurance sales should also be included.

▶ Resume Buzz Words

Accident
Accountability
Accounts Receivable
Act of God
Adhesion
Adjust
Adjustment
Advance
Agency
Agents
Aggregate
Aid
Amendment
Annuities
Annuity Plans
Annuity Products
Appraisal

Asset Accumulation
Asset-Based Lending/Financing
Assets
Attorneys
Audit
Auto Insurance Claims
Automobile Accident
Automobile Dealers
Automobile Insurance
Automotive
Basic Coverage
Benefits
Binding Agreement
Book Value
Borderline Risk
Branch Offices
Broad-Based Customer Group

Brokerage
Building Code
Capacity
Capital
Captive Agents
Care Plan
Carrier
Caseload
Cash Value
Casualty
Certificate
Charitable Health Care Corporation
Charter
Claims
Claims Management Services
Class
Clause
Clients
Closing Services
Collision
Commercial and Individual Financial Services
Commercial Clients
Commercial Insurance
Commission
Common Law
Compensation
Consolidation
Contingency
Contract
Convention
Convergence
Conversion
Countersignature
Coverage
Covered Loss
Credit Associations
Credit Insurance
Credit Life Insurance
Credit Report
Customers
Daily Report
Damage
Deductible
Dental Care Services
Dental Insurance Firm
Dependents
Descendent
Disability Coverage
Disability Income Insurance
Earned
Emergency Coverage
Endorsement
Enterprise
Equity
Escrow
Estate
Estate Planning
Exclusion
Expense
Extended
Fee
Field
Financial and Insurance Operations
Financial Services Group
Firm
First Party
Flat

Gain
Geographical Location
Gross
Group Health
Group Life
Group Pension
Guiding Principle
Hazard
Healthcare Delivery
Health Maintenance Organizations (HMO)
Health Plan Coverage
High Exposure Claims
Holding Company
Homebuyers
Homeowners
Indemnity Medical
Individual Life
Inevitable Accident
Injury
Inspection
Institutional Investments
Insurance Carrier
Insurance Products
Insurance Provider
Insurance Risks
Interest Rate
Investigation
Investment
Investment Planning
Investment Planning Company
Joint Coverage
Jurisdictions
Leaseholder
Lenders
Lending Organizations
Liabilities
License
Life Insurance
Limitations
Liquidation
Loss
Loss Prevention
Major Disasters
Malpractice Insurance
Market Value
Members
Mortgage
Multiline Financial Services
Multiperil
Multiple-Line
Mutual Funds
Mutualization
Natural Death
Negligence
Net Loss
Noninsurable Risk
Nonrenewal
Offices
Outsource Vendor
Overrides
Ownership
Payee
Pension
Pension Planning Markets
Performance Reports
Permanent Insurance
Personal Automobiles

Personal Injury
Personal Insurance
Personal Lines of Insurance
Policies
Policy Cancellation
Policy Writing
Policyholders
Portfolio
Power of Attorney
Premium Rate
Premiums
Prevention
Primary Coverage
Primary Insurers
Procedures
Product Portfolio
Professional Liability Insurance
Professional Medical Services
Proof of Loss
Property
Property and Casualty Reinsurance
Provider Reimbursement
Providers

Quota
Rates
Real Estate Brokers
Real Estate Transactions
Rebate
Records
Regional and Specialty Property and Casualty
    Insurers
Reinsurance Intermediary Facilities
Renewal
Retirement Planning
Risk Management Programs
Risks
Search and Examination Services
Securities
Selling
Services
Settlement
Severity
Special Accounts
Sum
Surety
Title Insurance

Legal and Protective Services

In these fields, buzz words highlight experience with interpreting and enforcing the laws. This includes supporting the legal system; patrolling and inspecting property to protect against theft, vandalism, and illegal entry; and ensuring the safety and security of persons who have been arrested, are awaiting trial, or who have been convicted of a crime and sentenced to serve time in a correctional institution. It also includes maintaining order, enforcing rules and regulations, and supplementing counseling.

▶ Resume Buzz Words

Administrative Hearings
Administrative Support Services
Advisory Committees
Advisory Opinions
Alarms
Ambulance
Antitheft System
Appeals Court
Appellate Briefs
Appellate Litigation
Applicants
Appointments
Appropriate Parties
Arbitrators
Arraignment
Assigned Areas
Attorney Appearance Records

Attorney-Client Conferences
Bail Agreements
Bail Motions
Bankruptcy
Bankruptcy Trustees
Brief
Budgeting
Building Security
Burglar Alarms
Bylaws
Camera Surveillance System
Campaign Activities
Capital Projected Costs
Care and Protection Cases
Case Files
Case Management Project
Case Research

Cell Checks
Citations
City Property
Civil Action
Civil Litigation
Civil Motions
Civil Pleadings
Civil Probate Court
Civil Proceedings
Civil Rights
Clerical Support
Client Forms
Client Needs
Client Scheduling
Client Service Plans
Clients
Client's Suit
Co-Counsel
Codes
Collective Bargaining Issues
Commercial Accounts
Commercial Law Department
Commissions
Committee Hearings
Communication Law
Community Outreach
Community Relations
Community Resources
Complaints
Complex Litigation
Computerized Information System
Conciliations
Conclusion of Law
Confidential Reports
Constituents
Contract Administration
Contract Law
Contractual Support
Copyright Registration and Licensing
Corporate Acquisitions
Corporate Compliance
Corporate Data
Corporate Documents
Corporate Financing
Corporate Law
Corporate Tax Standing
Corporate Votes
Correctional Institutions
Correspondence
Cost Analysis
Cost Records
Court
Court Proceedings
Court Reporter
Court Scheduling
Court Sessions
Court Transcripts
Courthouses
Courtroom
Courtroom Activity
CPR/First Aid
Crime Deterrence
Crime Prevention
Crime Zones
Criminal Action
Criminal Arrest Citations
Criminal Cases

Criminal Investigations
Criminal Law
Criminal Motions
Criminal Proceedings
Criminal Situations
Crisis Intervention
Custody/Traffic Direction Processes
Deadlines
Debtors
Defamation Claims
Defendants
Defense Attorney
Delegation of Tasks
Department of Corrections
Department Procedure
Departmental Goals and Direction
Deposition
Deposition Hearings
Discharge
Discharge Petitions
Discovery
Discovery Motions
Dissolution Plans
District Attorney's Office
District Court
Drafting Wills
Drafts
Elective Offices
Emergency
Emergency Situations
Emergency Transportation
Emotional Status
Energy Maintenance Program
Enlistment
Environmental Arenas
Environmental Litigation
Environmental Programs
Environmental Status
Evaluation
Evidence Information
Execution of Duties
Extensive Corporate Dealings
Facilities
Fact
False Advertising
False Claims
Final Payments
Final Settlement Statement
Financial Institutions
Financing Statements
Fingerprints
Fire Academy
Fire Fighting
Fire Prevention
Firearms
Firearms Qualified
Foot Patrols
Forensic Fire Photography
General Business Litigation
General Laws
General Patrol Responsibilities
General Practice
General Practice Law Firm
General Public
General Security Proceedings
Good Will
Government

Government Agencies
Governmental Communications
Grand Jury Testimony
Guard Forces
Guardianship
Guidance
Hearing Practice
High Crime Area
High Pressure Arenas
Hospital Transportation
Housing Area
Human Services
Immigration Case Conferences
In Custody
Incentive Programs
Incident Reports
Inmate Population
Inpatient Facilities
Inquiry Recording System
Insurance Claims
Insurance Companies
Intellectual Property Law
Interviewing of Witnesses
Investigation of Losses
Investigations
Involved Parties
Judicial Arenas
Judicial Lobbies
Justices
Juvenile Court
K-9 Handler
Labor Law
Labor Litigation
Labor Relation Issues
Larceny
Law
Law Enforcement
Law Enforcement Agencies
Law Firm
Law Office Accounts
Law Schools
Legal Counsel
Legal Opinions
Legal Research
Legislation
Legislative Bills
Legislatively Mandated Advisory Committee
Library Research
Licensing
Liens
Liquidation
Litigation Experience
Litigation of False Advertising
Loan Documents
Lobby
Local Agencies
Long-Term Care Issues
Loss Prevention
Maintenance Contracts
Major Felony Cases
Management Inspection
Management Labor Relations
Marriage Certificates
Material Handling
Media Relations
Mediations
Medical Documentation

Medium-Sized Law Firm
Memoranda
Memorandums of Law
Mental Health Law
Mentally Handicapped Clients
Misdemeanors
Modernization of Office Procedures
Money Orders
Monthly Logs
Mortgage Payment
Motions
Motor Vehicle Fraud
Municipal Buildings Security
Municipal Lien Certificates
Municipal Public Safety
Municipalities
Negotiation Strategies
Notarizing Legal Documents
Notice System
Official Records
On Foot
Outside Hospital Guard
Paralegal Services
Patients
Patrol
Peace
Perjury
Permitting Processes
Personal Effects
Physical Status
Plaintiffs
Plea Agreements
Policies and Procedures
Policing Functions
Polygraph Techniques
Population Counts
Post-Closing Functions
Powers of Arrest
Practice
Precedent Information
Pre-Disposition Conferences
Preparation of Cases
Pre-Trial Conference
Prioritize Assignments
Prisoner Visitation
Prisoners
Private Interests
Private Sector
Procedural Issues
Proceedings
Procurement Inspection
Production
Proper Operation
Properties
Property Cases
Property Matters
Proposed Findings
Prosecute
Protection
Provision of Security
Public Agency
Public Interests
Public Relations
Public Safety
Public Traffic
Public Utility Litigation
Purchasing Agent

Real Estate Law
Record Filing
Recording System
Records
Recruiting Efforts
Registration
Registration Process
Registry of Motor Vehicles
Repair Contracts
Reports
Requirements
Resident and Building Security
Respond to Alarms
Restructuring Transactions
Routine Patrol
Safety
Safety and Crime Prevention
Safety of Students
Safety Program
Safety/Self-Protection
School Security
Searches
Security
Security Programs
Security Supervision
Seminars
Service Contracts
Settlement
Small Claims Settlements
Social Trends
Special Prisoners
Special Projects
Special Radar Program
Specifications
State Agencies
State Enabling Statute
State Revenue Sharing
State Tax Liens
Statewide Moratorium
Strategy Planning
Subcontract

Substance Abuse Treatment Centers
Substantive Issues
Superior Court
Support System
Supporting Documents
Supreme Court Arenas
Supreme Court Decisions
Surveillance
Tax Bills
Testify
Third-Party
Title Insurance Forms
Title Searches
Titles
Trademark Licensing
Training Drills
Training Workshops
Transactional Experience
Transactions
Transfer
Treatment Programs
Trial
Trial Attorney
Trial Papers
Trial Preparation
Trial Proceedings
Uniformed Commercial Code
Union Members
Vandalism and Theft Deterrence
Vendors
Victims
Violating the Law
Volunteers
Weaponry Training
Witnesses
Work Schedules
Workload
Work-Study
Writing Skills

Marketing and Sales

Buzz words for positions in the fields of marketing and sales high-light experience with attracting customers, promoting businesses and increasing their public profiles, and closing deals. For these results-oriented positions, specific references to measurable accomplishments are most effective.

▶ Resume Buzz Words

4-Color Process
Account Acquisition
Account Balances
Account Locations
Account Performance
Accountable Documents
Accounting Noting Systems
Accounting Operations

Accounting Reports
Accounts
Accounts Receivables
Acquisition
Additional Business
Additional Sales
Adjusters
Adjustments

Administrative and Marketing Responsibilities
Administrative Policies
Administrative Procedures
Advertisement Placement
Advertisements
Advertising
Advertising Budget
Advertising Campaigns
Advertising Lineage
Advertising Positioning
Advertising Space
Advertising Strategy
Advertorials
After-Market Volume
After-Sales Support
Aggressive Work Flow Management
Analysis
Analysis of Current Accounts
Analysis of Old Accounts
Annual Ad Placements
Annual Division Sales
Annual Marketing Budget
Annual Purchases
Annual Sales
Annual Volume
Appointments
Area Trade
Assets
Assigned Sales Quotas
Average Annual Sales
Average Unit Sales
Awareness
Banking
Bank-Wide Advertising
Basement Store
Behavior-Based Research Projects
Benefits Administration Software
Biannual Sales Conferences
Billboard
Billing
Booking
Booking Agency
Booths
Branch Profits
Brand Initiative
Brochure Production
Brochures
Broker Accounts
Brokerage Concerns
Budget Controls
Budget Management
Budget Recommendation
Budgets
Business Accounts
Business Contacts
Business Expansion
Business Plan
Business Protocols
Business Relationships
Business Reviews
Business-to-Business Services
Buyers
Buying Trips
Camera Ready Ads
Cash Transactions
Catalogues
Centralized Reporting System

Claim Settlements
Claims Handling
Claims Service
Classified Advertising
Client Base
Client Confidence
Client Needs
Client Relations
Client Service
Clients
Closing
Closing Capabilities
Cluster Analysis
Cold-Call Sales-Generation Centers
Cold Calling
Collateral Materials
Collection
Color Brochures
Commerce
Commercial Products
Commercial Properties
Commission Checks
Commissions
Communication Audits
Communication Network
Company Development
Company Distribution Center
Company Management Structure
Company Procedures
Company Purchase Agreements
Company/Customer Personnel
Competitive Pricing
Competitive Ranking
Comprehensive Expertise
Computer Estimating Software Package
Concept Testing
Confidential Reports
Constituency Relations
Consulting Firms
Consumer Behavior Models
Consumer Goods
Consumer Oriented
Consumer Products
Contract Negotiations
Contract Options
Contracted Vendors
Contracts
Contractual Reversions
Controller
Cooperative Sales Strategy
Core Products
Corporate Accounts
Corporate Chain
Corporate Clients
Corporate Contacts
Corporate Field Contact
Corporate Financial Management
Corporate Objectives
Corporate Plans
Corporate Position
Correspondence
Cost Parameters
Cost-of-Lead
Counters
Creative Concept
Creative Ideas
Creative Services

Credit Checks
Current Pricing
Customer Base
Customer Buying Policies
Customer Follow-Up
Customer Inquiries
Customer Needs
Customer Package Specifications
Customer Relations
Customer Reservation Specification
Customer Satisfaction
Customer Satisfaction Measurement
Customer Service
Customer Service Procedures
Customer Service Techniques
Customer Specification
Customer Studies
Cycles
Daily Calendar History
Daily Deposits
Daily Interface With Clients
Daily Operations
Daily Reports
Daily Tax Title Receipts
Dealer Channels
Dealer Commission
Dealer Locations
Dealer Promotions
Decision Making Process
Deep Discount Stores
Department Procedures
Department Standards
Departmental Contracts
Design Concepts
Detailed Sales Forecasts
Determination of Costs
Development Projects
Direct Calls
Direct Claims Handling
Direct Liaison
Direct Mail Brochures
Direct Mail Promotions
Direct Mail Schedule
Direct Mail Strategy
Direct Marketing
Direct Sales
Display Techniques
Displays
Distribution
Distribution Disagreements
Diverse Specifications
Divisional Business Plan
Documentation
Dollar Volume
Domestic Calling Needs
Domestic Fares
Education Accounts
Elicit Interest
Employee Studies
Employee Training and Effectiveness Program
End-User Software
Engineering Solutions
Engineering Staff
Equipment Installation
Events Planning
Executive Relocations
Exhibit

Exhibit Posters
Exhibitions
Existing Accounts
Expense Account
Fabrication
Facilitate Sales
Factory Authorized Dealers
Field Coordination
Field Sales
Field Surveys
Final Itineraries
Finance
Financers
Financial Account
Financial Institutions
Financial Packages
Financial Statements
Financial Support Services
First-Time Buyers
Flyers
Focus Group
Follow-Through
Follow-Up
Forecast
Foreclosure Sales
Foreign Customs
Freelance Models
Fundraising Capabilities
Future Action
Future Sales
General Accounting Functions
General Management
General Supplies Purchasing
Goals
Government Allotments
Government Contractor
Gross Sales
High Exposure Claims
High Motivational Level
High-End Sales
Historical Data Planbook
Immediate Goals
Incentive Programs
Incoming Calls
Incoming Invoices
Increase Sales
In-Depth Questionnaires
In-Depth Sales Training
Individual Sales Leads
Industry Knowledge
Industry Research
Industry Trends
Information Requests
In-House Promotions
Initial Business Plan
Innovative Techniques
In-Print Advertising Campaigns
In-Print Marketing Campaigns
Installation of Systems
Installed Accounts
Instrument Development
Intake Forms
Interior Displays
Internal Strategic Planning
International Calling Needs
International Distributors
International Fares

Interviewing Techniques
Inventory
Inventory Control System
Inventory Products
Investment Properties
Involved Parties
Key Account Relations
Key Account Sales
Key Accounts
Large Scale Development
Large Scale Investments
Lead Analysis
Leads
Leasing
Legal Documents
Legal Requirements
Leisure Accounts
Letters of Intent
License Regulatory Issues
Licensees
Lines of Merchandise
Local Franchises
Local Promotions
Long Range Business Planning
Long-Term Contracts
Long-Term Goals
Loss Performance
Loss Prevention Programs
Loss Report Reviews
Low Turnover Rate
Major Accounts
Major Manufacturers
Major Wholesalers
Management Reports
Management Systems
Manufacturing Requests
Market Analysis
Market Conditions
Market Enthusiasm
Market Opportunities
Market Research
Market Segment
Market Share
Market Trends
Marketing
Marketing Campaigns
Marketing Effort
Marketing Expenses
Marketing Information
Marketing Materials
Marketing Plans
Marketing Promotions
Marketing Research and Analysis
Marketing Research Needs
Marketing Segmentation
Marketing Strategies
Marketing Support Operations
Marketing Technology
Mass Marketing
Mass Merchandising
Maximize Sales
Media Contracts
Media Coverage
Media Department
Media Events
Media Files
Merchandising

Merchandising Concepts
Merchandising Functions
Merchandising Materials
Merchandising Products
Merchants
Mid-Size Companies
Monthly Claims Quota
Monthly Communications Packages
Monthly Forecast
Monthly Planbook
Monthly Sales Plan
Multiethnic Population
Multimillion-Dollar Negotiations
Multivariate Techniques
Name/Logo Testing
National Account
National Probability Survey
National Sales Strategy
Nationwide Network
Negotiate
Net Operating Profit
Net Profit Margins
New Business Development
New Business Technology
New Clients
New Product
New Product Launch
New Product Research
Newsletters
Newspaper Ad System
Newspaper Inserts
Nonprofit Accounts
Ongoing Customer Relationships
Onsite Survey Groups
Open-Order Status Reports
Operating Plans
Operational Budgets
Operational Deadlines
Operational Procedures
Order Accuracy
Order Placement
Order Processing
Orders
Outlet Sales
Outside Sales
Outstanding Performance
Overall Market Strategy
Overall Sales Efforts
Parallel Exporting
Parallel Processing
Percentages
Performance
Performance Evaluations
Performance Incentives
Periodic Claims Reviews
Personal Account Information
Personal Relations
Pertinent Materials
Petitions of Foreclosure
Placement
Point-of-Sale Forecasting
Policy
Portfolio Objectives
Portfolios
Positioning
Positive Company Image
Post-Installation Analysis

Posters
Potential Business Applications
Potential Clients
Pre-Booked Sales
Prequalification
Press Clippings
Press Kits
Press Releases
Price
Price Selections
Pricing Data
Primary Emphasis
Print Licenses
Print Marketing
Print Production
Private Investors
Procedures
Procurement Negotiation
Product Awareness
Product Development Operations
Product Enhancements
Product Knowledge
Product Line Presentation
Product Merchandising
Product Packages
Product Presentations
Product Recognition
Product Requirements
Product Sales
Product Training
Product Usage
Production
Production Schedules
Professional Growth
Professional Sales
Profit Estimates
Profitable Line
Profitable Relationships
Program Commitment
Program Performance
Project Specification
Promotional Agencies
Promotional Concept
Promotional Copy
Promotional Events
Promotional Material
Promotional Strategies
Promotional Work
Promotions
Proof
Proposal Preparation
Proposals
Prospect Identification
Prospecting
Prospective Clients
Provision-of-Sales Services
Public Relations
Publicity Opportunities
Purchaser/User Studies
Qualified Clients
Qualified Prospects
Quality Performance
Quality Product
Quantitative Research Projects
Quarterly Budget Reports
Quarterly Forecasts
Quota Assignment

Quota Expectations
Quoting System
Radio Marketing
Rapid-Growth Organization
Rate Structure
Ratebook
Reactivation of Dormant Accounts
Real Estate Companies
Real Estate Development Division
Real Estate Sales
Real-Time Market Data
Recurring Revenue Agreements
Referral
Registration Data
Releases
Remote Market Information
Remote Markets
Remote Territory
Rental Contracts
Rentals
Research Laboratories
Resellers
Residential Consumers
Retail Buying
Retail Outlets
Retail Sales
Retailing
Revenue Streams
Round-Table Discussions
Salary Reviews
Sales Aids
Sales Appointments
Sales Campaigns
Sales Candidate
Sales Collateral
Sales Conventions
Sales Efforts
Sales Goals
Sales Objective
Sales Per Year
Sales Plan
Sales Presentations
Sales Priorities
Sales Production
Sales Productivity
Sales Programs
Sales Projections
Sales Promotions
Sales Results
Sales Scripts
Sales Services
Sales Support
Sales Techniques
Sales Volume
Sales/Marketing Copy
Sample Development
Seasonal Merchandise
Seasonal Planbook
Seasonal Planning
Selling Reports
Seminars
Service Accounts
Short Range Business Planning
Software Vendor
Source Selections
Space Ads
Special Advertising

Special Assignment
Special Events
Special Ordering
Special Requests
Special Seasonal Sales
Specialty Book Club Licenses
Sponsor Relations
Stock
Stock Areas
Stock Control
Stock Levels
Store Chains
Strategic Planning
Subcontractors
Subsidiary Rights Contracts
Subsidiary Rights Licenses
Subsidiary Rights Monies
Supplement Program
Support Networks
Support Services
Tally Sheets
Tapes
Target Accounts
Target Grids
Target Market
Technical and Cost Proposals
Technical Presentations
Technical Sales
Technical Sales Support
Tele-Interviewing
Telemarketing
Telemarketing Scripts
Telephone Techniques
Terms
Territory
Third-Party Distribution Channels
Timely Merchandising Delivery
Top Account Executives
Top Sales Performer
Total Client Satisfaction

Total Quality Implementation
Total Volume
Tour Schedules
Track Record
Trade Shows
Training Record
Transaction Data
Travel Orders
Union Labor
Unit Pricing
Unmarked Territory
Upwardly Mobile Buyers
User-Friendly
Valuable Application
Value of Claim
Vendor Programs
Vendors
Verbal Sales Skills
Vertical Market Framework
Viable Network
Visual Appeal
Volume Increase
Warehouse
Warehouse Accountability
Warehouse Administration
Weekly Planbook
Well-Traveled
Well-Established
Wide Range
Window Displays
Wire Trades
Working Knowledge
Working Relationships
Worksheet Program
Workshops
Workstations
Written Communication Skills
Yearly Sales Activity
Year-to-Date Sales

Printing and Publishing

Printing and publishing buzz words display experience and familiarity with content management, book and magazine production, printing environments, and applicable technologies and systems.

▶ Resume Buzz Words

Academia
Academic Books
Acquiring Authors
Acquiring Books
Adult Secondary and Primary Material
Advance
Advertising Specialties
Agents
Animation
Announcements
Annual Reports
Aptitude Tests
Art Design

Artwork Services
Authoring Process
Authors
Backlist
Billing and Payment
Billing Orders
Binders
Bindery Equipment
Binding
Block Printing
Boiler Plate
Book Manufacturing
Book Production

Brochures
Bundling
Business Forms
Business Stationery
Cable Television
Calligraphy
Camera-Ready Graphics
Catalog Copy
Catalogs
Character
Children's Books
Circulation
Color Correction
Color Forms
Commercial Printing
Communications Firm
Communications Systems
Consumer Magazine Publishing
Content Editing
Contract
Converting Process
Copyediting
Corporate Printing
Corporate Publishing System
Counting
Course Needs
Cover Copy
Custom Publishing
Customer Accounts
Customer Needs
Daily Newspapers
Data Entry
Data Manipulation Services
Database Development
Deal Sheet
Design
Detail-Oriented
Developing Books
Dictionaries
Digital Color
Digital Fonts
Digital Media Input
Direct Mailing
Directories
Distribution
Distribution Technology
Document Library Services
Document Management
Documentation Services
EDI (Electronic Data Interchange)
Editing
Editorial Calendar
Editorial Literary Services
Editorial Materials
Editorial Process
Editorial Vision
Educational Material
Electronic Archiving
Electronic Printer
Electronic Production
Electronic Publishing
Electronic Storage and Retrieval Systems
Electrotype
Encyclopedias
Engraved Plate
Engraved Rollers
Fiction

Fiction Book Publisher
Film
Financial Printing
Formats
Formatting
Fulfillment Services
Full-Color Process
Galleys
Guides
Handbills
Hardcover
High-Production Environment
High-Speed Digital Printers
High-Volume Photocopying
Illustrations
Imaging
Impression
Imprints
Independent Publishers
Information Management
Information Services
Informational Publications
Ink
Ink Jetting
Inked Type
Instructional Materials
Integrated Circulation Services
Internet Content Publishing
Inventory Management
ISO9002 Certification
Ivory Black
Laminating
Lampblack
Large Format
Laser Imaging
Layout
Legal Printing
Lettering
Libraries
Library Information Science
List Acquisition
List Management
Literary Fiction
Literary Manuscripts
Lithographic Stone
Local Distribution
Logos
Magazines
Mailing
Manuals
Market Research
Market Share Analysis
Market Studies
Marketing Collateral
Marketing Services Company
Markings
Mass Market Paperback
Matter
Media
Media Buying
Media Planning
Medical Books and Journals
Mission Critical Data
Movie
Multimedia Products
Multiple Machine Environments
Musical Piece

Negatives
Network-Affiliated TV Stations
New Title Development
News-Gathering
Newsletters
Newswire Service
Nonfiction
Nonfiction Book Publishers
Offset
Online Library
Online Sports Information
Outside Vendors
Package
Packaging and Finishing
Pagination
Pamphlets
Parcel Fulfillment
Perfect Bind
Periodicals
Photo Retouching
Photographic Image
Photography
Photosensitive Surface
Pickup and Delivery
Plates
Poems
Poetry
Post Press
PostScript Files
Presentations
Press
Presswork
Primary Source Material
Printed Material
Printing
Printing Frame
Printing House
Printing Ink
Printing Paper
Printing Press
Printing Wheel
Print-on-Demand
Print-Production
Production Costs
Production Environment
Production Process
Professional Production Services
Professional Testing Products and Services
Project Costs
Project Management Experience
Promotional Activities
Promotional and Premium Copies
Promotional Copy
Prose
Public Attention
Public Contact
Public Distribution
Publication Layout
Publicity
Published Work
Publisher
Quick Conversion
Quote Generation
Radio Data Terminals
Real-Time Financial Market Data
Replication Services
Reprints

Reproduction Process
Research
Retouching
Roll Systems
Royalties
Scanning
Schedules and Quality Guidelines
Scholarly Books
Science Textbooks
Seal
Sensitized Paper
Short Run Books
Single-Source Marketing Organization
Small Press Publishers
Software Packaging
Sorting
Specialty Publishers
Specs
Stacking
Stamp
Statistical Information
Stereotype
Subscriptions
Subsidiary Ledgers
Supplements
Targeting Strategies
Technical and Reference Books
Technical Manuals
Textbooks
Text Capture Services
The Press
Third-Party Publishers
Titles
Trade Publications
Trucking
Turnaround Time
TV Broadcasting Services
Typesetting
Typing Ability
Typography
University Presses
Verses
Warehousing Books
Web Publishers
Weeklies
Wire-O Books
Wood Block
Workflow
Yearbooks

Real Estate

Buzz words for positions in this field highlight experience acting as a medium for transactions between homebuyers and sellers. They should show knowledge in evaluating the construction of a home in order to estimate its market value; contacting individuals by phone, mail, or in person to interview and assist them in completing various forms; and verifying the information obtained and performing various processing tasks. This often includes knowledge of leasing laws, contracts, and mortgages.

▶ Resume Buzz Words

Abandonment
Acquisitions
Active Adult Communities
Adjustable Rate
Adjustment
Adult Retirement Communities
Advisory Services
Agency
Agreement
Apartment Buildings
Apartment Communities
Apartment Sales
Apartments
Applications
Applications Processing
Appraisals
Approvals
Asking Price
Asset Management Services
Asset Value
Assets
Assignment
Assisted Living Centers
Audits
Balance
Bankruptcy
Base Salary
Beneficiary
Bill of Sale
Binder
Blanket Mortgage
Bonds
Breach
Brokerage
Budget Forecasts
Buffer Zone
Building Code
Buying
By Owner
Capital Gain
Certificate of Title
Clause

Clients
Closing
Code of Ethics
Collateral
Colonial
Commercial
Commercial Office Space
Commission
Common Law
Company Policy
Complexes
Condominiums
Construction
Contingency
Contract
Conveyance
Corporate Investors
Corporate Office Buildings
Corporate Relocation Markets
Corporate Relocation Services
Corporation
Covenants
Credit
Credit History
Credit Report
Debt
Debt Structures
Deed
Deed in Lieu of Foreclosure
Default
Department Stores
Deposit
Design
Development
Direct Sales
Documents
Down Payment
Easement
Eminent Domain
Encroachment
Equity
Escrow

Estate
Ethics
Eviction
Exclusive Listing
Existing Properties
Fair Market Value
Financing
Firm
Fixed Rate
Fixture
Foreclosure
Full-Service Real Estate Development Firm
Fully Furnished
Gas Stations
Good Faith
Government Loan
Greater Area
Grocery Stores
Healthcare Facilities
Heir
Holding Company
Home Sales Transactions
Hotels
House
Housing Builder
Individual Investment
Industrial
Inflation
Installment Sales Contacts
Institutional Buildings
Institutional Investors
Insurance
Insurance Claims
Integrated
Interest
Interest Rate
Investment Trust
Investments
Joint Tenancy
Land
Lease
Lease-Up
Leasing
Leasing Goals
Leasing Operation
Lessee
Lessor
Leverage
License
Liens
Listing
Loans
Locations
Loft
Long-Term
Long-Term Care Services
Luxury Housing
Maintenance
Major Metropolitan Area
Management Firm
Market Research
Market Value
Marketing
Markets
Master Planning
Metropolitan
Mid-Priced Single-Family Homes

Mobile Homes
Mortgage
Mortgage Loans
Motels
Move-Ins
Multifamily Properties
Multifamily Property Management
Multitenanted Property
Notes
Nursing Homes
Office
Office Buildings
Open House
Owner Financing
Partial Payment
Performance Reviews
Personal Property
Plazas
Point
Power of Attorney
Pre-Approval
Prepayment
Pre-Qualification
Prime Rate
Principal
Private Investors
Project Development
Promissory Note
Properties
Property Acquisitions
Property Management
Property Service Records
Prospective Resident
Purchase Agreement
Purchases
Ranch
Rate Lock
Real Estate Brokerage
Real Estate Developer
Real Estate Firm
Real Estate Investment Trust
Real Estate Rentals
Real Estate Sales
Realty
Refinance Transaction
Refinancing
Related Services
Relocation Services
Remaining Balance
Rent
Rent Collection
Rent Rolls
Rental Units
Rentals
Repayment Plan
Resident Files
Residential
Residential Properties
Residential Real Estate
Residential Real Estate Consumers
Residential Relations
Resort Properties
Resorts
Restaurants
Retail
Reviews
Sales

Secured Loan
Securities Portfolio Management
Security
Security Deposit
Self-Administered
Self-Managed
Selling
Services
Shopping Centers
Site Reporting
Specializes
Structural Integrity
Studio
Subacute
Subdivision

Subsidiaries
Tax Credit
Taxes
Tenancy
Tenancy-at-Will
Third-Party Property Owners
Title
Title Insurance
Trailer Parks
Transactions
Turnover
Unit
Vacancies
Vendor Relations
Work Orders

Retail

Retail industry buzz words demonstrate experience in the sale of clothing, goods, or appliances, either directly to consumers or to the retail stores, or the buying of such products for sale in stores. They also demonstrate knowledge of customer service, handling transactions, complaints, and returns, and the management of a retail environment.

▶ Resume Buzz Words

Accessories
Accounts Receivable
Advertising
Advertising Programs
American Designers
Annual Circulation
Antiques
Apparel
Appliances
Art
Assortments
Audio Equipment
Automobiles
Automotive
Automotive Aftermarket Products
Automotive Manufacturers
Back Order
Baking Facilities
Barcode
Beauty Care Products
Bedroom Sets
Book Titles
Bookstores
Boutique
Branch
Brand Names
Building Materials
Buyback
Call Recording Devices
Camera Shop

Car Audio Systems
Cash On Delivery
Cash Register
Cash Register Tape
Cash Transaction
Casual Apparel
Catalog Retailer
Cataloger
Categories
Cellular Phones
Children
Children's Activewear
Children's Products
Christmas Products
City-Style Apparel
Classic Apparel
Clearance Sale
Clothing
Coatings
Collegiate Department Store
Company-Owned
Computers
Consumer
Consumer Advocate
Cookware
Co-Operative
Copy Center
Cost
Credit Card Transactions
Customers

Daily Sales Audit
Decorative Products
Delicatessen
Demo
Department Store
Department Store Merchandise
Design
Design Professionals
Desks
Dining Room Sets
Direct-Mail Software
Direct Marketing
Direct Selling
Discount Bookstore Chain
Discount Drugs
Discount Office Products
Discount Outlet
Discounted Prices
Distressed Goods
Doors and Windows
Dresses
Drug Store Products
Drugstores
Dry Cleaning
Electrical Supplies
Electronic Funds Transfer
Electronic Products
Electronics
End Caps
Exchange Policy
Exchanges
Fabric Retailer
Factory-Direct
Fad
Family Apparel
Fashion
Fashion Jewelry
Features
Floor Model
Focused Selection
Food Retailers
Food Service Distribution Businesses
Food Services
Footwear
Fragrances
Franchisees
Full-Line
Full-Line Department Store
Full-Price Stores
Furniture
Furniture Manufacturers
Gardening Products
Gas Stations
General Merchandise
Gift Certificate
Gift Products
Gift Receipt
Gifts
Global Retailer
Grocery Chains
Gross Margin
Hang Tag
Hardware
Headsets
Health and Fitness
High-Volume
Home and Safety

Home Audio Systems
Home Furnishings
Home Improvement Centers
Home Office Systems
Home Theater Speakers
Hosiery
Household Products
Housewares
Ice Cream
Ice Cream Manufacturer
Independent Dealers
Independent Operators
Independent Sales Representatives
Independently Owned
Industrial Maintenance Market
Initial Markup
International Designers
Inventory
Item Price Marking
Kiosk
Kitchen Furniture
Knitted Fabrics
Label
Layaway
Leading Retailer
Leased
Leisurewear
Licensed Franchises
Limited Warranty
Line Switches
Lingerie
Living Room Sets
Locations
Loss Prevention
Lumber
Mail-Order Retailing
Mail-Order Apparel
Mall
Mall-Based Retail Outlets
Management Support Designed
Mannequin
Manufactures
Markdown
Marketing
Marketing Research
Markets
Markup
Mass Merchandisers
Material
Meat Processing
Member-Owned
Men
Merchandise
Merchandising
Milk Processing Plant
Moderately Priced Merchandise
Music
Music Departments
National Direct Sales Company
Nationally Recognized Brands
Network
No Frills
Office Products
Off-Price Outlet Stores
Off-Price Retail
Online Sales
Original Equipment Manufacturers (OEM)

Outdoor and Garden Merchandise
Paint
Percentage
Personal Care Products
Photo Development Services
Photographic Equipment
Plumbing Supplies
Price Marketing
Price War
Prints
Private Labels
Product Line
Products
Promotion
Promotional Advertising
Promotional Discount
Quantity Discount
Ready-to-Assemble
Receipt
Refund
Related Support Facilities
Reserve Stock
Retail Chain
Retail Convenience Stores
Retail Drug Stores
Retail Fabric Stores
Retail Furniture Stores
Retail Locations
Retail Price
Retail Units
Retail Warehouse Stores
Retailer
Returns
Sales Forecasting
Sales Promotion
Seasonal Discount
Selected Home Furnishings
Serving Equipment
Shoe Departments
Site Location
Soft-Goods Products
Software
Specialty Catalog Retailer
Specialty Catalogs

Specialty Clothing
Specialty Fashion Store
Specialty Menswear
Specialty Paint and Wall Covering Stores
Specialty Retailer
Specialty Women's Clothing Retailer
Sportswear
Stereo
Store Chain
Store Credit
Store Items
Suggestive Selling
Super Drug Stores
Supermarket Chain
Superstores
Swimwear
Target Market
Telephone Productivity Items
Telephones
Televisions
Toys
Trade
Traffic Paint Market
Travel and Luggage
Trend
Tuxedo
Unit-of-Sale Method
Universal Product Code (UPC)
Used
Value-Priced
Various Industries
Video Rental
Videos
Warehouse Foods
Warehouses
Warranty
Wholesale
Wholly Owned Subsidiaries
Wide Assortments
Wide Variety
Women's Apparel
Women's Intimate Apparel
Work Clothing
Woven Fabrics

Science

For scientific positions, each particular field will have many specialized technical terms aside from those listed here. Science industry buzz words, in general, display experience with research and development. This includes research to develop new medicines; increase crop yield; improve the environment; study farm crops, animals, and living organisms; and explore practical use and knowledge of chemicals, as well as the atmosphere's physical characteristics, motions, and processes.

► Resume Buzz Words

Aberrations
Absolute Molecular Weight
Acreage Evaluation
Agrarian-Based Industries
Agriculture
Air Pollution
Algal Organisms
Amphibious Surveying Operation
Analysis
Animal Care
Animal Health Practices
Animal Husbandry
Animals
Annual Operating Budget
Aquaculture Projects
Arborists
Artificial Insemination Considerations
Assisted Animals
Bacteria
Bale
Beef
Bid Documents
Binary Stars
Biochemical Procedures
Biochemistry
Biological Research
Biological Sources
Blood Banking Procedures
Blood Components
Blood Products
Branching Data
Breeding
Briefing Papers
Briefings
Brillouin Scattering
Briquetting
Cadmium Telluride Gamma Ray Detector
Calculations
Carcinogenic Analysis
Cellular Structure
Ceramics
Chemical Synthetic Procedures
Chemicals
Chemistry
Classroom-Style Lectures
Cleanup Procedures
Coastline
Common Illnesses
Compositions
Comprehensive Management Plan
Computer Record Maintenance
Computerized Assays
Continuous Viscometer Detector
Contractual Services
Courses
Cows
Crop
Cross Breeding
Culture Facility
Cultures
Curation
Custom Instrumentation
Custom Test Equipment

Cutting
Daily Temperature
Dairy Cows
Dairy Produce
Dairy Production
Data
Deadline Pressure
Dental X-Ray Calibration
Designated Forecasts
Detailed Reports
Digital Equipment
Digital Recording
Dilutor System Analyses
Disciplines
DNA Research
DNA Sequence Analysis
Drainage
Dredge Materials
Dressage
Drilling Fluids
Ecological Sources
Ecosystem
Education
Effluents
Eggs
Electron Microscopy
Electronic Repair
Elementary Level
ELISA (Enzyme-Linked Immunosorbent Assay)
Environmental Issues
Environmental Protection
Environmental Science
Epithelial Cellines
Equipment
Expected Inherited Traits
Experimental Research
Experiments
Expertise
Exploration
Fabry-Perot Interferometer
Farm Equipment
Feed
Fermentor Microcarrier Cultures
Fertilization
Fibrinogens
Fibroblast
Field Support
Field Surveys
Findings
Firefighting Techniques
Fire Prevention
Fish
Fish Ponds
Fisheries
Flood Protection
Foaling
Forecasting Weather
Forecasts
Forestry
Forests
Fungal Cell Metabolism
Funnel Extractions
Gel Permeation Chromatography

Genetic Factors
Genetic Research
Genetics
Geological Aspects
Geological Background
Geophysical Crew
Geophysical Exploration Programs
Glacial Deposits
Grant Tracking Support
Grooming
Ground Water
Growth Parameters
Hay
Heat Treatment
Heavy Mineral Separation
Helium Neon Laser
Herbicides
Hormonal Assays
Horticultural Planting
Horticulture
Hospital Laboratories
Hubble Telescope
Humidity
Hurricanes
Industrial Wastes
Instrument Automation
Instrumentation
Inventory
Invertebrate
Irrigation
Isolation Schemes
Lab
Lab Samples
Labeling
Labor
Laboratories
Laboratory Inventory
Laboratory Operations
Laboratory Setting
Lamb
Lambing Season
Large-Scale Fermentation
Light Mineral Separation
Lightweight Aggregates
Lime Manufacturer
Livestock
Local Dairies
Lumber Projects
Magnitude
Mainframe System
Maintenance Schedules
Malformations
Manual Assays
Manufacture
Maps
Mares
Market
Materials
Materials Research
Mathematics Text
Mating Procedures
Mating Season
Measurements
Meat Processing Industry
Metals
Methodology
Microbiology Classes

Microcomputer Systems
Microprocessors
Mill Contractors
Mineral Content
Mineralogical
Minicomputers
Miniprep DNA Purification
Molecular Biological Problems
Molecular Biology
Monitoring Survey
Moon
Municipal Records
Mutations
National Chemistry Convention
Natural Disasters
Natural Habitat
Newborn Foal Diseases
Nonlinear Optics
Nucleic Acid Hybridization
Nucleotides
Oceanic Research
Oil Company Consortium
Old Stars
Organic Extractions
Organic Liquid Crystals
Organic Pigment
Organic Synthesis
Palletizing
Park Collection
Park Records
Particle Size Instruments
Patented Design
PCB
Perfusion System
Pest Control
Pest Control Program
Pesticides
Petrographic Technique
Petroleum Monitoring Programs
pH Adjustments
Physicians
Physics Labs
Pilot Plant Equipment
Planetary Surface Research
Planets
Plant Acquisition
Plant Alkaloids
Plants
Plasmid Constructions
Plasmid DNA Purification
Positron Annihilation Spectroscopy
Precipitation Level
Preparing Media
Private Sectors
Privately Funded Organizations
Process Experimentation
Produce
Produce Farm
Production Basis
Production Handling
Proper Calibration
Protein Assays
Protein Purification
Proteins
Pruning
Q-Switched Ruby Laser
Quality Control Systems

Radar
Radiosonic Equipment
Raw Material
Recombinant DNA Technology
Research and Development
Research Papers
Research Problems
Research Reports
Research Techniques
Ribosome Structure
RNA Component
Sanitation Procedures
Satellites
Science Texts
Scientific Crew
Scientific Seminars
Sea Transportation
Seasonal Climate Conditions
Seeds
Semiconductor Neutron Detector
Semiconductors
SI Mapping
Slides
Soil Samples
Soil Testing
Special Forecasts
Specialized Instrumentation
Specialized Test Equipment
Stars' Magnitudes
Steroids
Stimulated Sound Scattering
Studs
Study Subjects
Subsurface
Supernovae
Surface Stations
Surrogate Solutions
Surveying
Technical Applications
Technical Data
Technical Writing

Telescope
Temperature
Territorial Logging
Test Results
Tests
Textbook
T-Flasks
Thoroughbreds
Tilapia
Timber
Tissue Culture Glassware
Tissue Experiment
Total Maintenance Program
Toxicity Tests
Trace Organic Analysis
Traces
Transfusion
Tree Acquisition
Trees
Turf Management
U.S. Wildlife Department
Upper-Air Data
Upper-Air Stations
USDA Regulations
Vaccination Schedules
Vegetation
Veterinary Medicine
Viral Immunology Testing
Vitamins
Waste Disposal
Wastewater
Water Supply
Weather Balloon
Weather Conditions
Weed Control
Well Logging
Wet Chemistry
Wildlife
Wildlife Activities
Winds
Zoo

Service

These service industry buzz words highlight experience with providing high-quality customer service. This includes positions in food preparation, clerical work, retail, and the like.

▶ Resume Buzz Words

Academic Training
Account Adjustment
Accounting
Accounting Principles
Address Changes
Adjustments
Administrative Policies
Advice
Analysis of Services

Assisting Customers
Attractive Presentations
Automated Solutions
Banquets
Base Salary
Bill Maintenance and Reconciliation
Billing
Billing Process
Bookings

Booth Set-Up
Budget
Budget Worksheets
Business Conventions
Business Management
Business Practices
Business Protocol
Business System Support
Business System Training
Cash Control
Cash Deposits
Cash Intake
Cash Received
Cash Reconciliations
Cash Transactions
Cashiering
Centralized Management Systems
Check-In
Checkout
Client Base
Client Needs
Clientele
Clients
Cold Calling
Commercial Account Installation
Commitment to Excellence
Community Development
Complete and Thorough Service
Confidential Client Files
Conflict Resolution
Consulting with Guests
Consumer Services
Contract Negotiation
Corporate Accounts
Corporate Communication
Corporate Events
Corporate Foundations
Corporate Membership Packages
Correspondence
CPR
Credit Card Transactions
Credits
CRM Systems
Cross-Industry Marketing Efforts
Customer Assistance
Customer Care
Customer Loyalty
Customer Relations
Customer Service
Customer Support Environment
Customers
Daily Reports
Data Entry
Delivery Processes
Department Regulations
Design
Desserts
Develop and Maintain Client Relationships
Distributors
Diversity
Diversity of Professionals
Documentation
Drafts
Economies of Scale
Emergency Equipment
Emergency Evacuation Plan
Employee Performance

Employee Relationship Management
Employee Satisfaction
ERP Systems
Establish Rapport
Executive Guidelines
Existing Accounts
Facility Operations
Fast Food Industry
Field Inquiries
Field Support
Filing
Filing Invoices
Filing System
Filling Job Orders
Finance
Financial Experience
Financial Record Keeping
Financial Systems
Front Desk Operations
Frontend Systems
Guest Check-In
Guest Check-Out
Guest Complaints
Guest Mail and Faxes
Guestrooms
Guest Services
Guest Survey
Guests' Needs
Guidelines
Hospitality-Oriented
Human Resources
Incoming Calls
Increased Sales
Independent Worker
Instructions
Interpersonal Skills
Inventory
Job Applicants
Job Openings
Job Placement
Light Maintenance
List Management
Mailing Checks and Statements
Managed Care Industry
Management Reports
Management Systems
Marketing Initiatives
Marketing Office
Marketing Plans
Marketing Report
Marketing Strategies
Materials Costing Processes
Media Relations
Merchandising
Monitor
Monitored Payroll
Monitoring Delivery Personnel
Monthly Menu
Monthly Reports
Monthly Seminars
Multiple Accounts
Multiple Tasks
National Business Convention
New Associate Training Program
New Business Development
Office Operations
Office Responsibilities

Operational Deadlines
Operational Procedures
Operations
Ordering
Organization of Delivery Schedules
Outbound Calls
Overnight Operations
Passenger Boarding
Passenger Manifest
Passenger Safety
Passengers
Patient
Payroll
Performance
Performance Bonus
Personalized Client Interactions
Personnel
Personnel Assistance
Phone Interaction
Plan Design Features
Plane Reservations
Portioning
Practical Applications
Premium Refund
Prep Work
Preparation
Pre-Selected Client Groups
Presentation
Presentation of Goods
Prioritize Tasks at Hand
Problem Area
Problem Resolution
Problem-Solving
Procedures
Process Payments
Processing Returns
Production
Products
Professional Image
Professional Services Environment
Promotion
Promotional Demonstration Activities
Promotional Efforts
Promotional Events
Promotional Opportunities
Prospective Customers
Proven Track Record
Public Relations
Purchasing
Purchasing Procedures
Quality Control
Quick and Accurate Decisions
Realization of Customer Specifications
Receiving
Reconciling
Reconciling Commission Reports
Referral Service
Referrals
Register Control
Registers
Relationship Building
Relationship Building Skills
Rentals
Reporting Tools
Reports
Requisitions
Researching and Resolving Customer Inquiries

Reservations
Resolve Customer Complaints
Resolve Guest Grievances/Problems
Restaurants
Retail
Route-Oriented Industry
Sales Goals
Sales Programs
Sales Staff
Sales Support Services
Sales Territory Development
Sales/Marketing
Schedule of Shows
Scheduling
Seating Allocation
Selection and Referral Process
Seminar
Service Business Systems
Service Distributors
Service Opportunities
Service Procedures
Services
Shift Management
Shift Scheduling
Shipping
Shipping Errors
Shop Management
Show Expenses
Sourcing Network
Sourcing of Vendors
Special Functions
Special Interest Groups
Special Orders
Special Sales
Specialized Training
Staff Motivation
Staff Training
Standardized Processes
Stations
Strong Academic Background
Strong Communication Skills
Supermarkets
Supplies
System Support
Take Out
Team Member
Telemarketing
Telephone Bookings
Telephone Survey
Telex Bookings
Terminations and Commission Assignments
Three-Star Hotel
Time and Labor Solutions
Tour Arrangements
Tourist Information
Tracking Demands
Tradeshows
Training Program
Transactions
Transportation Coordination
Travel Problems
Troubleshoot
Typing
Weekly Volume
Weekly Work Schedule
Workflow
Workshops

Social and Human Services

Industry buzz words for these helping fields highlight experience with improving the emotional wellbeing of individuals in need; studying human behavior and mental processes to understand, explain, and change people's behavior; developing programs to provide for growth and revitalization of urban, suburban, and rural communities and their regions; and helping local officials make decisions on social, economic, and environmental problems. This also includes work in group homes and halfway houses, correctional, mental retardation, and community mental health centers.

▶ Resume Buzz Words

24-Hour Hotline
Academic Assistance
Achievement Test
Administrative Duties
Admissions
Adoption Purposes
Advocacy
After-School Program
Assessment of Clientele
Assignment of Children
Assisted Living
At-Risk Students
Behavior Modification
Behavioral Programs
Bicultural Experience
Bilingual
Campaign Fund Solicitations
Case Management
Case Presentations
Case Prevention
Case Studies
Child Advocate
Clarification Exercise
Client Need
Client Progress
Clientele
Clients
Clinical
Clinical Practices
Clinical Treatment Plans
Co-Directed
College-Prep Test
Commercial Development
Community Agencies
Community Development Group
Community Group Meetings
Community Mobilization
Community Outreach
Community Residents
Community-Based Agencies
Compliance

Concrete and Supportive Services
Conduct Assessment
Consultant Reports
Contact Development
Content Planning
Cooperative Experience
Counseling
Credit Management
Credit Program
Crisis Intervention
Crisis Situation
Curriculum Development
Curriculum Implementation
Curriculum Recommendations
Daily Living Skills
Department of Social Services (DSS)
Developmental Stimulation
Developmentally Delayed Clients
Diagnostic Evaluation
Difficult-to-Place Clients
Direct Assistance
Direct Patient Care
Discharge Planning
Disciplinary Problems
Discipline
Discussion Groups
Economic Analysis
Economic Development
Editorial Department
Education
Education for Families
Educational Institutes
Educational Testing
Effective Treatment Strategies
Efficient Daily Operations
Emotional Support
Enterprise Project
Evaluation of Mental Status
Extrinsic Motivation
Families at Risk
Families in Crisis

Family Life Education Group
Family Therapy
Feasibility Analysis
Foundation Fundraising
Fundraising
Grant Programs
Grant Proposals
Group Activities
Group Practice
Group Therapy Sessions
Home Studies
Hotline Calls
House Management
Housing Authority
Housing Development
Human Services
Hypothesis Testing
Individual Educational Programs
Individual Psychotherapy Sessions
Individual Social Work
Individualized Academic Instruction
Industrial Expansion
Industrial Retention
Informal Family Therapy
Information Referral
Initial Evaluation
In-Service Education
In-Service Training
Interdisciplinary Team
Intrinsic Motivation
Knowledge Management
Legal Resources
Legislative Documents
Local Organizations
Long-Term Treatment Plans
Maintenance Services
Managed Cases
Management Development
Mass Mailing Programs
Medical Charts
Multidisciplinary Education
Multidisciplinary Team
Negotiation
New Programs
Nonprofit Organization
Nursing Care
On-Call
One-on-One Meetings
One-to-One Basis
Outpatient Clinic
Outpatients
Outreach Clinical Services
Outreach Services
Outside Consulting
Parent Education Groups
Parent-Teacher Conferences
Patient Independence
Personal Practice
Petitions
Placement Services
Play Groups
Policies and Procedures
Policy Development
Position Case Study
Preventive Strategies
Primary Care
Private Agencies

Private Practice
Problem Diagnosis
Procedural Guidelines
Professional Development
Progress Charting
Project Development
Promotional Letters
Proposals
Protective Custody
Psychiatric Admissions
Psychiatric Assessment
Psychological Assistance
Psychological Testing
Public Agencies
Public Relations
Record Keeping System
Records
Recreation
Recruitment
Recruitment of Prospective Parents
Referral Requests
Referral Services
Regression Analysis
Relationship of Trust
Remedial Plans
Residential Program
Residential Treatment Facility
Routine Monitoring
Self-Image Enhancement
Seminars
Service Networks
Shelter
Situation Evaluation
Skill Utilization
Small Scale Enterprise
Social Assistance
Social Problems
Social Service Arena
Social Service Organization
Social Work
Special Service Network
Specialized Services
Status Reports
Students
Survival Skills
Task Force
Teaching Staff
Technical Assistance
Therapeutic Activities
Therapeutic Intervention
Therapeutic Plans
Treatment
Treatment Plans
Vocational Test
Workflow
Workshops
Youth Programs

Technical

Technical industry buzz words highlight experience with applying specialized knowledge of technology, systems, engineering, and science. Potential applications for technical skills and experience exist in virtually all industries, including transportation, building design and inspection, engine repair and maintenance, electrical systems design, and communications.

▶ Resume Buzz Words

Administration Lead
Air-Cooled Condenser
Aircraft Maintenance
Aircraft Power
Aircraft Towing
Alignment
Analog
Analytical Attributes
Annual Network Costs
Architectural Development
Architectural Landscape Design
Architectural Landscaping
Architectural Renderings
Architecture
Artistic Illustration
Assemble
Assembly Drawing
Attainment
Baffle Tiles
Battery Connections
Battery Disconnections
Blueprints
Boiler Hookup
Boilers
Bookkeeping
Building Codes
Building Inspection
Building Laws
Bulk Memory Cards
Burners
Cable Drawings
Calcium Silicate Block
Chart
Chimney
Civil Engineering
Codes and Standards
Commercial Buildings
Commercial Wiring
Commercials
Community Production
Completed Framing
Compliance Procedures
Component Drawing
Component Parts
Computer Aided
Computer Aided Design (CAD)

Computer Design Base (CDB)
Computer Product
Computer Programming
Computer Science
Computer Tradeshow
Computer Work Station
Conceptualization Stage
Concrete Design
Condenser
Condenser Head
Configuration Time
Continuing Engineering Functions
Control Chart
Cost Control
Craft Workers
Custom Construction
Custom Style
Customer Housing
Customer Service
Customer Support
Cylinder
Data Testing Standards
Database
Database Management
Datum Structure
Design Development
Development
Diagnostic Test
Digital Concept
Dimensioning System
Dimmer Board
Disassemble
Disk Interface
Distributor
Drafting
Drafting Technology
Drawing
Drawing Development and Detailing
Electrical
Electrical Regulations
Electrical Repairs
Electrical Technology
Electronic
Electronic Illustration
Electronics Technology
Emissions Certificate

Engine Cowl
Engineering
Equipment Application
Estimate
Experience
Exploded View
Exterior
External Credentialing Groups
Extrusions
Fabricated Complex Parts
Fabrication
Facility Justification of Systems and Networks
Federal Licensing/Certification
Field Drawing
Field Service
Field Service Engineer
Field Tested
Film Production
Final Inspection
Final Product Design
Final Recommendation
Final Release
Final Report
Fire Brink
Flat Patterns
Flight Officer
Flight-Line Launching
Flight-Line Recoveries
Floating Point Processors
Floor Framing
Flow Model
Fluid System Design
Footings
Foreman
Fuel Product
General Construction
General Repairs
Grading Safety Laws
Graph
Hand Tools
Hardware
Harnessing
High-Speed Logic Board
Hybrid Microcircuit Design and Drawing
Illustration
Image Memory Cards
In Process
Incoming Material
Information Distribution
In-Plant
Inspection
Inspection Area
Inspection Records
Inspection Technique
Insulator Skills
Interfacing
Interior Spaces
Internal Support
Internal Technical Operations
International Broadcasting
International Marketing Tool
Interpret Legal Requirements
Inventory
Landing Gear
Lights
Line Artwork
Lock Repair

Lubrication
Machine and Sheet Metal Parts Inspection
Machine Drawing
Machine Language Firmware
Machined
Machinery Support
Mainframe
Maintenance
Manufactured Products
Manufacturing
Mason Skills
Mechanical
Mechanical Aptitude
Mechanical/Electronic Detailing and Drawing
Microcomputer Industry
Microprocessor Principles
Military Construction
Military Hardware
Model Assembly
Model Construction
Model Part
Multilocation Companies
Multimedia Product
Network Design
Network Facility
Onsite Research
Operating Systems
Operational Discrepancy Logs
Operations
Overlay Applications
Parts Numbering System
Permanent Building Inspector
Permits
Photo-Typesetting
Piping
Plant Construction
Plumbing Regulations
Precision Inspection
Presentation
Presentation Graphics
Pressure Chamber
Pressure Fuel Oil Tank
Pressure Parts
Preventive Maintenance
Print Specification
Private Sectors
Procedure
Product Development
Product Performance
Product Reliability
Production
Program Logs
Program Management Techniques
Program Sources
Project Leadership
Project Management
Project Scheduling Priority System
Project Superintendent
Promos
Proposal
Prototype System
Public Sectors
Public Service Announcements
Public Works
Pump
Quality Assurance
Quality Workmanship

Radio-Television-Film Technology
Real Estate Development Layout
Reconfiguration
Refueling
Refurbished Technology
Regulations
Regulatory Compliances
Repair
Research
Research Data
Residential Electrical Needs
Residential Heating Needs
Residential Plumbing Needs
Residential Wiring
Retaining Walls
Revision Cycle
Routing Sheet
Sample Part
Sand Casting
Satellite Feeds
Schematic Capture
Scoop Lights
Service Manual
Servicing
Sheet Metal Drawing
Sheet-Metal Layout Inspection
Sheet-Metal Fabrication
Single Location Companies
Site Survey
Software
Software Enhancements
Specifications
Stairway
Standards
State Building Codes
State Rules and Regulations
Station Organization
Strategic Alliance
Streamlined Procedures
Strict Quality Control
Structural Steel Work
Studio Camera
Studio System
Sub-Assembly
Submit Reports

Submittal
Successful Development
Surface Ship Propulsion System
System Design
System Recommendation
System Test
System Test Board
Tactical Research
Technical Drawing
Technical Illustration
Technical Writing
Telecommunications
Television Production
Template
Terminal
Territory Management
Test Date Format
Test Equipment
Test File
Test Results
Testing Program
Testing Time
Topographical Survey
Track Trends
Transmitter Logs
Troubleshooting
Turbines
Variances
Verbal Specification
Video Adjuster Boards
Video Conference
Video Latch Boards
Video Sync Boards
Well Developed
Wing Tips
Wiring
Wiring Lamps
Working Audit
Working Drawing
Workstation Product Lines
Worldwide Television Deregulation
Writing Diagrams
Zoning Laws
Zoning Safety Laws

Transportation and Travel

In the transportation and travel industries, buzz words highlight experience with conveying passengers or goods, providing or controlling means for transportation, and coordinating or advancing the travel of others. They also include knowledge of various transportation methods, either from the customer service side or the transporting side.

► Resume Buzz Words

Air Compressor
Air Express Network
Air Freight
Air Tank
Aircraft
Aircraft Fittings
Airframe Services
Airport Code
Airport Facilities
Airport Transfers
Airports
Alignment
Area School Bus Company
Assembly
Automated Control Systems
Automated Guideway Transit
Automatic Train Control
Average Weekday Traffic
Aviation Industry
Baggage Check
Barges
Berthing Facilities
Boarding Pass
Boxcars
Brake Shoes
Bulk Freight Shipping
Bulk Transportation
Bus Service
Buses
Business Meetings
Business Trips
Cab Signaling Equipment
Cabin Cleaning
Cam Buckles
Canal System
Canopy Platform
Capacity
Capital Asset Financing
Car Maintenance
Car Rental Agreement
Car Repair
Cargo Handling
Cargo Restraint Equipment
Cargo Services
Carrier
Carry-On
Charter Bus Service
Charter Services
Chemicals
City-Funded
Cleaning Planes
Coal Cars
Code System Emulators
Commission
Commission Sales Agents
Commodities
Common Carrier Freight Line
Common Carrier Trucking Firm
Communities
Commuter Train Lines
Complete Packaged Transportation Service
Computerized Aircraft Maintenance Services
Confirmation
Connecting Flight
Connections

Constituent Agencies
Construction Aggregate
Construction Services
Container Freight Station Operations
Containerized Cargo Distribution System
Contracting Services
Control Systems
Corporate Clients
Corporate Rate
Covered Hoppers
Cruise Line
Cruise Speed
Customs Brokerage
Deep-Sea and Coastal Towing
Dinner/Theater Events
Direct Flight
Direct Services
Discount Fairs
Dispatch Computer
Distribution
Districts
Domestic Offices
Domestic Travel
Double Stack Intermodal Facilities
Drop-Off Locations
Dwell Time
Electronic Controls
Elements
Emergency Air and Truck Freight Services
Emergency Road Services
Engine Services
Engineering Consulting
Equipment Housings
Equipment Management Services
Executive Travel
Expedited Air and Truck Freight Services
Express Services
Express Transportation
Extensive Commuter Passenger Service Rail-
  road Operations
Fare
Flat Rate
Fleet
Fleet Financing
Floor Jack
Foreign Travel
Freight Cars
Freight Forwarding
Freight Handling
Freight Service Railroad Operations
Freight Traffic
Fueling Planes
Full-Service
Global Transportation
Ground-Handling
Group Rate
Guideway
Heavy Rail Transit
High-Speed Rail
Highway Trailers
Highways
Household Goods
Import/Export Brokerage
Inbound Marine Shipping
Independent Contractors

Industrial Development
In-House Capabilities
Inspections
Insurance
Integrated Logistics Programs
Intermodal Cars
Intermodal Distribution Company
International Air and Ocean Freight Forwarding
   Services
International Air Carrier
International Travel
Interstate Freight Carrier
Into-Plane Fueling
Jumper Cables
Land Shippers
Lease Types
Leasing Company
Light Rail Transit
Limousine Transportation Services
Loading Standards
Loading/Unloading
Local Service
Lock-Out Tools
Locomotives
Logistics
Main Lines
Mainline Railways
Maintenance
Major Cities
Major Lessor
Major Markets
Marine Divisions
Marine Towing
Marine Transportation
Maritime Academies
Mass Transportation
Microprocessor-Based Automatic Train Control
Mileage
Modification Services
Motor Carrier
Motor Freight Carrier
Motorists
Moving
Moving Company
Nonrail Holding Company
O/C Buckles
Off-Road Divisions
Oil Transportation
Operator Consoles
Original Equipment Products
Outbound Marine Shipping
Overseas Forwarding
Packages
Park-and-Ride
Passenger Car Heating and Air Conditioning
   Equipment
Passenger Railroad Operators
Passenger Service
Passing Track
PC-Based Systems
Peak Hour
Peak Period
Peak Season
Petroleum Transport
Pipelines
Plastic Resins
Platform

Positioning Tunnel and Bridge Segments
Pressure Differential Cars
Private Customers
Public Benefit Corporation
Public Transportation Firm
Rail Cars
Rail Networks
Rail Signal
Rail Transportation
Railcar Equipment
Railcars
Railroad Industry
Railroad Operations
Railroad Speed Indicating/Pacesetting Controls
Railroad Tracks
Railway Freight Cars
Ramp Services
Regulations
Relay-Based Automatic Train Control
Relays
Replacement Products
Reservation
Route System
Routes
Rush Hour
Safety Policies and Procedures
School Bus Contractor
Secondary Main Lines
Self-Propelled Vehicles
Self-Unloading Bulk Carriers
Ship Docking
Shippers
Shipping Agency
Ships
Shoring Beams
Sightseeing Activities
Signals
Spare Parts Inventory
Special Projects
Specialized Transportation Services
Specialty Cars
Standby
Station
Steam Generators
Steel Products
Storage Services
Storage Tanks
Subways
Switch Machines
Switching Track
Tank Cars
Tank Storage Terminals
Terminal
Ticket Broker
Tire Iron
Tow Services
Track
Track Circuits
Tractors
Traditional Freight Forwarding
Transit Rails
Transportation Services
Travel
Travel Agency
Travel Demand
Trips
Trolleys

Truck Rental Company
Truck Transportation
Trucking
Trucking Company
Truckload Transportation Services
Tugs
Turnaround Time
Vacations
Van Transportation Company
Vehicle Leasing Companies
Vehicles
Vital Processors
Vital Timers
Volume

Warehouse Space
Warehousing
Warehousing Facilities
Wayside
Weddings
Wheel Services
Wheels
Winches
Work Equipment
Workstation-Based Systems
Worldwide Supply Chain Solutions
Yachts
Yard Track

Visual and Performing Arts

These buzz words for the visual and performing arts concentrate on those positions for creative artists. Arts buzz words highlight experience with creating art and with entertaining an audience through performance art, theater, and music. This includes organizing and designing articles, products, and materials; portraying people, places, and events; communicating ideas, thoughts, and feelings; making words come alive by creating a visual and oral presentation based on written words in a script; expressing ideas, stories, rhythm, and sound; and creating dance interpretations.

▶ Resume Buzz Words

Accessory
Act
Advertising
Airbrush
Album Tour
Apparel
Architectural Design
Artist Shop
Artistic Feasibility
Artwork
Ballet
Black and White
Book Illustration
Bound Printed Material
Broadway
Brochures
Business and Art Professional
Cable Program
Calligraphic Artwork
Camera Ready Art
Charts
Choreography
Classical Ballet
Classical Piano
Color
Color Film Development

Color Promotional Samples
Comedy Sketch
Commercial Art
Commercials
Computer Art
Contemporary Ballet
Corporate Design
Corporate Portrait
Costume Design
Costumes
Creative Analysis
Creative Dance
Creative Planning
Dance Studio
Dealer Sell Sheets
Debut Album
Departmental Database Network
Design
Design Logos
Diagram
Diagram Maps
Direct Lighting
Display Technique
Drum Technician
Extra
Fabric

Fashion Design
Fashion Show
Feature Film
Fine Arts
Freestanding Insert Ads
Freehand
Freelance
Front Window Display
Gallery Logo
Garment
Hand-Design
Header Cards
Illustration
Improvisational Workshop
In the Round
Independent Record
Interior Design
Interior Finish
Japanese Motif Sketch Design
Large Format View Camera
Laser Printing
Layout and Design
Lighting
Lighting Effects
Lighting Equipment
Location
Location Photography
Mail Marketing Pieces
Major Label
Makeup
Marketing Brochure
Marketing Lists
Material
Mechanical Paste-Up
Mechanical Stages
Mechanicals
Method Style of Acting
Model
Modern Ballet
Modern Dance
Music Director
Music Format
Musical
Narrative Sketch
New York Stage
Onstage
Operational Deadlines
Orchestra
Orchestral Experience
Pastels
Paste-Up
Pattern
Pattern Making
Performance
Performer
Photo Essay
Photography
Photography Sessions
Playwright's Text
Point-of-Sales Material
Portfolio
Portrait
Positive and Negative Images
Prerelease
Printing
Printing Process
Producer
Production Report

Promotional Campaign
Promotional Event
Promotional Photography
Promotions
Props and Backgrounds
Proscenium Arch
Prototype Design
Published
Radio Chart
Recital
Reprint Titles
Reproduction Camera
Road Crew
Road Tour
Runway Show
Scene
Script
Seasonal Floor Set
Set
Shelf Talkers
Showcase
Sing
Sketch Comprehensives
Slide Materials
Slideshow
Small Format View Camera
Soft Sheets
Sound
Sound Technician
Sound Work
Special Effects
Stage Direction
Stage Management
Staging
Stand-Up Comedy
Stanislavski Style of Acting
Stat Camera
Structure
Studio Art
Studio Assignment
Stylized Lettering
Superstructure
Tailor
Tap
Teaching
Tear-Off Pads
Technical Art
Technical Report
Theater Production
Theatrical Direction
Three Color Brochures
Tickets
Top-10 Selling Record
Trade Promotions
Traditional Art and Drawing
Traditional Painting and Drawing
Type Layout
Vendor
Video
Visual Audit
Visual Checklist
Visual Criteria Standardization
Visual Presentation
Wardrobe
Window Display

Commonly Used Action Verbs

Accounting and Finance
Acted
Actuated
Adjusted
Administered
Allocated
Analyzed
Anticipated
Appraised
Assessed
Audited
Balanced
Budgeted
Calculated
Compiled
Completed
Composed
Computed
Conserved
Controlled
Corrected
Created
Determined
Developed
Entered
Established
Estimated
Expanded
Filed
Forecasted
Generated
Implemented
Improved
Maintained
Managed
Marketed
Measured
Monitored
Netted
Oversaw
Passed
Performed
Planned
Posted
Prepared
Programmed
Projected
Provided
Qualified
Reconciled
Recorded
Reduced
Researched
Resolved
Retrieved
Reviewed
Settled
Supported
Utilized
Worked

Administrative
Arranged
Assisted
Budgeted
Collected
Conducted
Coordinated
Created
Designed
Developed
Distributed
Edited
Executed
Facilitated
Filed
Handled
Implemented
Improved
Managed
Monitored
Organized
Performed
Planned
Prepared
Prioritized
Produced
Provided
Recorded
Resolved
Scheduled
Secured
Served
Serviced
Solicited
Sorted
Supervised
Tested
Translated
Utilized

Aerospace
Analyzed
Assisted
Designed
Developed
Engaged
Engineered
Established
Evaluated
Generated
Led
Manufactured
Performed
Planned
Prepared
Production
Provided
Recommended
Researched
Supplied
Tracked
Wrote

Apparel, Fashion, and Textiles
Checked
Created
Designed
Developed
Established
Featured
Finished
Generated
Handled
Licensed
Managed
Manufactured
Oversaw
Printed
Processed
Produced
Purchased
Received
Sold
Supervised
Tailored
Wove

Architecture, Construction, and Engineering
Built
Completed
Conceptualized
Conducted
Constructed
Controlled
Designed
Drafted
Drew
Generated
Managed
Outlined
Oversaw
Planned
Prepared
Programmed
Proposed
Renovated
Researched
Scheduled
Served
Supervised
Surveyed
Transported

Arts, Entertainment, Sports, and Recreation
Acted
Analyzed
Competed
Conceptualized

Created
Developed
Directed
Managed
Organized
Oversaw
Planned
Produced
Promoted
Provided
Supervised

Automotive

Accessorized
Assessed
Built
Certified
Customized
Diagnosed
Distributed
Drove
Explained
Formed
Improved
Installed
Managed
Manufactured
Performed
Produced
Repaired
Replaced
Serviced
Showed
Sold

Biotechnology and Pharmaceuticals

Applied
Compared
Contributed
Coordinated
Designed
Determined
Directed
Discovered
Disseminated
Facilitated
Generated
Guided
Identified
Implemented
Labeled
Leveraged
Maintained
Managed
Performed
Planned
Processed
Provided
Received
Sampled
Tracked
Trained
Utilized

Communications

Acted
Administered
Aided
Assisted
Conducted
Controlled
Coordinated
Created
Developed
Directed
Drafted
Edited
Evaluated
Generated
Identified
Implemented
Interviewed
Managed
Operated
Ordered
Organized
Oversaw
Performed
Planned
Produced
Promoted
Proofread
Publicized
Received
Recommended
Reported
Researched
Resolved
Scheduled
Served
Solicited
Supervised
Typed
Wrote

Computers and Mathematics

Adapted
Analyzed
Assisted
Calculated
Contributed
Controlled
Correlated
Created
Defined
Designed
Developed
Directed
Engineered
Evaluated
Formulated
Functioned
Identified
Implemented
Installed
Instituted
Led
Maintained

Managed
Monitored
Performed
Presented
Processed
Programmed
Provided
Published
Researched
Resolved
Scrutinized
Suggested
Supplied
Supported
Translated
Updated
Upgraded
Wrote

Education and Library Sciences

Administered
Aided
Arranged
Articulated
Assisted
Assumed
Budgeted
Cataloged
Chaired
Compiled
Computerized
Conducted
Coordinated
Created
Designed
Developed
Directed
Ensured
Facilitated
Generated
Handled
Hired
Initiated
Instructed
Interviewed
Managed
Organized
Participated
Performed
Planned
Prepared
Provided
Purchased
Recorded
Recruited
Researched
Reviewed
Scouted
Served
Supervised
Taught
Trained
Transferred
Tutored

Worked
Wrote

Engineering
Analyzed
Applied
Assembled
Assisted
Conducted
Designed
Developed
Directed
Engineered
Established
Evaluated
Initiated
Inspected
Manufactured
Modified
Monitored
Observed
Operated
Oversaw
Participated
Performed
Planned
Prepared
Provided
Represented
Researched
Reviewed
Revised
Scheduled
Served
Supervised
Supported
Trained
Utilized
Worked
Wrote

Executive and Managerial
Administered
Analyzed
Appointed
Approved
Assigned
Attained
Authorized
Chaired
Considered
Consolidated
Contracted
Controlled
Converted
Coordinated
Decided
Delegated
Developed
Directed
Eliminated
Emphasized
Enforced
Enhanced
Established

Executed
Generated
Handled
Headed
Hired
Hosted
Improved
Incorporated
Increased
Initiated
Inspected
Instituted
Led
Managed
Merged
Motivated
Navigated
Obtained
Organized
Originated
Overhauled
Oversaw
Planned
Presided
Prioritized
Produced
Recommended
Reorganized
Replaced
Restored
Reviewed
Scheduled
Secured
Selected
Streamlined
Strengthened
Supervised
Synchronized
Systematized
Terminated

Food and Beverages/ Agriculture
Acquired
Bred
Controlled
Developed
Displayed
Distributed
Ensured
Exported
Harvested
Imported
Improved
Managed
Manufactured
Marketed
Organized
Oversaw
Planted
Produced
Researched
Sold
Supplied
Worked

Government
Campaigned
Delegated
Demonstrated
Dispatched
Investigated
Lobbied
Managed
Organized
Participated
Practiced
Processed
Raised
Researched
Served
Settled
Supervised
Supported
Updated
Volunteered

Health and Medical
Acted
Administered
Advised
Alleviated
Allocated
Analyzed
Arranged
Assessed
Assisted
Assumed
Attended
Collaborated
Completed
Conducted
Conferred
Constructed
Consulted
Coordinated
Created
Dealt
Demonstrated
Determined
Developed
Directed
Dispensed
Distributed
Drafted
Educated
Encouraged
Ensured
Established
Evaluated
Facilitated
Fielded
Filled
Formed
Functioned
Geared
Generated
Handled
Hired
Identified
Implemented
Initiated

Instructed
Interviewed
Invited
Lectured
Led
Maintained
Managed
Monitored
Motivated
Observed
Organized
Oriented
Participated
Performed
Planned
Prepared
Presented
Priced
Produced
Purchased
Ran
Received
Recommended
Recorded
Redesigned
Required
Requisitioned
Researched
Reviewed
Scheduled
Selected
Served
Serviced
Specialized
Started
Structured
Supervised
Supported
Taught
Trained
Typed
Updated
Used
Utilized
Worked
Wrote

Hotels and Restaurants

Adhered
Assisted
Communicated
Ensured
Escorted
Established
Greeted
Hired
Maintained
Managed
Monitored
Participated
Provided
Recommended
Scheduled
Supervised
Trained
Worked

Human Resources

Administered
Advised
Analyzed
Assign
Assisted
Conducted
Coordinated
Counsel
Delegated
Developed
Entered
Established
Evaluated
Expanded
Facilitated
Hired
Improved
Interpreted
Interviewed
Investigated
Logged
Maintained
Managed
Monitored
Motivated
Organized
Paid
Participated
Performed
Placed
Prepared
Professionalized
Reconciled
Recruited
Reduced
Researched
Resolved
Responded
Reviewed
Revised
Screened
Served
Signed
Solved
Spearheaded
Supervised
Terminated
Trained
Verified

Insurance

Computed
Created
Delivered
Developed
Estimated
Evaluated
Filed
Implemented
Interacted
Negotiated
Processed
Recorded
Sold
Updated

Legal and Protective Services

Actuated
Advised
Argued
Conducted
Coordinated
Designed
Directed
Initiated
Interviewed
Negotiated
Patrolled
Practiced
Prepared
Presented
Prosecuted
Protected
Represented
Retained
Served
Supervised
Trained

Marketing and Sales

Coordinated
Created
Designed
Devised
Directed
Edited
Executed
Generated
Implemented
Initiated
Interacted
Maintained
Managed
Operated
Organized
Planned
Prepared
Sold
Supervised
Updated

Printing and Publishing

Acquired
Advertised
Announced
Conceived
Declared
Disclosed
Divulged
Edited
Executed
Issued
Maintained
Negotiated
Prepared
Printed
Proclaimed
Produced
Promulgated

Proofed
Read
Revealed
Trafficked
Wrote

Real Estate
Advised
Appraised
Assessed
Bought
Calculated
Conducted
Contracted
Directed
Explained
Handled
Negotiated
Obtained
Processed
Refinanced
Reviewed
Showed
Sold
Specialized
Toured
Updated
Worked
Retail
Bought
Catalogued
Excelled
Explained
Filled
Helped
Inventoried
Managed
Marketed
Operated
Ordered
Organized
Oversaw
Priced
Scheduled
Served
Shipped
Sold

Science
Built
Completed
Conducted
Designed
Developed
Diagnosed
Ensured
Evaluated
Examined
Filtered
Handled
Monitored
Originated
Performed
Processed
Promoted

Recorded
Researched
Sterilized
Supported
Tested

Service
Arranged
Assisted
Conducted
Demonstrated
Designed
Developed
Ensured
Evaluated
Generated
Handled
Ordered
Performed
Prepared
Provided
Received
Served
Trained
Utilized

Social and Human Services
Administered
Assessed
Assisted
Coordinated
Counseled
Established
Evaluated
Handled
Initiated
Led
Managed
Observed
Organized
Provided
Responded
Reviewed
Served
Specialized
Streamlined
Taught
Treated
Worked

Technical
Assigned
Communicated
Conducted
Created
Designed
Developed
Edited
Evaluated
Interpreted
Modified
Outlined
Programmed
Promoted

Researched
Services
Started
Tested
Trained
Updated
Used
Utilized
Worked

Transportation and Travel
Conducted
Confirmed
Contacted
Coordinated
Drove
Enforced
Filed
Flew
Handled
Instructed
Mapped
Operated
Performed
Planned
Prepared
Programmed
Scheduled
Sold
Transported
Traveled

Visual and Performing Arts
Achieved
Acted
Advertised
Assisted
Built
Choreographed
Communicated
Conceived
Coordinated
Created
Designed
Directed
Drew
Focused
Illustrated
Managed
Organized
Oversaw
Painted
Performed
Planned
Played
Produced
Revised
Sculpted
Served
Sewed
Shot
Staged
Videotaped
Worked
Wrote

Appendix A: Job Board Giants and Niche Sites

THE JOB SEEKER WHO FAILS to make use of the Internet's most popular job boards and niche sites is doing her job search a major disservice. These Internet resources have become a major source of recruiting for almost all employers. A job board is a website that lists job postings by employers and resumes offered by job seekers. Although each site has different methodologies, both the employer and the candidate can identify good prospects based on their needs. Some job boards are generic and offer a wide range of employment opportunities by industry, job title, location, and earnings. At the time of this writing, the three most popular general job board giants are: *www.monster.com*, *www.careerbuilder.com*, and *www.hotjobs.yahoo.com*. You can visit *www.weddles.com/awards/index.htm* for a list of the User's Choice Awards for the best job boards.

Many job seekers choose to set up a search agent at the boards, which means they are regularly e-mailed openings that match a specific criteria according to parameters they set up for themselves. If you see a position that appeals to you, click the link that allows you to reply to the opening and send your resume. Do not rely on the job board or the employer to find you on the site, even if you have a resume posted there. Be proactive and go after the openings that seem the best match for your skills and career goals.

Niche sites are exactly as they sound and are typically sites that are devoted to a specific industry, earning capacity, or geographic region. Some popular niche sites include: *www.absolutelyhealthcare.com*, *www.allretailjobs.com*, *www.jobs4hr.com*, and *www.talentzoo.com*, which is for advertising and media professionals. If you want to make your job search more focused, you might find greater success with the niche boards.

Appendix B: Effective Action Verbs and Adverbs

HOW YOU WRITE YOUR RESUME is just as important as what you write. In describing previous work experiences, the strongest resumes use short phrases beginning with action verbs and positive adverbs. Below are some of those you might want to use. These lists are not all-inclusive, but they should help you when you are trying to add variety and forcefulness to your descriptions of your job experiences and your abilities.

400 Action Verbs

Accelerated
Accentuated
Accomplished
Achieved
Acted
Activated
Actuated
Adapted
Addressed
Adjusted
Administered
Advanced
Advertised
Advised
Advocated
Aided
Allocated
Amplified
Analyzed
Answered
Anticipated
Applied
Appointed
Appraised
Approved
Arbitrated
Arranged
Ascertained
Assembled
Assessed
Assigned
Assisted
Assumed
Attained
Audited
Augmented
Authorized
Awarded
Balanced
Began
Boosted
Briefed
Broadened
Budgeted
Built
Calculated
Captured
Cataloged

Centralized
Chaired
Charted
Checked
Clarified
Classified
Coached
Collaborated
Collected
Combined
Communicated
Compared
Compiled
Completed
Composed
Computed
Conceived
Conceptualized
Condensed
Conducted
Conferred
Conserved
Consolidated
Constructed
Consulted
Contacted
Continued
Contracted
Contributed
Controlled
Convened
Converted
Conveyed
Convinced
Cooperated
Coordinated
Corresponded
Counseled
Created
Critiqued
Cultivated
Customized
Debugged
Decided
Defined
Delegated
Delivered
Demonstrated
Described

Designated
Designed
Detected
Determined
Developed
Devised
Diagnosed
Diagrammed
Directed
Discovered
Dispatched
Dispensed
Displayed
Dissected
Distributed
Diverted
Documented
Drafted
Drew
Earned
Edited
Educated
Effected
Eliminated
Emphasized
Employed
Encouraged
Enforced
Engineered
Enhanced
Enlarged
Enlisted
Ensured
Entered
Entertained
Established
Estimated
Evaluated
Examined
Executed
Expanded
Expedited
Experimented
Explained
Explored
Expressed
Extended
Extracted
Fabricated

Facilitated
Fashioned
Filed
Finalized
Fixed
Focused
Forecasted
Formed
Formulated
Fostered
Found
Founded
Fulfilled
Furnished
Gained
Gathered
Generated
Governed
Grossed
Guided
Handled
Harmonized
Headed
Heightened
Helped
Hired
Honed
Hosted
Hypothesized
Identified
Illustrated
Imagined
Implemented
Improved
Improvised
Incorporated
Increased
Indexed
Influenced
Informed
Initiated
Innovated
Inspected
Inspired
Installed
Instituted
Instructed
Integrated
Interacted
Interpreted
Interviewed
Introduced
Invented
Inventoried
Investigated
Invited
Involved
Issued
Joined
Judged
Kept
Launched
Learned
Lectured
Led
Lifted
Listened
Located

Logged
Maintained
Managed
Manipulated
Marketed
Matched
Maximized
Measured
Mediated
Merged
Mobilized
Modified
Monitored
Motivated
Navigated
Netted
Observed
Obtained
Opened
Operated
Orchestrated
Ordered
Organized
Originated
Outdid
Outlined
Overcame
Overhauled
Oversaw
Paid
Participated
Passed
Performed
Persuaded
Photographed
Piloted
Pinpointed
Pioneered
Placed
Planned
Played
Posted
Predicted
Prepared
Prescribed
Presented
Preserved
Presided
Prevented
Printed
Prioritized
Processed
Produced
Professionalized
Programmed
Projected
Promoted
Promulgated
Proofread
Proposed
Protected
Proved
Provided
Publicized
Published
Purchased
Qualified
Questioned

Raised
Ran
Rated
Reached
Realized
Reasoned
Received
Recommended
Reconciled
Recorded
Recruited
Reduced
Reestablished
Reevaluated
Referred
Regulated
Rehabilitated
Reinforced
Reinvigorated
Related
Remodeled
Rendered
Reorganized
Repaired
Replaced
Reported
Represented
Researched
Reshaped
Resolved
Responded
Restored
Restructured
Resupplied
Retrieved
Revamped
Reviewed
Revised
Revitalized
Routed
Saved
Scheduled
Screened
Searched
Secured
Selected
Separated
Served
Serviced
Settled
Shaped
Shared
Signed
Simplified
Simulated
Sketched
Sold
Solicited
Solved
Sorted
Spearheaded
Specialized
Specified
Spoke
Sponsored
Staffed
Standardized
Started

Streamlined
Strengthened
Structured
Studied
Substituted
Suggested
Summarized
Supervised
Supplied
Supplemented
Supported
Surpassed
Surveyed
Sustained
Synthesized
Systemized
Targeted
Taught
Terminated
Tested
Tightened
Totaled
Tracked
Traded
Trained
Transcribed
Transformed
Translated
Transmitted
Transported
Traveled
Tutored
Uncovered
Undertook
Unified
United
Updated
Upgraded
Used
Utilized
Validated
Verbalized
Verified
Vitalized
Volunteered
Weighed
Widened
Won
Worked
Wrote

400 Adverbs
Absolutely
Accommodatingly
Accordingly
Accurately
Actively
Acutely
Adamantly
Adeptly
Adequately
Adroitly
Advantageously
Affably
Affectingly
Affectionately
Affirmatively

Aggressively
Alertly
Ambitiously
Amicably
Amply
Analytically
Appraisingly
Appreciatively
Appropriately
Artfully
Articulately
Artistically
Assertively
Assuredly
Astutely
Attentively
Authoritatively
Automatically
Autonomously
Avidly
Beamingly
Beautifully
Becomingly
Befittingly
Believably
Bravely
Brightly
Brilliantly
Busily
Calmly
Candidly
Capably
Carefully
Caringly
Casually
Cautiously
Ceremoniously
Charmingly
Cheerfully
Cheerily
Civilly
Cleanly
Cleverly
Closely
Coherently
Colorfully
Comfortably
Comfortingly
Commandingly
Communicatively
Comparatively
Competently
Competitively
Completely
Composedly
Comprehendingly
Concisely
Conclusively
Confidentially
Confidently
Congenially
Conscientiously
Consciously
Conservatively
Consistently
Conveniently
Convincingly
Coolly

Cooperatively
Cordially
Correctively
Courageously
Courteously
Creatively
Critically
Decidedly
Decisively
Definitely
Deftly
Deliberately
Delicately
Delightedly
Delightfully
Demonstrably
Dependably
Descriptively
Determinedly
Devotedly
Dexterously
Dignifiedly
Diligently
Diplomatically
Directly
Discreetly
Distinctly
Divinely
Doggedly
Dramatically
Drastically
Eagerly
Earnestly
Easily
Educationally
Effectively
Effervescently
Efficiently
Effortlessly
Elaborately
Elegantly
Eloquently
Emphatically
Encouragingly
Energetically
Engagingly
Enjoyably
Enthusiastically
Evenly
Exactingly
Experimentally
Expertly
Explicitly
Expressively
Extensively
Exuberantly
Faithfully
Favorably
Fearlessly
Fervently
Fiercely
Firmly
Fittingly
Flexibly
Fluently
Fluidly
Fondly
Forcefully

Forcibly
Foresightedly
Formally
Frankly
Freely
Freshly
Gaily
Gallantly
Gamely
Generously
Genially
Gently
Genuinely
Gleefully
Good-Naturedly
Gracefully
Graciously
Gradually
Grammatically
Gratefully
Handily
Happily
Harmoniously
Heartily
Heedfully
Helpfully
Honestly
Honorably
Hopefully
Hopingly
Humbly
Imaginatively
Immaculately
Independently
Indirectly
Industriously
Informatively
Ingeniously
Inquisitively
Insightfully
Insistently
Instinctively
Instinctually
Instructively
Intellectually
Intelligently
Intelligibly
Intensely
Intently
Interestedly
Intrepidly
Intricately
Intriguingly
Intuitively
Inventively
Jauntily
Jocularly
Jointly
Jovially
Joyfully
Judiciously
Justly
Keenly
Kindly
Knowingly
Laboriously
Liberally
Lightly

Logically
Loyally
Lucidly
Mannerly
Masterfully
Maturely
Meaningfully
Mechanically
Merrily
Methodically
Meticulously
Mindfully
Minutely
Moderately
Modestly
Naturally
Neatly
Nicely
Nimbly
Nobly
Noncompetitively
Obediently
Obligingly
Observantly
Occasionally
Officially
Openly
Optimistically
Outrageously
Overwhelmingly
Painstakingly
Particularly
Passionately
Patiently
Peacefully
Perceptively
Perfectly
Perkily
Perpetually
Perseveringly
Persistently
Persuasively
Physically
Plainly
Playfully
Pleasantly
Pleasingly
Pointedly
Politely
Positively
Potently
Practically
Precisely
Preparedly
Professionally
Proficiently
Profoundly
Progressively
Promptly
Properly
Proudly
Prudently
Punctiliously
Purposefully
Quickly
Rapidly
Rationally
Readily

Realistically
Reasonably
Reassuringly
Receptively
Reflectively
Refreshingly
Regularly
Reliably
Repeatedly
Resolutely
Resoundingly
Resourcefully
Respectably
Respectfully
Responsibly
Responsively
Rigorously
Robustly
Routinely
Satisfactorily
Securely
Selectively
Self-Assuredly
Selflessly
Sensibly
Sensitively
Seriously
Sharply
Shrewdly
Significantly
Silently
Simply
Simultaneously
Sincerely
Single-Handedly
Skillfully
Smartly
Smoothly
Snappily
Solidly
Soothingly
Sophisticatedly
Soundly
Sparingly
Spiritedly
Splendidly
Spontaneously
Stalwartly
Stately
Steadfastly
Steadily
Stoutly
Straightforwardly
Strategically
Strictly
Strongly
Studiously
Stupendously
Sturdily
Stylishly
Substantially
Successfully
Superbly
Supportively
Surely
Sympathetically
Systematically
Tactfully

Tastefully
Technically
Tenaciously
Thoroughly
Thoughtfully
Tirelessly
Tolerantly
Tremendously
Triumphantly
Trustingly
Trustworthily
Truthfully
Unabashedly
Unaffectedly
Unassumingly
Unblinkingly
Uncritically
Understandingly
Unemotionally
Unequivocally
Unfalteringly
Unflinchingly
Unselfishly
Unsettlingly
Unusually
Unwaveringly
Unyieldingly
Uprightly
Urgently
Usefully
Valiantly
Valorously
Verbally
Vibrantly
Victoriously
Vigilantly
Vigorously
Voraciously
Warmly
Watchfully
Welcomingly
Wholeheartedly
Willfully
Willingly
Wisely
Zealously
Zestfully

Index

Acceptance letters, 106
Accomplishments
    listing, 44–45
    personal vs. professional, 101
Accountant, 119–21
Account executive, 119
Accounting analyst, 121
Accounting and finance
    action verbs, 235
    buzz words, 164–68
Accounting assistant/intern, 121
Accounting manager, 54, 58, 121–22
Accounting technician, 122
Action verbs, 235–39, 241–43
Address changes, 107
Administration
    action verbs, 235
    buzz words, 168–70
    field, 115–16
Administrative assistant, 8, 17, 31, 39, 41, 48, 49, 67, 74, 122–23
Administrative judge, 10, 17, 31
Administrator, 123
Admissions and enrollment management, 48, 49, 52
Admissions counselor, 39, 44, 45
Adverbs, 243–45
Advertising, 123–24
Advertising sales associate, 39, 41–42, 45
Aerospace
    action verbs, 235
    buzz words, 170–72
Agriculture
    action verbs, 237
    buzz words, 193–95
Alumnus, networking note to, 76–77
Analyst, 10, 17
Apparel, fashion, and textiles
    action verbs, 235
    buzz words, 172–74
Applications programmer, 14
Architect, 124
Architecture
    action verbs, 235
    buzz words, 174–77
    field, 116
Art assistant, 124
Art instructor, 125
Arts and entertainment
    action verbs, 235–36, 239
    buzz words, 177–79, 233–34
    field, 116
Assistant curator, 8, 17, 31

Assistant editor, 9, 25, 32
Assistant hospital supervisor, 21, 32
Assistant personnel officer, 15
Associate desktop publisher, 11, 17, 25, 32
Associate editor, 39, 45
Athletic director, 21
At-home parents, 82, 88
Audio visual coordinator, 139–40
Audiovisual specialist, 39, 44, 46
Auditing analyst, 126
Auditor, 126
Audit trainee, 125
Automotive
    action verbs, 236
    buzz words, 179–81
Auto salesperson, 67, 71, 74

Bakery manager, 143
Bank branch manager, 126–27
Bank manager, 67, 71, 74
Bank teller, 127
Barback, 127
Bartender/bar manager, 127
Biomedical engineer, 15, 36
Biotechnology
    action verbs, 236
    buzz words, 182–83
Blogs, 5
Bookkeeper, 54, 56, 127–28
Brand manager, 128–29
Broadcast letters, 3, 38, 47–52
Budget analyst, 129
Bullet points, 24–31
Busboy, 129
Business, 116
Business consultant, 15

Campaign assistant, 129
Campus interviews, 4
Campus police officer, 11, 17–18, 32, 130–31
Career changers, 82–83, 88–89, 95
Career fairs, 4
Career objectives, 112
Career path, lack of clear, 86, 92
Case manager, 18, 32, 129–30, 138
Case worker, 130
Chef, 40, 46, 54–56, 58–59
Chief financial officer, 10, 22, 67
Child care assistant director, 11, 21–22, 32
Chiropractor, 48, 49–50, 52
Civil litigation specialist, 131
Claims adjuster, 10, 25–26, 32
Claims processor, 54, 58

Clinical research nurse, 26
Clinic therapist, 131
Closing paragraph
    of cover letter, 5
    in networking letters, 74–76
    phrases for, 31–37, 45–47, 51–52, 58–59, 63–64
    in special situations, 94–98
Cold contact letters, 4, 38, 39–41
Commercial business development officer, 126
Communications
    action verbs, 236
    buzz words, 183–85
    field, 116
Computers and mathematics
    action verbs, 236
    buzz words, 185–87
Computer software designer, 40, 42, 46
Computer systems analyst, 131–32
Conference coordinator, 21
Confidentiality, 12–13, 63
Confidential job postings, 3, 14–16
Construction
    action verbs, 235
    buzz words, 174–77
    field, 116
Contact information, 163
Continued education, phrases emphasizing, 22
Coordinator, special events, 132
Cosmetologist, 12, 26
Counseling and mental health services intern, 132
Counseling psychologist, 132–33
Counselor, 133–34
Cover letter phrases
    for closing paragraphs, 31–37, 45–47, 51–52,
        58–59, 63–64, 74–76, 94–98
    for contacting employment agencies, 54–59
    for contacting executive search firms, 60–64
    for contacting targeted employers, 38–52
    for introductory paragraphs, 8–16, 39–41,
        47–49, 54–56, 60–61, 80–87
    for job posting responses, 8–37
    for qualification and motivation paragraphs,
        16–31, 41–45, 49–51, 56–58, 61–63, 71–73
    in special situations, 80–98
Cover letters
    content of, 4–5
    to employment agencies, 53–59
    for networking, 65–79
    questions to ask before writing, 6
    reviewing sample, 1–2
    things not to say in, 99–102
    types of, 3–4
    writing essentials, 1–7
Credit manager, 48, 50, 52
Customer service manager, 23, 33
Customer support representative, 67–68, 74

Dental assistant, 55–57, 59, 134
Dental clinic director/instructor, 135
Dental hygienist, 12–13, 27, 33, 134–35
Dental trainee/extern, 135
Dentist, 135–36
Dentistry department manager, 18, 33
Director of information services, 60, 61–62, 63–64
Director of public works, 12, 23, 33
Drafts, of cover letter, 2

Editor, 12, 27, 33, 68, 136
Editorial assistant, 40, 46
Education
    action verbs, 236
    buzz words, 187–89
    field, 116
Educational background, weaknesses in, 85, 98
Elementary school teacher, 40, 42, 46
Employer identified job postings, 3
Employment agencies, 3, 53–59
Employment history
    gaps in, 86, 90, 96
    military, 87, 91–92, 97
    at one company, 81, 87–88, 94
    overseas, 87, 92–93, 97
    part-time, 86, 97
Engineering
    action verbs, 235
    buzz words, 174–77, 190–91
    field, 116
Engineering technician, 136
Enthusiasm, phrases conveying, 8–9
Event planner, 13, 27–28, 33
Executive and managerial
    action verbs, 237
    buzz words, 192–93
Executive assistant, 55, 57, 59
Executive recruiting, 147–48
Executive search firms, 3, 60–64
Experience, phrases conveying, 9–10

Facebook, 5
Faculty member, networking note to, 77
Features reporter, 18
Field finance manager, 9, 28
Film archivist, 34
Finance, 117
Finance assistant, 136–37
Finance manager, 68, 74–75
Financial analyst, 40, 42, 46
Fired/laid off candidates, 85–86, 90, 96
Follow-up communications, 103–07
Fonts, for resumes, 111
Food and beverages
    action verbs, 237
    buzz words, 193–95

Freelancers, 83–84, 91, 96
Freight supervisor, 48, 50, 52
Friend of the family, networking note to, 77–78
Fundraiser, 9, 34, 42
Future contact, 35–36

Gemologist, 21, 34
Government
    action verbs, 237
    buzz words, 196–98
    field, 117
Guidance counselor, 137

Health
    action verbs, 237–38
    buzz words, 198–200
Health and human services, 117
Home economics department coordinator, 9, 22, 34
Homemakers, 82, 89, 95
Hospital administrator, 18, 34
Hospitality
    action verbs, 238
    buzz words, 200–201
    field, 117
Hotel manager, 11, 34
Human resources
    action verbs, 238
    buzz words, 201–03
    field, 117
Human resources director, 137–38
Human services
    action verbs, 239
    buzz words, 226–27
HVAC technician, 14, 22

Informational interviews, 105
In-house positions, 81, 88, 94–95
Insurance
    action verbs, 238
    buzz words, 203–05
Interest, phrases conveying, 8–9, 23–24
International buyer, 11, 34
International controller, 68, 75
Interviews
    follow-up communications, 104
    request for, 31–35
Introductory paragraphs
    in cold contact letters, 39–41
    of cover letter, 4–5
    in networking letters, 66–71
    phrases for, 8–16, 39–41, 47–49, 54–56, 60–61
    for special situations, 80–87
Investigator, 138
Investment banking analyst, 46

Job boards, 240
Job candidates
    fifty-plus-years-old, 81, 89–90, 95
    fired/laid off, 85–86, 90, 96
    for in-house positions, 81, 88, 94–95
    out-of-workforce, 81–82, 88, 89, 95
    recent graduates, 84–85, 93–94, 97–98
Job descriptions, reviewing, 1–2
Job offers, rejecting, 106
Job postings
    letters of application in response to, 3
    phrases to use when responding to, 8–37
    reviewing, 1–2

Key points, identifying, in cover letter, 2
Keywords, 13–14

Laboratory technician, 138
LAN coordinator, 138
Language instructor, 137
Law, 117–18
Legal administrator, 55, 59
Legal and protective services
    action verbs, 238
    buzz words, 205–08
Legal assistant, 18, 35, 57
Legal associate, 15
Legal intern, 139
Legal secretary/legal assistant, 139
Letterhead, 111
Letters of application, 3
Letters of introduction, 3–4
Letters of recommendation, 36–37, 104
Librarian, 16, 47, 139–40
Library science
    action verbs, 236–37
    buzz words, 187–89
Lies, 161
Lists, 44–45
Loan officer, 28, 146–47

Management consultant, 60, 62, 64, 140
Management consulting analyst, 43
Managerial
    action verbs, 237
    buzz words, 192–93
Marketing
    action verbs, 238
    buzz words, 209–13
    field, 118
    phrases for, 141–42
Marketing assistant, 68–69, 71–72
Marketing director, 40, 43
Marketing/sales executive, 50–51, 52
Marketing specialist, 69, 72, 75, 128–29
Market research, 140–41

Materials, phrases calling attention to submitted, 12
Mathematics
    action verbs, 236
    buzz words, 185–87
Media, 116
Medical
    action verbs, 237–38
    buzz words, 198–200
Meeting planner, 12, 35
Military experience, 86–87, 91–92, 97
Mortgage/loan officer, 69, 72, 75, 127
Motivation paragraphs
    in cover letter, 5
    in networking letters, 71–73
    phrases for, 16–31, 41–45, 49–51, 56–58, 61–63
    in special situations, 87–94
Multimedia specialist, 9, 35
Mutual funds broker, 41, 44–45, 47

Nanny, 142
Networking letters, 65, 66–76
Networking notes, 4, 65–66, 76–79
Newspaper intern, 9, 35
Niche job sites, 240
Nurse, 69, 75
Nurse practitioner, 142–43

Occupational health manager, 19
Office manager, 131
Office receptionist, 28–29, 35
Operations manager, 16, 36, 60, 62, 64
Optics researcher, 51, 52
Overseas employment history, 87, 92–93, 97

Park maintenance supervisor, 11, 23
Part-time employment history, 86, 97
Past employer, networking note to, 78
Pastry chef, 143
Patrolman, 144
Payroll supervisor, 69, 72, 75
Performing arts
    action verbs, 239
    buzz words, 233–34
Personal connections, 14
Pharmaceuticals
    action verbs, 236
    buzz words, 182–83
Pharmaceutical sales, 16, 37
Pharmacist, 23–24, 35
Phone number changes, 107
Photographer, 13, 19
Physical therapy aid, 144
Plant manager, 61–64
Political staffer, 19, 35
Portfolios, phrases calling attention to, 11
Preschool director, 37

Printing and publishing
    action verbs, 238–39
    buzz words, 213–15
Product developer, 19–20
Production assistant/intern, 144
Production manager, 70, 72–73
Production quality control manager, 13, 36
Professional growth, 21–22
Professional society colleague, networking note
    to, 79
Professional society officer, networking note to, 79
Professor, 144–45
Program coordinator, 13
Programmer, 145
Project administrator, 160
Promotional assistant, 145
Publicist, 70, 73, 146
Publicity assistant, 146
Public relations assistant/associate, 29, 36, 43, 47,
    125
Public relations manager, 145–46
Publisher's assistant, 20, 36
Purchasing agent, 29, 37

Qualification paragraphs
    in cover letter, 5
    in networking letters, 71–73
    phrases for, 16–31, 41–45, 49–51, 56–58, 61–63
    in special situations, 87–94

Radio station producer, 157
Real estate
    action verbs, 239
    buzz words, 216–18
Real estate loan officer, 146–47
Real estate sales, 147
Recent graduates, 84–85, 93–94, 97–98
Recruiting manager, 147–48
References, 36–37, 104
Referrals, 104–05
Rehabilitation therapist, 148
Rejection, response to, 105–06
Relocation, 24
Research and development position, 55, 57, 59
Researcher, 36
Resignation letter, 107
Restaurant manager, 148–49
Restaurant manager trainee, 20, 36
Restaurants
    action verbs, 238
    buzz words, 200–201
Resumes
    action verbs for, 235–39, 241–43
    buzz words for, 164–234
    checklist for, 114–15
    competencies and capabilities on, 113

distribution of, 114
first draft, 113
format of, 110–11
objectives on, 112
organization of, 112
phrases directing attention to, 20–21
phrases for, 119–60
qualifications and achievements on, 113
reviewing sample, 109–10
things not to say in, 161–63
writing essentials, 109–18
Resurrection letters, 105
Retail buyer, 149
Retail buzz words, 218–20
Retail sales manager, 149–50
RIGHT formula, 1–2

Salary requirements, 101–02, 162
Sales
action verbs, 238
buzz words, 209–13
field, 118
Sales account executive, 150–51
Sales account manager, 151
Sales/customer services representative, 55–56, 58, 59
Sales representative, 151–52
School and community counseling, 41, 43, 47
Science and technology
action verbs, 239
buzz words, 220–23
field, 118
Search professionals, 53
Secretary, 70, 73, 76, 152
Security, head of, 152
Security guard, 58
Senior accountant, 61, 63, 64, 119–20
Senior HVAC technician, 14, 22
Senior vice president (banking), 48–49, 52
Service industry
action verbs, 239
buzz words, 223–25
Site location supervisor, 14
Skills, phrases conveying, 10–11
Small business owners, 83, 90–91, 96
Social networking sites, 5
Social services
action verbs, 239
buzz words, 226–27
Social worker, 29–30, 153
Special situations, 5, 80–98
Sports and recreation
action verbs, 235–36
buzz words, 177–79
Staff accountant, 70, 76
State administrator, 24, 37
Store manager, 37, 153–54

Student clinician, 154–55
Student teacher, 155
Successful track record, phrases conveying, 9–10, 23
Systems engineer, 155
Systems manager, 155–56
Systems programmer, 156

Targeted employers, phrases to use when contacting, 38–52
Teacher, 40, 42, 46, 156, 157
Teaching assistant, 156–57
Technical
action verbs, 239
buzz words, 228–30
Technical writer, 14, 30
Technology and operations, 118
Telecommunications specialist, 71, 73, 76
Telemarketer, 30–31, 157
Television camera operator, 20, 35
Television producer, 157
Television production assistant, 43–44
Thank-you notes, 37, 103–06
Thesis statement, 4
Training, phrases emphasizing, 22
Transcripts, 36–37
Translator, 37
Transportation and travel
action verbs, 239
buzz words, 230–33
Travel agent, 10, 24
Travel consultant, 157–58
Tutor, 158
Twitter, 5

Underwriter (insurance), 158–59

Veterinary assistant, 159
Visual arts
action verbs, 239
buzz words, 233–34
Voicemail greetings, 111–12
Volunteer experience, 162

Waiter, 160
Withdrawal from consideration letters, 106
Witness advocate, 160
Work force, re-entering, 81–82, 88, 89, 95
Writer, 13, 19, 136, 160
Writing process
for cover letters, 1–2
for resumes, 109–14